In Memory of Frederick J. Hoffman (1909–67)

"Earth, receive an honoured guest"

Contents

Preface

An earlier form of this book appeared in French as *Configuration critique de Samuel Beckett* (M. J. Minard, Lettres Modernes, 1964). The contributors to that volume rethought their original essays and made changes in their texts in the course of preparing the present English versions. The majority of these critics are bilingual like Samuel Beckett and handle the problems of "self-translation" with exemplary ease.

The present collection contains three previously unpublished essays by Raymond Federman, John Fletcher, and Ruby Cohn; they were written especially for *Samuel Beckett Now*. I need not comment on the credentials of these three gifted Beckett critics.

We have tried here for variety and versatility, perhaps at the expense of a unified point of view. The essays represent agreeable and useful differences of approach, ranging from close textual study to more detached wanderings into literary history and biography. One might suggest that Beckett's career resembles a triptych, with two relatively slender panels (the plays and the poetry) flanking and enclosing an imposing central panel (the novels). (There are of course those who would disagree with this estimate of the drama.) The present volume is structured to acknowledge this tripartite division, with the main emphasis on the novel and a somewhat lesser attention given to the plays and the poetry.

Frederick Hoffman's essay surveys the major fiction from *Murphy* through *The Unnamable* and offers a valuable passageway to the more specialized essays of Raymond Federman, Robert Champigny, David Hayman, and John Fletcher (all of which concentrate on aspects of the French trilogy). Raymond Federman's study uses some of the tools he worked with in his study of the early fiction, *Journey to Chaos;* he refines upon them and enlarges their application as he applies them to the more mature Beckett. John Fletcher's reading of *Molloy* strikes me as being more exciting and less conventional than the one he offered in his *The Novels of Samuel Beckett.* David Hayman comes to Beckett after many years devoted to Joyce, especially to *Finnegans Wake,* while Robert Champigny comes via the French existentialists. The mythic patterns and structural complexities which Hayman uncovers in *Molloy* reflect his Joycean training just as Champigny's concern with the semantic and philosophical possibilities of the narrative "I" in *The Unnamable* reflects his preoccupation with a first-person confessional tradition in the French novel typified by Sartre's *Nausea.*

Lawrence Harvey's essay on *Echo's Bones* is one of the rare attempts to study Beckett's poetry. He not only studies the poetry close up, in good "new critical" fashion, but also brings to bear essential biographical information: a rare accomplishment for any student of poetry as even Brooks and Warren would—perhaps reluctantly—admit.

Ruby Cohn and Rosette Lamont both touch on aspects of the drama until now virtually unnoticed. Their essays display a sanity and restraint absent from so much of the Beckett criticism that darkens the pages of the drama quarterlies.

The remaining three essays indulge more in literary theorizing and confrontation. Germaine Brée and Edith Kern are interested in defining a proper ambience for Beckett's world. Germaine Brée passes by the Pythagoreans, Dante, and Descartes, among others, on her way to characterizing Beckett's "grands articulés." Edith Kern deals with two seemingly different literary climates: the rational and the ordered world of the eighteenth century and the absurdist, irrational twentieth century. She brings together representatives of the two centuries who bear an uncanny resemblance, Swift and Beckett.

Bruce Morrissette's is an essay in literary confrontation. He studies very closely Robbe-Grillet's changing reactions to

Beckett as revealed first in the *Godot* piece which appeared in
the February 1953 *Critique* and later in the more substantial
1957 essay which eventually became part of Robbe-Grillet's
collection *For a New Novel*. Morrissette, the author of the most
distinguished book on Robbe-Grillet, cleverly brings the two
experimenters together in close juxtaposition and reveals new
aspects of each writer's achievement. Morrissette is perhaps the
only critic in the collection who is less than a confirmed
Beckettian, and it is refreshing to see his more Robbe-Grilletian
optics at work.

One of the contributors to this book died just after he gave
me the present version of his essay. Frederick J. Hoffman was
the author not only of an excellent study of Samuel Beckett but
also of some twenty other books and some three hundred scholarly articles and reviews. His finest book, *The Mortal No*,
belongs in the company of Erich Auerbach's *Mimesis* and
Northrop Frye's *Anatomy of Criticism*. Fred Hoffman's unique
gift for literary interpretation places all of us who knew him in
his debt.

I wish to thank M. Michel J. Minard for allowing us to use so
much material from the *Configuration critique de Samuel
Beckett* in the present volume. The final section of my introduction appeared in an earlier form as "Crritic!" in the December
1966 *Modern Drama*. I am grateful to Professor A. C. Edwards,
editor of this distinguished journal, for allowing me to use this
material in its present form; I am also grateful to Professor
Ruby Cohn for first commissioning the article.

Frederick Hoffman's essay originally appeared as part of his
book, *Samuel Beckett: The Language of Self* (1962) . I wish
to thank Mr. Vernon Sternberg and the Southern Illinois
University Press for allowing me to reprint this chapter in the
present volume: Frederick J. Hoffman, "The Elusive Ego:
Beckett's M's" from *Samuel Beckett: The Language of Self*
(© 1962 by Southern Illinois University Press, reprinted by
permission.)

An earlier version of David Hayman's essay appeared in *Six*

Contemporary Novels: Introductory Essays in Modern Fiction, edited by W. O. S. Sutherland and published in 1962 by the Humanities Research Center, University of Texas; I am grateful for the occasion to acknowledge my thanks.

I should like to thank Mr. Barney Rosset and Grove Press for kind permission to quote from the following works of Samuel Beckett: *Waiting for Godot,* translated by the author (© 1954 by Grove Press) ; *Proust* (© 1957 by Grove Press) ; *Murphy* (© 1957 by Grove Press) ; *Endgame,* translated by the author (© 1958 by Grove Press) ; *Watt* (© 1959 by Grove Press) ; *Krapp's Last Tape and Other Dramatic Pieces, Act without Words* I and II, both translated by the author (© 1957 by Samuel Beckett and © 1958, 1959, 1960 by Grove Press) ; *Happy Days* (© 1961 by Grove Press) ; *How It Is,* translated by the author (© 1964 by Grove Press) ; *Stories and Texts for Nothing,* translated by the author and Richard Seaver (© 1967 by Samuel Beckett and Grove Press) ; *Molloy,* translated by Patrick Bowles in collaboration with the author (© 1955 by Grove Press) ; *Malone Dies,* translated by the author (© 1956 by Grove Press) ; *The Unnamable,* translated by the author (© 1958 by Grove Press) ; *Poems in English* (© 1961 by Samuel Beckett and Grove Press) . I should also like to thank Mr. Barney Rosset and Grove Press for kind permission to quote from Alain Robbe-Grillet's *For a New Novel,* translated by Richard Howard (© 1965 by Grove Press) .

Finally, I am grateful to Thomas Donovan for helping me to prepare the manuscript for the publisher and to Peter B. Brunner for help with reading proofs.

MELVIN J. FRIEDMAN

samuel   beckett   now

Note

Since the Grove Press (New York)
English-language editions of Samuel
Beckett's works are readily available,
all page references in the present
volume to the works of Samuel
Beckett, unless noted otherwise, refer
to Grove editions. Also for the
convenience of the reader, the page
references to these editions, *Waiting
for Godot* (1954), *Proust* (1957),
Murphy (1957), *Endgame* (1958),
Watt (1959), *Krapp's Last Tape and
Other Dramatic Pieces* (1960;
includes *All That Fall, Embers,* and
Act without Words I and II), *Happy
Days* (1961), *How It Is* (1964),
Stories and Texts for Nothing
(1967), *Molloy* (1955), *Malone Dies*
(1956), and *The Unnamable* (1958),
appear within parentheses in the
text. If it is not clear from the text
which of Beckett's works is being
cited, the page reference will be
preceded by a short title within the
same set of parentheses.

Introduction

The editor of a collection of criticism on a single writer is usually faced with two possibilities: discussing, in introductory fashion, the author's work or an aspect of it; surveying the principal tendencies of the critical and scholarly writing devoted to him. The first seems, in the case of Samuel Beckett, a pointless exercise. We have passed beyond the stage of acknowledging the achievement of the Irish writer who has taken up permanent residence in Paris—which is usually the aim of such an introductory essay. Beckett criticism has reached such an enviable and almost unbelievable level of sophistication that any kind of overview of his life and works is at least ten years out-of-date. (I wrote such an essay myself ten years ago: "The Achievement of Samuel Beckett," *Books Abroad,* Summer 1959.) It is clear, then, that we should concentrate on the second possibility.

Despite the fact that Samuel Beckett has been writing with some consistency since the early 1930s, genuine critical interest in him dates only from the 1950s. The first articles of any substance in English have been published since about 1954, and these early ones (such as Edith Kern's "Drama Stripped for Inaction: Beckett's *Godot,*" *Yale French Studies,* no. 14) are largely concerned with the plays. It is not really until the Beckett issue of *Perspective* in 1959 that we have a substantial body of essays devoted to the novels. A glance at Ruby Cohn's checklist in this special Beckett issue reveals that the Irish-born writer was far from being the critics' favorite among contemporary writers. Most of the items mentioned (this bibliography lists essays in a variety of languages, including

English, French, and German) are relatively short and tend mainly to be extended book reviews or survey articles. Ruby Cohn's introduction to the Autumn 1959 *Perspective* is interesting because of certain biographical insights—she is among the first to puncture the myth of Beckett's unapproachability—and some very sane judgments of the work, especially the novels. Her introduction is followed by a series of articles which concentrate principally on the fiction and use a thematic rather than a technical or structural approach. Three of the essays point out the Cartesianism in Beckett and underscore the philosophical basis of the novels.

After 1959 Beckett ceases to be (to use Cyril Connolly's expression) a "condemned playground" for critics. Attempts have been made to place him in congenial literary surroundings and to explain his debts to earlier writers. Kenneth Allsop tried to place him in the company of the then faddish "Angry Young Men" in *The Angry Decade* (1958), whereas a variety of other critics have tried to see his novels as examples of the *nouveau roman*. From Martin Esslin on, the tendency has been to view Beckett's plays as part of the theater of the absurd. The earlier writers whose names have frequently been linked with Beckett are Dante, Sterne, Swift, Proust, Joyce, Kafka, and Céline; the philosophers are so numerous that we can merely say that they extend from the pre-Socratics through the Logical Positivists, and include Descartes and Leibniz.

As Beckett continues to gain literary respectability these influence-hunting games will doubtless expand and more explanations will be offered for the genesis and direction of his experiments. Critics have been faced since the early 1950s with Beckett's astonishing bilingualism. One can look to the Irish phase of his work which produced *More Pricks Than Kicks, Murphy, Watt,* and such later plays as *All That Fall* and *Happy Days,* then turn to a very different literary climate which produced the French trilogy, *En attendant Godot, Fin de partie,* and *Comment c'est.* In many ways there is a sharp difference between the works written in English and those written in French. The levity (often assumed) of the first group makes us think of Swift, Sterne, and Joyce, but the more somber tone of the second recalls Dostoevsky, Kafka, and the French existentialists. Thus Beckett seems to present two distinct literary mentalities—and consequently his critics have come up with every variety of ingenious solution to the enigmas posed by his work.

His choice of names, for example, has caused considerable speculation. By deflating the importance of names, by attaching tags of anonymity to most of his characters (calling them by such stock Irish surnames as Murphy, Molloy, and Malone), he has helped bring about a startling revolt from the Victorian notion of suggestive and whimsical names. Critics have fondly played with the *M* and *W* which are the initial letters of so many of the characters in the novels; there is little agreement except for the assurance that Beckett's insistent use of the same two consonants is not capricious.

The fascination with objects, what J. Robert Loy in a *PMLA* article has called "things," is another aspect of Beckett which has intrigued his commentators. The famous sixteen "sucking stones" of *Molloy*, the pencil stub in *Malone meurt*, the bicycles and umbrellas which recur everywhere in his work are symptoms of an almost primitive addiction to totemistic practice. Hugh Kenner, for example, calls the Beckett-man-on-a-bicycle a "Cartesian centaur," which gives this new condition of movement special metaphorical properties.

Beckett the "self-translator" has inspired commentaries by some of his most gifted critics, from Hugh Kenner and Ruby Cohn to John Fletcher. They have studied the English and French versions of the novels and plays, determined the reasons for their differences, and characterized Beckett's style in the two languages. Fletcher's succinct statement is worth quoting: "He writes spare, but idiomatic French, with somewhat idiosyncratic punctuation and rhythms that are his own, basically Irish, transposed. His early English is dense, allusive, clever; his later style imitates the spareness of his French, but is unmistakably and beautifully Irish . . ." (*Samuel Beckett's Art,* 1967) .

These are a few of the unusual aspects of Beckett's work which have intrigued his commentators. To explain the "man behind the work," there has been an attempt at biography, some of it quite capricious and unauthorized. Peggy Guggenheim's *Out of This Century* (1946) surrounded Beckett with a cloak of indolence; she referred to him obliquely as Oblomov, after Goncharov's inactive hero. The gossipy tone of these intensely female memoirs could do little to advance Beckett's reputation or help the cause of his future biographers. Peggy Guggenheim repeated much of the same material in her later *Confessions of an Art Addict* (1960) and this time referred to him directly as Samuel Beckett. She repeated verbatim such intriguing statements as, "Ever since his birth, he had retained a terrible memory of life in his mother's womb."

Richard Ellmann, in his *James Joyce* (1959) , built on several interviews with Beckett and was able to document the personal relationship with Joyce (already alluded to by Peggy Guggenheim) . Interviewing Beckett ceased to be a rarity about the time Ellmann published his Joyce biography and Ruby Cohn edited the special issue of *Perspective.* Among the more revealing "biographical" documents are Alan Schneider's "Waiting for Beckett" in the Autumn 1958 *Chelsea Review,* Tom Driver's "Beckett by the Madeleine" in the Summer 1961 *Columbia University Forum,* Gabriel d'Aubarède's "En attendant Beckett" in the 16 February 1961 *Nouvelles Littéraires,* and "The Talk of the Town" item in the 8 August 1964 *New Yorker.*

Book-length studies of Beckett have from the beginning revealed valuable biographical insights. Hugh Kenner explains in the preface to his 1961 study that his book "could not have been written without its subject's assistance" although it is

clearly not "an authorized exposition." Kenner is fond of
throwing in such personal touches as, "on leaving Mr. Beckett's
apartment I became confused in the courtyard, and applying
myself to the wrong door, instead of the street I blundered into
a cul-de-sac which contained two ash cans and a bicycle." John
Fletcher's *The Novels of Samuel Beckett* (1964) profits
immensely from his meetings with Beckett; Fletcher manages
to slip in, quite unobtrusively, the biographical in the midst of
the critical.

If one were to write a history of Beckett criticism, one would
be faced with a vacuum in the thirties and forties. While
Beckett was reviewing three books of fugitive interest—Ezra
Pound's *Make It New*, Giovanni Papini's *Dante Vivo*, and
Sean O'Casey's *Windfalls*, all in the Christmas 1934 *Bookman*
—his own *More Pricks Than Kicks*, published the same year,
was passing practically unnoticed. *Murphy* suffered a similar
neglect when Beckett was busy reviewing a lesser work, Denis
Devlin's *Intercessions*, for the April–May 1938 *Transition*.
There seems to be a certain irony in the fact that as soon as
Beckett gave up book-reviewing and essay-writing outside
interest in his own work began. The "Three Dialogues,"
conversations that Beckett exchanged with Georges Duthuit in
the pages of *Transition Forty-nine* (1949), represents his last
sustained critical effort. Two years later there appeared the
remarkable early piece by Maurice Nadeau, "Samuel Beckett:
l'Humour et le néant," in the August 1951 *Mercure de France*.
Georges Bataille wrote perceptively on *Molloy* in the 15 May
1951 *Critique,* and Bernard Pingaud did an even more
searching review in the September 1951 *Esprit*. Alain
Robbe-Grillet followed less than two years later with his
now-famous study of *En attendant Godot* in the February 1953
Critique. Then American critics, who have since virtually
usurped the field from the French, started to explore the
labyrinthine corners of Beckett's work—and the period of
neglect was at an end. We should not forget the historical

importance also of Niklaus Gessner's Zurich thesis of 1957, devoted entirely to Beckett.

Samuel Beckett was fifty-five and still known principally as the author of *Godot* (despite the efforts of the early French critics and the contributors to the special issue of *Perspective* to alert attention to the novels) when the first book on him appeared. Hugh Kenner's *Samuel Beckett: A Critical Study* relies heavily on impressionistic criticism, forcibly supported by biographical detail gleaned directly from conversations with Beckett. The manner and style of the book seem remarkably in tune with Beckett's own manner and style. Kenner achieves a kind of thematic unity by finding a dual image of "Cartesian clown" and "Cartesian centaur" running through Beckett's *oeuvre*.

Frederick J. Hoffman's *Samuel Beckett: The Language of Self* (1962) uses an approach which combines literary history and criticism, mainly in an effort to place Beckett in congenial surroundings and study the major work in detail. Thus Hoffman derives Beckett from a genealogical line which begins with the nineteenth-century Russians, such as Dostoevsky and Goncharov, and ends with Kafka. The premise of his book is that modern literature has moved from metaphysics to epistemology; his main concern, finally, is to " 'locate' Beckett within the modern history of the self's language." Hoffman's method allows him a close examination of the indispensably relevant Beckett texts, those which profit from "the Russian-to-Kafka metaphors and the Descartes-to-Joyce techniques."

Ruby Cohn's *Samuel Beckett: The Comic Gamut* (1962) resorts to close examination of Beckett's language, themes, and dramatic and fictional techniques. She uses Bergson's categories in *Le Rire* as an organizing device for her material, especially in her discussion of the English-writing phase of Beckett's career (from *Whoroscope* through *Watt*). Ruby Cohn's book is a superior example of the "reader's guide" approach; the author is attempting to conduct the specialist—her study is

clearly not designed for the beginner—through the labyrinth of
Beckett's work. Unlike Hoffman, she is not interested in
placing Beckett in any kind of literary setting; unlike Kenner,
she generally eschews both philosophical and biographical
considerations. Her immediate concern is with the text.

Josephine Jacobsen's and William Mueller's *The Testament
of Samuel Beckett* (1964) is the first of the book-length studies
that is theologically oriented. The authors intelligently proceed
from Beckett's comment in his Proust monograph: "Style is
more a question of vision than of technique"; they tell us: "we
are interested in his craftsmanship primarily as it serves as a
vehicle for his vision, what we have called his 'testament.' " We
are assured that the ideal reader of Beckett must have more
than a passing acquaintance with the Gospels and the Mass.

John Fletcher's *The Novels of Samuel Beckett* (1964) gives
the fiction a systematic close reading. There is a design to each
chapter: a brief biographical sketch of Beckett at the period of
composition of the work in question; a detailed plot summary,
even when the plot is as elusive as it is in the *Textes pour rien*
or *Comment c'est;* a full-scale analysis taking into account
technique, philosophical basis, characterization, and other
critical views either in agreement with or in opposition to his
own theories. *The Novels of Samuel Beckett* has a leisurely,
calmly-paced quality as Fletcher examines the fiction, in strict
chronological order, from the previously unknown, jettisoned
manuscript *Dream of Fair to Middling Women* through
Comment c'est.

Fletcher recently brought out a second book, *Samuel
Beckett's Art* (1967). It contains essays (many of them
previously published) on the poetry, criticism, drama, fictional
background of the novels, sources and influences, and Beckett's
command of French. Fletcher justifies the second book on the
grounds that "so far the content of his [Beckett's] writings has
received rather more attention than it either merits or requires,
to the detriment of the form. Beckett is, indeed, an artist for
whom form and shape are prime considerations. . . ." He

concludes this study with the valuable suggestion that Beckett stands at the end of the Symbolist movement and, in a sense, is composing its "epitaph."

Raymond Federman's *Journey to Chaos: Samuel Beckett's Early Fiction* (1965) begins with a convincing study of *Comment c'est,* based on the assumption that it is "an experiment in willful artistic failure." Federman takes his cue from Beckett's admiring statement about the painter Bram van Velde who was "the first to admit that to be an artist is to fail, as no other dare fail, that failure is his world. . . ." *Comment c'est* is the launching point for a detailed examination of the early prose from *More Pricks Than Kicks* through the French *Les Nouvelles.* Federman is the first Beckett critic who seems intent on defining the writer's fictional aesthetic. He is interested in defining a kind of "rhetoric of fiction" and offers a useful system of opposites to account for the dissolution of reality in favor of "absurdity," of the omniscient author in favor of a staccato first-person who speaks for both author and hero. Readers who have been nurtured on Henry James's prefaces, Percy Lubbock, and Wayne Booth should profit from Federman's approach.

Ludovic Janvier's *Pour Samuel Beckett* (1966) restores considerable sophistication to the study of Beckett in France, a sophistication which was previously noticeable only intermittently in short pieces by Maurice Nadeau, Alain Robbe-Grillet, Jean-Jacques Mayoux, Bernard Pingaud, and Claude Mauriac. Janvier is the first critic writing in French who manages a full-scale study of Beckett worthy of the work of Ruby Cohn, Frederick Hoffman, John Fletcher, and Raymond Federman. He insists in his prefatory note, "C'est hors des catégories et des mauvaises questions qu'il faut, d'abord, lire Beckett." After rejecting most of the conventional readings of Beckett he proceeds on his own. Just as Kenner's book seemed to have the appropriate Beckettian mannerisms so Janvier's staccato rhythm seems precisely right for its subject.

German criticism of Beckett has passed beyond the early essays in *Akzente* and has reached enviable sophistication in the past few years. A trilingual edition of the plays published in Frankfurt in 1964, *Dramatische Dichtungen in drei Sprachen,* may have had something to do with this heightened and increasingly mature interest in Beckett. In the years following its publication, Hugh Kenner's Beckett book appeared in German translation (1965) ; Jean-Jacques Mayoux (a distinguished French critic of Joyce and Beckett) brought out a book in German, *Über Beckett* (1966) ; and Konrad Schoell contributed *Das Theater Samuel Becketts* (1966). In 1967 Ulf Schramm published a fascinating comparative study, *Fiktion und Reflexion: Überlegungen zu Musil und Beckett.* Unfortunately for Beckett enthusiasts most of the book concerns Musil; Beckett is relegated to a sixty-page section at the end. This book lacks the neat tripartite structure of Hugh Kenner's *Flaubert, Joyce and Beckett: The Stoic Comedians* in which Beckett is given equal space with Flaubert and Joyce. Ihab Hassan manages an intriguing rapprochement between Beckett and Henry Miller in his *The Literature of Silence: Henry Miller and Samuel Beckett* (1967). They are both seen as walking the tightrope of anti-literature, touching on "the two major movements of the twentieth century, Surrealism and Existentialism, without yielding to either."

The remaining Beckett studies are "series" books which have built-in limits of space and approach. Nathan Scott's *Samuel Beckett* (Studies in Modern European Literature and Thought, 1965) derives the author from a largely French tradition: Symbolism, Surrealism, and the *Nouveau Roman.* Baudelaire, Rimbaud, and Lautréamont offer Beckett a kind of ideological basis; Breton and Eluard offer "a kind of demiurgic passport to this uncharted and distant region"; Robbe-Grillet and his "school" offer the metaphor, they "stick to zero." Scott's superb brief study has in common with *The Testament of Samuel Beckett* an enlightened theological interpretation, which we often associate with *The Christian Scholar* and which is nurtured on the teachings of Paul Tillich and Reinhold Niebuhr.

William York Tindall, in a forty-eight-page pamphlet (the prescribed length for essays in the series, Columbia Essays on Modern Writers), manages a sensible and balanced appraisal of Beckett—with an orientation toward the fiction, probably shaped by his earlier essay, "Beckett's Bums" (*Critique: Studies in Modern Fiction,* Spring–Summer 1958). Tindall's years spent with Joyce clearly offered him a direction for his 1964 examination of Beckett.

Richard Coe's *Samuel Beckett* (Writers and Critics series, 1964) takes its cue from "Three Dialogues," the conversations exchanged between Georges Duthuit and Beckett. Coe is concerned primarily with two comments which Beckett makes about the painter Bram van Velde: in his work "there is nothing to paint and nothing to paint with"; he is "the first to admit that to be an artist is to fail, as no other dare fail. . . ." (With the second, of course, he comes very close to Raymond Federman, although the emphases of the two books are otherwise very different.)

André Marissel's *Beckett* (Classiques du Vingtième Siècle) is the earliest of the series books (1963) and in fact seems more elementary and introductory than the others; perhaps because it is the first book-length study of Beckett in French (if one excludes the curious monograph of Huguette Delye). Marissel would agree with Nathan Scott that Beckett inhabits a "zone of zero"; he even conjures up Roland Barthes' theory of "le degré zéro de l'écriture" to document his point. He characterizes Beckett's heroes in a most fortunate way: he borrows Claudel's famous description of Rimbaud, "mystique à l'état sauvage." Marissel's short study ends with a very thoughtful chapter, "Pour ou contre Beckett?"

Pierre Mélèse's *Beckett* (1966) appears in a new series, Théâtre de Tous les Temps. It is the "introduction and sampler" kind of thing that the French do so well. There is a lengthy introduction to the man and his work and then an elaborate series of "Textes et Documents," including the inevitable "Samuel Beckett par lui-même," "Témoignages," and "Panorama critique." The volume ends with various charts and a strikingly incomplete bibliography. Jean Onimus's *Beckett* (1968) is still another French series book; it is an addition to the successful Les Écrivains devant Dieu critical library. A prominent Italian series, Civiltà Letteraria del Novecento, has added Renato Oliva's *Samuel Beckett: Prima del silenzio* (1967), and the English Contemporary Playwrights Series, has brought out Ronald Hayman's *Samuel Beckett* (1968).

The most versatile anthology of criticism devoted to Beckett is undoubtedly the volume in the Prentice-Hall series Twentieth Century Views, edited by Martin Esslin. Esslin's introduction is a model of clarity and coherence. The reprinted essays, by Ruby Cohn, Hugh Kenner, Jacqueline Hoefer, Eva Metman, John Fletcher, A. J. Leventhal, Maurice Nadeau, Alain Robbe-Grillet, Jean-Jacques Mayoux, Dieter Wellershoff, Günther Anders, and others, represent some of the best criticism done in the four countries which have taken Beckett most seriously: America, Great Britain, France, and Germany. The approaches are almost as various as literary study allows: the eccentrically Jungian approach of Eva Metman could hardly be more different from the scrupulously documented approaches of Ruby Cohn and John Fletcher. Esslin offers a delightful bonus in reprinting the long-out-of-print "Three Dialogues" from *Transition Forty-nine* (which is obviously a key document in Beckett study).

Beckett's English publisher, Calder and Boyars, brought out a one-hundred-page volume in his honor in 1967: *Beckett at 60: A Festschrift*. The word *festschrift* has come to have academic overtones in recent years because it is usually the name given to a volume of essays honoring a professor who is about to retire from his university post. (Perhaps Beckett's

1966 appointment as an honorary fellow of the Modern
Language Association of America gave his publishers the
notion for the title; in any case, it does carry with it a certain
irony.) The collection is interestingly put together in three
sections: (1) reminiscences, containing short essays by, among
others, A. J. Leventhal (a long-time friend and author of
several fine pieces on Beckett), Maria Jolas (the widow of
Eugene Jolas and with him founder of *Transition*), Jérôme
Lindon (Beckett's French publisher at Les Editions de
Minuit), and John Fletcher (author of two books and many
essays on Beckett); (2) critical examinations, containing essays
by Martin Esslin and Hugh Kenner; (3) tributes, containing
brief eulogies by a variety of distinguished people, mainly
concerned with the theater, such as Harold Pinter,
Arrabal, and Madeleine Renaud. *Beckett at 60: A Festschrift*
seems to carry with it fair warning that we are dealing with the
greatest living writer (as many of us have suspected for some
time) and that his career is by no means over.

We can look ahead now to at least two major events in
Beckett scholarship. One is the annotated bibliography by
Raymond Federman and John Fletcher to be published by the
University of California Press. The other is the long-awaited
study by Lawrence Harvey (the author of a handful of the best
essays on Beckett) to be published by the Princeton University
Press.

The view we have offered of Beckett criticism tends to be
fragmentary and incomplete because an overwhelming amount
has been written in the last fifteen years. The only way we can
achieve any depth is by studying the approaches to a single one
of his works. The history of *Godot* criticism is doubtless the
most fascinating.

Beckett's 1952 play *En attendant Godot* has produced a
heated and sustained colloquy which is still not ended; it is
comparable to the critical dialogue engendered by Eliot's *The
Waste Land* and Hopkins's "The Windhover." The

comparison is especially apt when one realizes how many of Beckett's commentators, beginning with Horace Gregory, have insisted that he is a poet and that his is a "poetry of intensification" (to use the expression of Josephine Jacobsen and William Mueller). *The Waste Land* is probably less to the point because Eliot did supply a set of "program notes" to ease the problems of interpretation. *Godot,* like Hopkins's sonnet, stands rather as a kind of playground of critical controversy, wide open to conflicting and often mutually exclusive readings. Hopkins offered a crucial key to his poem by dedicating it to "Christ Our Lord" but Beckett has maintained his accustomed interpretive silence; the broadest hint he seemed willing to offer was his remark to Alan Schneider (*Chelsea Review,* Autumn 1958), "I am interested in the shape of ideas."

Godot and "The Windhover" will always have a secure place in literary history if only because they were the subjects of the two most active letter-writing campaigns, within recent memory, in the pages of the august London *Times Literary Supplement. La querelle de Godot* started innocently enough with a typically unsigned review, in the 10 February 1956 issue, with a title borrowed from Milton, "They Also Serve." A variety of letters appeared in response to the review between 24 February and 6 April. The letter writers finally started arguing hotly among themselves—for example, the poet and critic William Empson (author of a mild and judicious letter of 30 March) received a seemingly unwarranted reproof from a Mr. John J. O'Meara (6 April) who ended by suggesting, "the New Criticism is just the thing for him [Empson]." This was a harsh reproof for the author of *Seven Types of Ambiguity,* which was at one time one of the bibles of the American New Critics. A certain decorum was restored by the *TLS* editorial of 13 April 1956 ("Puzzling about Godot"); an attempt was made to tread a middle ground and to suggest that the letters printed represented only a small sampling of what at the time seemed an endless correspondence. The *TLS* editorialist ended on a pleasantly conciliatory note: "The extraordinary interest which this play has aroused from so many points of view, and at so many levels, suggests that a healthy hunger for novelty is not so dead in us as we may have feared." It is particularly ironic that this exchange should have been printed in the *TLS* whose "neverfailing toughness and impermeability" were admired by Beckett's Molloy. "Even farts made no impression on it."

Other literary periodicals which have opened their pages to rejoinders have had similar experiences when *Godot* was involved. Bernard Dukore published his "Gogo, Didi, and the Absent Godot" in the February 1962 issue of the new journal *Drama Survey* and was greeted a year later (February 1963) with a lengthy reply by Thomas Markus who felt Mr. Dukore had tied too much of *Godot* "in a neat Freudian parcel." Dukore replied in his own defense in the May 1963 issue; an editor's note at the end of his piece warned readers that no more rejoinders would be published on this subject. *The Kenyon Review* had a similar experience with Ward Hooker's "Irony and Absurdity in the Avant-Garde Theatre" (Summer 1960) when Martin Esslin felt obliged to ride his distinctive hobby-horse in a commentary revealingly entitled "The Absurdity of the Absurd" (Autumn 1960) ; this brief essay offers a convenient "overture" for Esslin's *The Theatre of the Absurd,* published the following year. The always controversial *Village Voice* printed its share of responses to *Godot* pieces by Jerry Tallmer and Norman Mailer.

The above is symptomatic of the failure of critics to reach any kind of agreement about Beckett's play. The commentators on *Godot* have had an unpleasant habit of tripping over one another's toes in their urgency to elucidate the play and to find some of their own problems solved in it. It will be difficult, if not impossible, to classify these critics by linking them to the more fashionable "schools" of literary criticism. The New Critics have never shown much interest in drama and so they have studiously avoided Beckett's play; they have preferred the elaborate cadences of modern poetry to the "silences" of *Godot.* The myth critics have found relatively little in it to their liking. The Chicago Aristotelians and the Freudians have kept their peace. The New Humanists have also kept silent—a silence which they have awkwardly maintained for some time when confronted with any form of the avant-garde. Yet the approaches of some of these "schools" have been used intermittently in the study of *Godot,* but not with the systematic persuasion of one committed blindly to a series of *données* or to a critical method. Occasionally a "professional" will turn up to offer a specialized reading, such as Eva Metman with her Jungian approach in "Reflections on Samuel Beckett's Plays" (*The Journal of Analytical Psychology,* January 1960).

Yet Beckett has maintained the almost uncompromising approval of his fellow writers. Beginning with Jean Anouilh's now-celebrated pronouncement on the first performance of *Godot* in 1953 ("It has the importance of the first Pirandello presented in Paris by Pitoëff in 1923"), the reaction of playwrights has clearly been in Beckett's favor. Tennessee Williams, Thornton Wilder, and William Saroyan were all fervent admirers, as Leonard Pronko has reminded us. Novelists were at least as enthusiastic—perhaps because Beckett had started his career in their midst and brought to his plays certain credentials of the fiction writer. Robbe-Grillet's pioneering essay on *Godot* is still one of the most discerning analyses of Beckett's theater. The novelist Herbert Gold was not only himself completely taken by *Godot* but remarked on the curious effect it had on another American novelist: "Norman Mailer was so stimulated that he wrote a series of columns in *The Village Voice* explaining that it was all about impotence, and when the publishers of the newspaper fired him for his pains, he paid for a full-page advertisement to have one last despairing say on the subject." (*The Nation,* 10 November 1956) Colin Wilson in his *The Strength to Dream: Literature and the Imagination* (1962) spares Beckett the embarrassment of being placed in one of Wilson's neat critical cubbyholes and admits that "there are flashes of a Rabelaisian wit" in Beckett's work. Claude Mauriac welcomes Beckett to the ranks of the *alittérateur* and admires the "silence" and "fascinating poverty" of *Godot.*

Beckett did not reciprocate these gestures of approval. He has said nothing about the work of other writers since his appreciative essay on Joyce in 1929, his monograph on Proust in 1931, and his reviews in *The Bookman, Criterion, Dublin Magazine,* and *Transition* in the 1930s. The "silence" of *Godot* has apparently proved contagious and seems to have silenced Beckett's critical voice. Hence one must be especially impressed by the spontaneity of these responses to *Godot.* Such noteworthy writers as Alain Robbe-Grillet and Claude Mauriac in France, Colin Wilson and William Empson in England, Norman Mailer and Tennessee Williams in America have become fervent *godotistas* (to use Kenneth Tynan's expression).

The majority of *Godot*'s commentators have been concerned with the religious problems suggested by the play, and many have taken refuge behind the fashionable notion of existentialism. Charles McCoy in his *"Waiting for Godot:* A Biblical Appraisal" *(Florida Review,* Spring 1958) urges that we distinguish between "nihilistic existentialism" and Christian existentialism and insists that the latter (from Kierkegaard to Paul Tillich) offers one of the essential keys to Beckett's play. Martin Esslin also leans strongly toward Kierkegaard as a shaping influence on Beckett (see his introduction to the Twentieth Century Views *Samuel Beckett*), yet he insists elsewhere on the Sartrean (nihilistic existentialism) side of *Godot:* "Although Beckett himself is not aware of any such influence, his writings might be described as a literary exposition of Sartre's Existentialism" ("Godot and His Children: The Theatre of Samuel Beckett and Harold Pinter," in William Armstrong, ed., *Experimental Drama,* 1963). Most of the other critics who have acknowledged the existentialist in *Godot* seem to lean toward the Sartrean interpretation. Thus Jacques Guicharnaud remarks that "the Sartrian analysis of the 'others' gives the existentialist theatre its basic drama. The vision of man in *Godot* is similar to it: a perpetual series of rebounds, in which man is constantly thrown back into his solitude" (*Modern French Theatre from Giraudoux to Beckett,* 1961). Frederick Hoffman seems generally in agreement with this position when he speaks of the "existentialist comedy" in *Godot,* "a genre not ordinarily associated with the philosophies of Sartre *et al.,* but in this case indispensably linked" (*Samuel Beckett: The Language of Self,* 1962). Katharine M. Wilson in her letter of 2 March 1956 to the *Times Literary Supplement* is also on the side of Sartre: "*Waiting for Godot* exactly fulfils Sartre's definition of an existentialist play as one which sets out to present the contemporary situation in its full horror so that the audience, finding it unendurable, may feel forced to remedy it." Finally, Robbe-Grillet's insistence on the Sartrean categories of *être-là* and *présence* in *Godot* is essential to his interpretation of the play.

Edith Kern, in her "Drama Stripped for Inaction: Beckett's *Godot,*" somewhat qualifies the existentialism in the play by mentioning that "unlike Sartre, Beckett's characters are never 'en situation.'" She also introduces the word "absurdity" and uses it in much the way that Camus used it in his *Myth of Sisyphus.* Jacobsen and Mueller in their "Samuel Beckett's Long Saturday: To Wait or Not to Wait?" (included in Nathan Scott, ed., *Man in the Modern Theatre,* 1965) begin their treatment of *Godot* by defining the absurd in convincing detail and relating the notion to Beckett's play. They acknowledge a debt to Esslin's *Theatre of the Absurd,* which was the first attempt to link Camus' term to the drama of Beckett, Ionesco, Adamov, Genet, Arrabal, Tardieu, and others.

Esslin accepts the philosophies of Sartre and Camus as being basic to *Godot* but is careful to indicate that the plays of these two dramatists are markedly different from Beckett's play: the difference is in the *form.* The texture of *Waiting for Godot,* with all its dramatic irregularities, mirrors its ideological base, whereas the theater of Sartre and Camus remains formally very staid and traditional. Ruby Cohn has further qualified Esslin's position by positing the presence in *Godot* of "the absurdly Absurd": "In this play form and content, absurdity and Absurdity, are organically interrelated; in this play there is coalescence of the Absurd, being-in-the-world, and the human condition" ("The absurdly Absurd: Avatars of Godot," *Comparative Literature Studies,* 1965).

The critics of *Godot* who have adopted the existentialist or "absurdist" interpretation are raising some of the same questions (in a more literary context) which the "New Theologians" have been fashionably involved in of late. The Bishop of Woolwich's *Honest to God* (1963) brought to the fore a controversy in the church about God's divinity; this book popularized a position already maintained by Dietrich Bonhoeffer, Rudolf Bultmann, Paul Tillich, and others. The secularized "wasteland" of *Godot,* with its theme of futile waiting, offers a convincing metaphor for this revolution in the church. If one reads *Godot* as "la farce du Sans-Dieu" (André Marissel's term) one is in the secularized climate the Bishop of Woolwich spoke about. The change in the "image of God" which *Honest to God* pleaded for is very much in line with a statement made by another of *Godot*'s critics: "Never since the 'Death of God' has man been so close to his god, or shall we say in this case to his idol" (Gabriel Vahanian, "The Empty Cradle," *Theology Today,* January 1957—Vahanian himself is the author of two books on the death-of-God controversy: *The Death of God: The Culture of Our Post-Christian Era* [1961] and *Wait without Idols* [1964]).

Frederick Hoffman differs: "the suggestions of a remote theological being fail to attract the inhabitants of Beckett's world. . . ." When Ruby Cohn (*Samuel Beckett: The Comic Gamut*) says that Beckett "mocks the whole classico-Christian tradition in *Godot,*" we find a more extreme statement of this position. G. E. Wellwarth is more defiantly aggressive: "those who profess to see in Beckett signs of a Christian approach or signs of compassion are simply refusing to see what is there" ("Life in the Void: Samuel Beckett," *The University of Kansas City Review,* October 1961) . Kenneth Hamilton, the author of articles on Beckett in *Queen's Quarterly* and *Dalhousie Review,* has summed up the view of these critics in the title of a recent book—which has nothing to do with Beckett—*God Is Dead.* (A story announced in bold print on the cover of the Summer 1966 *Carleton Miscellany* should also attract some attention: "I Remember the Day God Died Like It Was Yesterday.")

The critics whom Wellwarth accuses of "refusing to see what is there" have perhaps attracted more attention than those I have already discussed. When G. S. Fraser wrote his famous unsigned "They Also Serve," he took the unpopular position of reading *Godot* as a "modern morality play, on permanent Christian themes." Godot, for him, "stands for an anthropomorphic image of God." The symbols of the tree and tattered clothes of the tramps have distinctly Christian relevance for Fraser. He mentions *Godot* in the same breath as *Everyman* and *Pilgrim's Progress.* The interpretation he offers would probably not exclude a work like Hopkins's "The Windhover," which we observed to have much the same critical destiny as *Godot.*

Ronald Gray, in his *"Waiting for Godot:* A Christian Interpretation" (*The Listener,* 24 January 1957) , agrees essentially with the position taken by Fraser. He is among the first to suggest that Godot does indeed come "in the shape of Pozzo (and Lucky) ." Charles McCoy, in his *Florida Review* article, restates the Christian basis of the play, insisting on its biblical aspects. He agrees with Fraser that the tree, which has leaves in the second act, represents the Cross. He somewhat enlarges on Gray's position by asserting: "That for which Gogo and Didi wait does arrive. It is they who miss the appointment." Ward Hooker, in his *Kenyon Review* piece, suggests that "the play is a religious allegory." Heinz Politzer, in "The Egghead Waits for Godot" (*The Christian Scholar,*

March 1959) , thinks of *Godot* as a parable. He also calls it "the anti-mystery play of our time . . . one of the few experimental dramas in which Christ has won out over Oedipus as well as Priapus and Narcissus." Even Martin Esslin (in his essay in the Armstrong collection) , after stating the Sartrean position, comes around to admit "its basically religious quality." Other critics, including Wallace Fowlie *(Dionysus in Paris)* , Allan Lewis *(The Contemporary Theatre)* , and Jerry Tallmer (essays in *The Village Voice)* , arrive at the same position. Jacobsen and Mueller, in *The Testament of Samuel Beckett* (as we have seen above) , reinforce the critical stand of all who give the play a religious or biblical reading: "One might truthfully say that to a reader completely ignorant of the Gospels and the Mass a heavy proportion of Beckett would be totally lost."

The extremes suggested by G. E. Wellwarth and G. S. Fraser are typical of the range of interpretation possible in treating *Godot.* Nothing concerned with the play has aroused more lively and interesting controversy than the source of Beckett's title. Richard Coe has told us that in an earlier version the play was called simply *En attendant.* Martin Esslin makes clear in *The Theatre of the Absurd* that "the subject of the play is not Godot but waiting." Alec Reid echoes this sentiment in his "Beckett and the Drama of Unknowing" *(Drama Survey,* October 1962) . Even though there is general agreement that Godot is of less consequence than "waiting," the curiosity of most critics has led to innumerable conjectures about the source of Godot. Beckett was of little help when he told Alan Schneider in his *Chelsea Review* piece: "If I knew, I would have said so in the play." Robbe-Grillet, following Beckett's cue, asserted in a mild and restrained voice, almost in a prophetic attempt to show up the foolishness of pinning Godot down too concretely: "Godot is that character for whom two tramps are waiting at the edge of a road, and who does not come" *(For a New Novel,* 1965) . Yet the Godot-hunters, ignoring the implicit advice of Beckett and Robbe-Grillet, have remained indefatigable. They have played every variety of word game in their attempt to unravel the mystery that Beckett obviously wished to preserve. Thus Jacobsen and Mueller have seen a portmanteau word formed from the English *God* and the French *eau* (water). Jean-Jacques Mayoux ("Le Théâtre de Samuel Beckett," *Etudes Anglaises,* October–December 1957) reminds us that *Godo* is spoken-Irish for God. Hugh Kenner ingeniously connects the name with his own deservedly famous theory of the "Cartesian centaur" by conjuring up the name of a French racing cyclist whose last name is Godeau; Kenner has Beckett's authority on this interpretation, at least to this extent: "It may calm the skeptical reader to know that my knowledge of this man comes from Mr. Beckett." Edith Kern ("Drama Stripped for Inaction") prefers the French suffix *ot* as qualifying in a diminutive and amusing way the English word *God;* the analogy is always there with Charlot, the Frenchman's fond and somewhat intimate way of referring to Charlie Chaplin. Nathan Scott feels, on the contrary, that the *ot* is "intended to negate *God*" and uses an analogy drawn elsewhere from Beckett's work: Molloy's reference to his mother as "Mag," with the *g* intended as a consonant strong enough to obliterate the concept of motherhood.

So much for the possibilities of the name Godot. The source for the complete title has caused similar unrest. Eric Bentley's suggestion is perhaps the most convincing we have. Harmlessly tucked away in a brilliant review of *Godot* (*The New Republic,* 14 May 1956) is Bentley's reference to Balzac's *Mercadet.* In this almost forgotten play the return of a person named Godeau is anxiously waited for; the frustration of "waiting" is as much a part of *Mercadet* as it is of *Godot.* Martin Esslin heartily applauded Bentley's suggestion and so have a variety of other commentators. Two have analyzed the connection at some length: Harry Butler in *Romance Notes,* Spring 1962; S. A. Rhodes in *The French Review,* January 1963. Rhodes ends his "From Godeau to Godot" revealingly: "The nineteenth century social satire [*Mercadet*] gives place to a twentieth century mystery play [*Godot*]."

Although *Mercadet* has engaged more critical attention than any other source, the case Robert S. Cohen (*Modern Drama,* February 1964) makes for Simone Weil's *Waiting for God* is almost as convincing. Cohen cleverly brings biography and literary history to his aid by pointing out that Beckett and Simone Weil were at the Ecole Normale Supérieure at the same time and might have known each other, and that *Waiting for Godot* appeared a year after the posthumous publication of *Waiting for God*—so an influence by Weil on Beckett is plausible. Cohen joins Heinz Politzer and Günther Anders in calling *Godot* a parable (Anders calls it a "negative parable") and places himself in the camp of Ronald Gray, G. S. Fraser, and Charles McCoy by referring to it as a "religious allegory": "*Waiting for Godot* can then be understood as a religious allegory with the catechism provided by Simone Weil."

Charles McCoy, holding fast to his theory that the Christian existentialists are the shaping influence on *Godot,* has pointed to Paul Tillich's meditation on "Waiting" in *The Shaking of the Foundations* as a possible source. He also mentions a line from Goethe which Martin Buber quotes at the beginning of *I and Thou:* "So, waiting, I have won from you the end: God's presence in each element." Kenneth Tynan (*Curtains*) and G. S. Fraser (*The Modern Writer and His World*) both point to Odets' *Waiting for Lefty.* Fraser even mentions that Odets' name might have obliquely suggested Godot.

There is probably no phase of *Godot* commentary which has amused Beckett quite as much as this. (One can almost hear him pronouncing his favorite expletive, "crritic!" as he responds to these many conflicting suggestions.) I offer my own addition to the imposingly long list, partly tongue-in-cheek, partly with the seriousness with which Bentley proposed *Mercadet* and Robert Cohen proposed *Waiting for God.* Knopf published a strangely haunting book about the Great Depression in 1935, Tom Kromer's *Waiting for Nothing.* The book was virtually forgotten soon after its publication; its problems seemed not to interest the new generation of Americans. The chances are that Beckett did not know the book and that the similarities between it and *Godot* are pure coincidence. Yet the affinities, especially between chapter 11 and Beckett's play, are striking. Here are some of Kromer's remarks: "Where are they going? I do not know. They do not know." "Tomorrow they will huddle around their fires, and the next night, and the next." "We are here. We are here because we have no other place to go." "What is a day to us, or a month or a year? We are not going any place." "I can still walk. That is something." These comments do not have the ontological or metaphysical quality of Beckett's, yet *Godot* seems, quite unwittingly, to have caught something of the ambience of the American depression which Tom Kromer is intent on describing.

The structure of *Godot* is the next concern which has crucially caught the fancy of the critics. Eric Bentley, in his *New Republic* article, has spoken of its being "undramatic but highly theatrical." Bentley somewhat qualifies this view when he remarks later in *The Life of the Drama* (1965) that we should speak of it "not as *un*dramatic, but as a parody of the dramatic." Parody is an apt word in a discussion of Beckett because most of his work represents an elaborate and systematic pastiche of every variety of intellectual exercise—from philosophical systems to vaudeville routines.

Ruby Cohn is preoccupied with structure in her "Waiting Is All" (*Modern Drama,* September 1960) ; she is particularly interested in Beckett's notion of "symmetry to suggest a static design." She skillfully shows how Beckett's dramatic method eventually ends in "the destruction of the very symmetries he has created." (John Fletcher, in *Samuel Beckett's Art,* feels that it is the "asymmetrical structure" of *Godot* "which accounts for much of its power.") Ruby Cohn dismisses the possibility of dividing the play into Aristotle's beginning, middle, and end.

The Aristotelian "unities" have preoccupied a number of *Godot*'s critics. Wallace Fowlie (*Dionysus in Paris*) points out that its "close adherence to the three unities is a clue to the play's dramaturgy." Hugh Kenner mentions that one of the three forerunners of *Godot* is Greek drama (the other two are the Noh drama and *commedia dell'arte*). Allan Lewis, in his *Contemporary Theatre,* insists: "The form of the play is rigorous and classical, observing all unities." Bernard Dort raises a dissenting voice in his short piece in *Les Temps Modernes* (May 1953) ; he feels that the play represents "l'envers d'une pièce classique," with the unities being more apparent than real.

Beckett calls *Godot* a tragicomedy in the English version, yet in the original French is content to refer to it as a "pièce en deux actes." In the most recent book on the subject, Karl S. Guthke's *Modern Tragicomedy* (1966), the author chooses to give *Godot* only passing mention—taking his cue, perhaps, from Beckett's failure in the French to acknowledge the play as tragicomedy. Several close students of Beckett, however, make good use of his suggestion in the English version. Jacobsen and Mueller, in their "Samuel Beckett's Long Saturday," point out the "constant simultaneity of tragedy and comedy" in *Godot*. David Grossvogel in his *Four Playwrights and a Postscript* (1962) speaks of it as being "part tragedy, part comedy. Its barrenness situates the tragedy. . . . The construct makes possible the comedy. . . ." Ruby Cohn (*Samuel Beckett: The Comic Gamut*) connects Beckett's use of the term with Sir Philip Sidney's "mungrell Tragy-comedie" mentioned in his *Defence of Poesie.*

Not much has been said about the modest play-within-a-play in *Godot*. When Gogo and Didi decide, in the midst of a stifling period of boredom, to *do* Pozzo and Lucky, we are not far from the second act of *Henry IV,* part 1, when Prince Hal and Falstaff decide to have a mock colloquy in the courtly manner of King Henry addressing the seemingly wayward Hal, who is heir to the throne. The connection is probably not as far-fetched as it might at first seem if one takes seriously Roy Walker's provocative "Love, Chess and Death" (*Twentieth Century,* December 1958), which establishes every variety of

Shakespearean tie with *Endgame:* it concentrates on *The Tempest* (as does Ruby Cohn in her discussion of *Endgame*) but also suggests parallels with *Richard II* and *Richard III*.

Much attention has been given to the differences between Vladimir and Estragon. The commonplace solution is to make Vladimir the soul and Estragon the body (in good, uncomplicated Cartesian fashion). Ruby Cohn partly rejects this too-easy interpretation in her book and shows that the mental Vladimir (with his hat and bad breath) and the physical Estragon (with his boots and stinking feet) keep their identities fairly separate in the first act but tend to merge, as distinctions blur, in the second act. She points to the increasing "disintegration of the dichotomy" as the play develops. Ruby Cohn's is clearly the best discussion of this subject.

Although critics generally agree on Beckett's curious latter-day saints, Estragon and Vladimir, they are far apart on Pozzo and Lucky. The easiest solution offered for this "couple" is that they represent master and slave. Variations on this suggest the relationship between capital and labor (Colin Wilson, Vivian Mercier, J.-J. Mayoux, Gabriel Vahanian) or wealth and the artist (Wolcott Gibbs). One of the most original—and certainly most pleasantly eccentric— interpretations is Lionel Abel's suggestion (*Metatheatre,* 1963) that Pozzo represents James Joyce and Lucky, Samuel Beckett. Abel finds Lucky's "think" (Richard Coe's noun) to be a parody of Joyce. He extends the interpretation into *Endgame*, finding Joyce in Hamm and Beckett in Clov. Up to this point Abel is an agreeably "lonely wanderer" in *Godot* criticism. Then he enters a familiar terrain by suggesting that Pozzo is Godot (through a circuitous route passing by the Beckett-Joyce relationship).

Vivian Mercier mentioned that Pozzo was Godot, in an early essay, "A Pyrrhonian Eclogue," published in the Winter 1955 *Hudson Review*. He managed to introduce the possibility of a Viconian cycle into the play, "in which history repeats itself every evening." (Vico was, of course, familiar to Beckett from the period of his youthful essay on Joyce's *Work in Progress*, "Dante . . . Bruno. Vico . . Joyce.") C. Chadwick's *"Waiting for Godot:* A Logical Approach" (*Symposium*, Winter 1960) offers seemingly irresistible proof of why Pozzo must be Godot. Chadwick's "logic" usually runs something like this: "Godot is God, Pozzo is Godot, Pozzo is therefore God and since Pozzo is nothing but a tyrant and a slavedriver so too is God." Wylie Sypher convincingly characterizes Pozzo as the Old-Testament God, "the tyrant-divinity," in the first act and the New-Testament God, "injured, crucified, helpless," in the second act (*Loss of the Self in Modern Literature and Art*, 1962).

On the other extreme from this is Walter Strauss who, in his "Dante's Belacqua and Beckett's Tramps" (*Comparative Literature*, Summer 1959), calls Pozzo "a kind of anti-Godot." Frederick Lumley (*Trends in Twentieth Century Drama*) and Robbe-Grillet are also thoroughly convinced that Pozzo cannot possibly be Godot; Robbe-Grillet, for example, speaks of "this Pozzo, who is precisely *not* Godot."

Norman Mailer (*Advertisements for Myself*, 1959), who has rather crankily insisted that *Godot* is all about impotence, feels that Lucky holds the key to the play—especially in his long monologue. He is convinced that Vladimir and Estragon have destroyed their chances of finding Godot because "they have abused the link which is Lucky." He even suggests the possibility that Lucky himself may be Godot. Charles McCoy comes close to this position: "Pozzo's menial, Lucky, in some ways suggests the biblical figure of the Christ."

These are some of the concerns which have occupied *Godot*'s critics. Although the play has not captured the fancy of any of the more committed "schools" of literary criticism, there has been the occasional essay directed toward a specialized approach. Thus Bernard Dukore's "Gogo, Didi, and the Absent Godot" uses Freudian terminology, whereas Eva Metman's "Reflections on Samuel Beckett's Plays" falls back on Jungian categories. The myth critics would find Robert

Champigny's "Interprétation de *En attendant Godot*" (*PMLA*, June 1960) sympathetic to their position. The Marxist critics would enjoy the remarks of the various commentators who found the Pozzo-Lucky relationship a struggle between capital and labor, yet in the end they would have to dismiss the play because it is uncompromisingly *hors de situation*. The Bergsonian critics—who feel the urgency of explaining literature in terms of "human" and "psychological" time— should be delighted with Ross Chambers' "Beckett's Brinkmanship" (*AUMLA: Journal of the Australasian Language and Literature Association*, May 1963) .

Ruby Cohn has recently rendered the *godotistas* a valuable service by bringing together a fine selection of new *Godot* criticism in the December 1966 *Modern Drama* and by editing *Casebook on "Waiting for Godot"* for Grove Press (1967) . The casebook reprints the early, often unprepared responses to Beckett's 1952 play as well as a selection of the later mature critical writing; it also contains two new essays.

The graffiti observed in a New York City subway station by the *Village Voice* correspondent expresses the feeling of a play-going generation which has had too much of a good thing: "Godot, Go Home." Although I cannot seriously agree with the late John Gassner's sentiment, I should like still to quote it: "To my mind *Waiting for Godot* is a touching and beautiful little play that has been blown up beyond all sensible proportions by our recently fashionable obsession with works that invite explication. To a *parvenu* intelligentsia it would seem that a work of art exists not for its own sake but only for the possibilities of interpreting it" (*Theatre at the Crossroads*, 1960) .

MELVIN J. FRIEDMAN

POSTSCRIPT. The announcement was made after this book went to press that Samuel Beckett was awarded the 1969 Nobel Prize in literature, accompanied by the strangely worded citation: "for his writing, which—in new forms for the novel and drama—in the destitution of modern man acquires its elevation." Beckett has suddenly been besieged on all sides by the rhetoric which has become an inevitable part of the award. I can only wonder at his response to the concluding remark made by Karl Ragnar Gierow, secretary of the Swedish Academy, in a radio commentary on the subject: "From that position, in the realms of annihilation, the writing of Samuel Beckett rises like a miserere from all mankind, its muffled minor key sounding liberation to the oppressed and comfort to those in need." Beckett has always honored Paul Verlaine's wise suggestion "prends l'éloquence et tords-lui son cou!" He has worked toward a spareness and accentless prose—realized superbly in *Comment c'est*. He is among those who agree with Norman O. Brown that silence is the "mother tongue." There is an irony, then, in his being honored with such an embarrassing flourish of rhetoric.

But the intentions of the Swedish Academy are honorable. Many mistakes have been made since the first Nobel literary award was made in 1901; the choice of Beckett is clearly not one of them. The surprise is that the award has been so long in coming to the only writer who belongs genuinely to both Irish and French literature.

M. J. F.
November 1969

The Elusive Ego: Beckett's M's

Frederick J. Hoffman

Beckett's *Murphy* (1938) begins in a world of "the nothing new" (1). It is in many respects a record of very old, traditional issues, and of ancient means of solving them. It is also a comic novel, in the tradition of the buffoon of pathos, striving for an adjustment to a situation that is beyond his powers of tolerance but within the range of his rationalizing intellect. The resolution is *in intellectu;* it is also in terms of a homemade, improvisational mysticism. Like all other Beckett characters, Murphy has reasons for doing what he does, and these reasons are persuasive and engaging.

The "nothing new" of his world argues a rock-bottom situation. Murphy's needs are elemental, though not instinctively felt. He is discovered, in London, in "a medium-sized cage of north-western aspect commanding an unbroken view of medium-sized cages of south-eastern aspect" (1). There is, in short, no view at all; the physical aspect is dreary indeed, boxed in and geometric and impoverished. However, Murphy is not like the characters of Beckett's later novels. He commands both an inner and an outer prospect, and he is able clearly to differentiate between them. The inner world is not merely a "retreat" from the outer. Nor does he remove to it simply for reasons of timidity, but from a firm conviction of its self-evident superiority.

When his rather less than beloved Celia first discovers him, Murphy is lying face down on the floor of his "cage," his rocking chair—to which he is bound by scarves—on top of him. "Losing no time in idle speculation Celia undid the scarves and

Frederick J. Hoffman, now deceased, was Distinguished Professor of English at the University of Wisconsin, Milwaukee.

prised the chair off him with all possible speed. Part by part he subsided, as the bonds that held him fell away, until he lay fully prostrate in the crucified position, heaving." (28)

In this variant of the pratfall, Murphy's imperfections are initially seen. He is, after all, a fallible human, a prisoner of his body, which is in turn a prisoner in its "cage." The comic paradox is simply this: that Murphy seeks repose according to a fixed set of principled determinations. They are both philosophical and literary: a homespun Cartesian rationale, a faith in the Antepurgatory of Belacqua. These are not mutually exclusive but complementary. In neither does Murphy speculate upon the existence of a supreme being. He is not interested in God; for whereas God has been assumed in the Cartesian universe, He is out of Murphy's reach, and he must therefore improvise his own extensions of self beyond mortal limits.

One may speculate upon Murphy's antecedents: in Dostoevsky's underground, Goncharov's Oblomov, Joyce's Leopold Bloom. The line of descent is there, but Murphy is uniquely a Beckett hero whose literary heritage is indifferently small. He is a reductive agent who brings both theological and metaphysical issues down to the simple devices of body, using matter to escape both. He argues indispensably the separation of body and mind. In stressing mind, Murphy hopes to overcome expected limitations of body. Interrupting his attempt to communicate with infinity, Celia has brought him a large black envelope which contains his *schema universalis,* his "thema Coelis" compiled by Ramaswami Krishnaswami Narayanaswami Suk. This proves a guide both to a specific finitude and to its link with infinity, to which Murphy is peculiarly and individually heir. (32–33)

The principles of Murphy's life are inordinately simple. They are sensed by him, exposited by others. Both Neary and Wylie, compatriots in Dublin, explain the "Doctrine of the Limit." It argues, to begin with, a clear dualism: Matter extended simply compounds itself and inflames the appetite for extension; the "quantum of wantum" (57) compounds, is invariable, is self-destructive. But the proportions remain fixed. " 'Humanity is a well with two buckets,' said Wylie, 'one going down to be filled, the other coming up to be emptied' " (58). The escape is through impelling the mind, through forcing a way into its infinite extension. Murphy doubts the veritable meaning of infinity and will settle for a measurement that is at least comparable to it in provoking the imagination. The rocking chair, the scarves that bind, the absolute or nearly absolute repose, the rhythm of swaying back and forth, the dim light fading into darkness are all means of moving from matter to the clear spaces of mind. Suffusing all are the nuances of shadow and darkness which represent the transition from corporeality to transcendence. "There was not much light, the room devoured it, but [Celia] kept her face turned to what there was. The small single window condensed its changes, as half-closed eyes see the finer values of tones, so that it was never quiet in the room, but brightening and darkening in a slow ample flicker that went on all day, brightening against the darkening that was its end. A peristalsis of light, worming its way into the dark" (66).

Celia has other plans for Murphy. She is ambitious for him, wants him to be "respectable." She is his link to "blooming buzzing confusion" (29). But while Murphy goes out into it, on his perfunctory job-hunting, she is herself seduced by the ritual of the rocking chair. It is, after all, a symbol superior to the Market, "where the frenzied justification of life as an end to means threw light on Murphy's prediction, that livelihood would destroy one or two or all three of his life's goods" (67). Despite everything, she began to understand his purposes, while he—in search of a specious respectability—simply testified to the error of hers: "He had not the right gem to ensure success, indeed he had no gem of any kind" (75).

Instead, Murphy's ambitions are limited to Belacqua's "post-mortem situation." Not confident of his powers of circumventing mortality, Murphy chooses the rocking chair and Belacqua's shelf in Antepurgatory. He visualizes the "embryonal repose" of Dante's friend,

> looking down at dawn across the reeds to the trembling of the austral sea and the sun obliquing to the north as it rose, immune from expiation until he should have dreamed it all through again, with the downright dreaming of an infant, from the spermarium to the crematorium. He thought so highly of this post-mortem situation, its advantages were present in such detail to his mind, that he actually hoped he might live to be old. Then he would have a long time lying there dreaming, watching the dayspring run through its zodiac, before the toil up hill to Paradise. [78]

There is something curiously untheological in this adaptation of Dante's vision. Murphy has reduced the role of God and His religion to a condition beyond himself; they are integers in a larger calculus, but he would prefer a metaphor which describes a means of postponing their responsibility. That God will manifest Himself to Murphy is a definite prospect, but He has no record of intervening in quotidian meditations. Murphy's status is an anticipation of that enjoyed by subsequent Beckett heroes. They are at once engaged in puzzling over the resources of the body for continuance and for resisting decay, in meditation over available notions of creativity, in prolonging existence in the very act of defining it. Murphy's Belacqua fancy is, therefore, an early speculation over the problem of "waiting for Godot."

There is no denying that Murphy is a "religious man," but this phrase must be understood in the Beckett lexicon. He is religious, as was Joyce's Bloom, in being intensely and nervously interested in last things—above all, in seeking the repose that must come to all men with the resolution of human ambivalences and grotesqueries. But he is religious within limits; one feels that secularism is closing in on him and that rational persuasions concerning transcendence are a long way toward deterioration. This "seedy solipsist" (82) maneuvers his way through the intricacies of an ordinary life, minutely calculating his petty advantages and taking minuscule risks to gain time and remain upright (or, better, right side up). He has the clown's appearance and his view of metaphysics; he counts the specks of dust in the beam of light he has tried to sweep into a dustpan.

Murphy's chief opportunity is given him through lucky chance. He is hired on a temporary basis in the Magdalen Mental Mercyseat, a haven for distraught egos. It is the ultimate refuge from the blooming buzz; Suk had warned him to "Avoid exhaustion by speech," because he had been blessed with "Intense Love nature prominent, rarely suspicioning the Nasty, with inclinations to Purity" (32). The contrast of sanity and lunacy is implied; Murphy goes his own way in defining each, and the inhabitants of the M.M.M. are, almost all of them, "sane" if the word means anything at all. Beckett's descriptions of lunacy follow a time-honored habit: The "bright spirits" are inside, having withdrawn to the inside from the chaos outside. Those who are not in are either sadist exploiters of those who are or spirits trying to resolve the antinomies of the outside.

Within the M.M.M., imperfect as they seem, are the resources for quiet meditation. Beckett, aware that Murphy's new position will encourage speculation, pauses in chapter 6 to describe his mind, or rather his mind as "it felt and pictured itself to be." It seemed to him "a large hollow sphere, hermetically closed to the universe without." It was not therefore deprived, but rather enjoyed the advantage of dualistic immunity. "Nothing ever had been, was or would be in the universe outside it but was already present as virtual, or actual, or virtual rising into actual, or actual falling into virtual, in the universe inside it" (107). Dualism therefore encouraged warm inner meditation, immune from the "blooming buzzing confusion," since "the mental experience was cut off from the physical experience, its criteria were not those of the physical experience, the agreement of part of its content with physical fact did not confer worth on that part" (108).

The splitting of body from mind has its own pathos, but it is also an inestimable advantage. The very frailty of the body encouraged experiments in transcendence. Although there was intercourse between body and mind, Murphy did not find it a matter of supreme concern: "He neither thought a kick because he felt one nor felt a kick because he thought one." There was perhaps "a non-mental non-physical Kick from all eternity, simply revealed to Murphy in its correlated modes of consciousness and extension, the kick *in intellectu* and the kick *in re*. But where then was the supreme Caress?" He was not much disturbed about the possibility of "supernatural determination," but devoted his efforts to exploiting the advantages of the dualism. This task involved underrating the body and setting up its physical circumstances as nearly ideally suited to meditation, protecting the mind from the risk of its suffering the "vicissitudes of the body" (109).

Pursuing this aim, Murphy finds himself again and again in need of physical rest—a surcease of movement—so that the threat to the mind is not actualized. Murphy's aging may therefore be described as a gradual achievement of relief from the troubles of matter in motion. The progress toward quiescence is described in terms of three zones: light, half-light, dark. In the first there are forms with parallels in matter; a basic curiosity in Beckett's men has to do with the physical bodies, illuminated in more or less intensity, which occupy spaces, or "the elements of physical experience available for a new arrangement" (111). In the half-light are "the forms without parallels." Here the light recedes, leaving the gray which is Beckett's dominant color. To move away from the light that defines objects, into the dusk that neutralizes them, is to enter an area of twilight pleasure, "the Belacqua bliss and others scarcely less precise." These are pleasures in unextended being—that is, without spatial location and arrangement.

They are what Murphy seeks in his rocking chair, but they are
transitional to the third, the condition of "non-Newtonian
motion": no objects, no space, but "a flux of forms, a perpetual
coming together and falling asunder of forms" (112).

Taking these three conditions in order, one may say that the
first involves the risk of body (corruption, growing weakness,
the move toward death) ; the second is a state of obscurity but
relaxation from danger; the third is an absolute condition, in
which the responsibilities of body are totally surrendered, and
an absolute freedom reigns of unobstructed forms. The
rocking-chair rhythms are transitional; the scarves fix his
body, so that it will not irrelevantly move. Above all, these
speculations require warmth. Murphy refuses to help his friend
Ticklepenny unless he will be given heat. Considerable
ingenuity is required before a gas-jet in the W.C. can be used to
bring warmth to Murphy's garret. Within it and the wards of
M.M.M., the heat and the forms (of the mind) assault their
inhabitants.

The wards themselves have a suggestive design: they hint
weakly of sacrifice and the metaphors of theology, but they
bespeak principally of bodily deterioration, the rags and
abscesses of a deficient humanity: "The wards consisted of two
long corridors, intersecting to form a T, or more correctly a
decapitated potence, the three extremities developed into
spacious crutch-heads, which were the reading-, writing- and
recreation-rooms or 'wrecks,' known to the wittier ministers of
mercy as the sublimatoria" (166).

One needs to observe that, in all of this semicomic history,
there is also a deep pathos. Beckett is giving us in this early
novel a prior view of his disinherited and disenchanted world.
The comedy is in appearances, but the appearances are
themselves pathetic because they assume the lowest common
denominator of dignity and human resources. The great
majority of the patients "preferred simply to hang about doing
nothing" (166). This "nothing" is one of the three forms of

negation in Beckett's work: it is the "nothing new" to which
Murphy awakens in the beginning; it is the nothing in which
Vladimir and Estragon exist in *Waiting for Godot,* trying to fill
it or to "occupy" it, by any means at their disposal; but it is also
the void to which the defective Cartesian mind aspires, the
semidarkness of Belacqua's waiting, the total darkness of
Murphy's free forms.

The comedian-victim of the M.M.M. is in basic rapport with
Murphy. Not only does he not mind being their male nurse; he
enjoys the task. He shares their fears of the "nothing new"; but
each of them, like him, has sought the merciful, stasis refuge
from the "blooming buzzing confusion." Murphy's fate is to be
destroyed by an accident which occurs to the mechanism of the
Cartesian W.C. The gas-jet, formerly used to light the way to a
universal sewer, now linked by a series of wires and chains to
Murphy's radiator, falls apart, and Murphy is translated
entirely from this world to the next, his bodily substance
turned to ashes, which are in turn accidentally distributed over
the floor of a London pub (275).

So endeth Murphy, always suspicious of the capacities of
physical substance to sustain the mind, now entirely lost in the
detritus of space. In his life he had diligently avoided the
confused inadequacies of the world, but he was at last to fall
victim to a "mechanical mistake" and his ashes let loose
because of human error. The novel admirably points to
archetypal subheroics. The Beckett man is engaged restlessly in
an undiminished effort to define himself; the physical odds
against him increase as the energy of his effort grows. He is a
prisoner of the rusting cage of his body, the dispiriting
"underground" of his habitation. He does not defy reason but
gingerly though unavailingly uses it. He ends in something less
and more than disaster. The suspicion is that what he is
striving to define is "nothing," and that what he is "waiting
for" is annihilation. But he can't go on, he must go on, he will
go on, and at the same time puzzles over the meaning of can't,
must, and will.

Watt (written in 1944, but not published until 1953) is an epistemological farce. What Murphy tries to accomplish by rhythms and stillness, Watt seeks through talk. His peculiar rationality is a stuck-needle Cartesianism, in which the possibilities of language and reason are exploited nervously and feverishly. As Jacqueline Hoefer has described it, "His mind appears to be a kind of untiring logic-machine which dutifully reshuffles into seemingly endless logical combinations the scanty facts of physical experience which Watt's senses supply." [1]

Further, the mystery of Beckett's naming is given an interesting nudge. Watt is clearly a pun on What, as the master he appears to serve is Knott, a Joycean fusion of itself with Not; so that the Watt-Knott of the novel is at the center of its speculation, with Watt offering the processes of inquiry and Knott the ambiguous nonanswer. Knott also occasionally seems to suggest the evasive confusion of Kafka's *The Castle*. He leaves unanswered the questions of his existence and the manner in which he should or might be served. Does he "not" exist, or is the matter of his existence a "knotty" mystery? But Knott is after all in part the product of Watt's rationality; in trying to define himself, Watt "creates" Knott, so that he may serve him and in serving him justify himself. *Ex nihilo nil.* The substance of Knott is nothing if not contained in Watt's mind.

Speculation concerning Beckett's namings is a fatal temptation. The *W* of Watt's name is an inverted *M;* we leave the *M* of Murphy's Magdalen Mental Mercyseat (where he occupies a "chair," in which he is finally discovered dead) , to encounter the *W* of Watt. Subsequently, we encounter Molloy, Moran, Malone, and other minor creations (Mahood, Macmann, etc.) ; but Malone's name is itself one of two words, in the only title of Beckett's novels that has two substantial words: *Malone meurt.* The *eur* sound joins the *ur* of Murphy, or approximately; the *or* of Moran is the sound of

1. "Watt," *Perspective* 11 (Autumn 1959) : 167.

the noun *mort* to which *meurt* belongs as verb. The *n* sound of
Knott is like the double *n* of *The Unnamable*. In this
last-named novel, the Unnamable, who is either each of all the
others or the creator of all of them, or no-name, thinks of his
final "creation" as Worm. And in *Worm* all of the implications
in the other names are contained: the *or* of Mort, the *W* of
Watt, the *m* (which is here the last letter of a word that
represents the full span from *womb* to *tomb*, or from
spermarium to *crematorium*) . If the Unnamable is the creator
of all these, he is also linked to Knott, *ex nihilo nil*, or the
"god-given godhead" of what Joyce calls this "farraginous
chronicle."

These echoes and conjunctions suggest a dispossessed Adam,
or an *homme isolé* who is responsible for his own creations, yet
ultimately puzzled and confused by them. An atmosphere of
uncertainty (Beckett's "absolute absence of Absolutes")
dominates the scene. Each of Beckett's characters improvises
existences (his own, God's, the world's) as he goes on; he must
improvise as well his relationships to these improvisations. As
the Unnamable begins by saying, "Where now? Who now?
When now? . . . Keep going, going on, call that going, call that
on" (3) .

But these elaborations are scarcely all evident in *Watt*.
Beckett's hero is here engaged in an intense though limited
meditation. It involves the statement of all possible rational
combinations and possibilities and the selection of none. As
Christine Brooke-Rose has so ably put it, the "weird almost
mathematical style in *Watt* [is] a style with a slightly legal
flavour, a style based on permutations of possibilities. For not
only does any one action have numerous explanations, but
metaphysically speaking there are also numerous other possible
actions which, though not actualized by us in any one instance,
exist nevertheless in a timeless mind." [2] Above all, *Watt* is a
testimony of language, a comedy of *je parle*. The physical

2. "Samuel Beckett and the Anti-Novel," *London Magazine* 5 (December
1958) : 41–42.

setting is not nearly so elaborate as that of *Murphy;* nor is there any of the melodrama that heightens the earlier book. Later in his career, Beckett was to write *Act without Words,* I and II; here he gives us, almost, a words-without-acts equivalent.

Watt is on the edge of being the caricature comedian. His smile makes a doubtful impression: "To many it seemed a simple sucking of the teeth" (25) . He had an elaborately precise and deliberate walk, a "funambulistic stagger" (31) .

Watt's way of advancing due east, for example, was to turn his bust as far as possible towards the north and at the same time to fling out his right leg as far as possible towards the south, and then to turn his bust as far as possible towards the south and at the same time to fling out his left leg as far as possible towards the north, and then again to turn his bust as far as possible towards the north and to fling out his right leg as far as possible towards the south, and then again to turn his bust as far as possible towards the south and to fling out his left leg as far as possible towards the north, and so on, over and over again, many many times, until he reached his destination, and could sit down. [30]

This is the mechanical action of the clownish tightrope walker, or of the comedian who plays a drunk trying to describe the sober straight line. Unaccountably, Lady McCann, perhaps exasperated by the twisting, jerky motion, throws a stone which lands on Watt's hat and then falls to the ground—a providential escape, for Watt has a poor-healing skin. But he takes no notice of the aggression and walks on as though it has not happened (32) . This reaction, like others, is typical of Watt's denial of what happens outside his mind. He is adamantly fixed within the habits of his mind, and his actions and deliberations are a testimony to a diligent self-possession. When he arrives at his destination, he feels the joy of all-in-one-piece identity:

When in a word he will be in his midst at last, after so many tedious years spent clinging to the perimeter. These first impressions, so hardly won, are undoubtedly delicious. What a feeling of security! They are transports that few are spared, nature is so exceedingly accommodating, on the one hand, and man, on the other. . . . He removes his hat without misgiving, he unbuttons his coat and sits down, proffered all pure and open to the long joys of being himself, like a basin to a vomit. [41]

Watt tries to match his words to the physical confusion about him, exploring his world in detail, "millions of little things moving all together out of their old place, into a new one nearby, and furtively, as though it was forbidden" (43). In truth, Watt's actions are a mechanical repetition of "the whole bloody" quotidian business (47). "The ordinary person eats a meal, then rests from eating for a space, then eats again, then rests again, then eats again, then rests again, then eats again, then rests again, then eats again, then rests again, and in this way, now eating, now resting from eating, he deals with the difficult problem of hunger, and indeed I think I may add thirst, to the best of his ability and according to his state of fortune" (52).

This set of acts is a design of humdrum, which is matched by a torrent of talk and debate, the question shredding the reality into minute parts, dividing and classifying trivial combinations of practical and rational possibility. Watt moves funambulistically, in his mind as in his body: he queries identity in the act of practicing it. The deliberate application of his mind to the most trivial problems leads to the larger question of self as a composite of trivialities that in turn leads to the still larger question of God, or Watt is Knott. In so moving toward the definition of the ultimate certainty, Watt offers an ingenious view of rational creativity: "For the only way one can speak of nothing is to speak of it as though it were something, just as the only way one can speak of God is to speak of him as though he were a man, which to be sure he was, in a sense, for a time, and as the only way one can speak of man, even our anthropologists have realised that, is to speak of him as though he were a termite" (77).

In the service of Knott, Watt speculates upon the Watt-ness of Knott's pots; the true nature of potness escapes him, and "it was just this hairbreadth departure from the nature of a true pot that so excruciated Watt" (81). And his need of "semantic succour" was at times so great "that he would set to trying names on things, and on himself, almost as a woman hats" (83). For Watt's struggle is with the knowledge of phenomena, and of its flow of succession and repetition: "for the coming is in the shadow of the going and the going is in the shadow of the coming, that is the annoying part about it" (57).

The net effect of Watt's deliberations is that of a circle in search of its center; he thinks himself as center, but is not sure, so that the process is an endless enclosing of circles moving about centers. As Miss Hoefer has said in her *Perspective* article, "A circle seems to be the right symbol for Watt's world, for it so forcefully asserts a limit—solipsistic, self-contained, and inescapable" (176). He observes reality, but only to deny it as existing except in terms of his "system," which consists of a succession of prattle: "Je parle sans cesse; donc je suis, peut-être." So, in considering the picture in Erskine's room, he thinks it to represent "a circle and its centre in search of each other, or a circle and its centre in search of a centre and a circle respectively" (129).

In some respects, this is a parody of the pretentious rhetoric and delusive logic of conventional philosophical thinking, using words and concepts as a clown uses balls or the circles of a bicycle. Watt's deliberate rhetoric, as his name, is as much a comic inversion of conventional talk as is the speech of Lucky (*Waiting for Godot*) or the stock-in-trade of Ionesco's plays. There is an important difference, however. Watt is in earnest; his rigmarole is an honest attempt to define the wattness of things as he can both apprehend them and participate in them. He goes all the way, to become involved in an elaborate consideration, first of the reality of things, then of the reality of the words he uses to define their possibilities, finally of their source and cause.

Beckett has claimed that his best work, all that he values, was written between 1945 and 1950.[3] This would exclude *Murphy*

3. Ruby Cohn, "Preliminary Observations," *Perspective* 11 (Autumn 1959): 123.

and *Watt* but include the trilogy of novels, three *nouvelles,* and the *Texts for Nothing.* He underestimates the value of his first two novels, as comic creations and as anticipations of major concerns in the trilogy. There are some conspicuous changes: The trilogy is directly narrated by its characters (the "I" becomes extraordinarily complex as the certainty of self-definition diminishes) ; they are less involved in the rudiments and more concerned over ultimate questions of being; in being less clearly and overtly characterized, they are more complex and their feverish search for precision is a more powerful and moving engagement.

Here too, for the first time, the full weight of the question of responsibility comes into play. The "I's" of the trilogy are a fluctuant mass of self, moving and fading and reemerging as specific selves, diminishing and enforcing their strengths, as the strength of declamation and the power of doubt struggle for dominance. Although *Murphy* and *Watt* are parodies of epistemological issues, the trilogy is directly involved with the question of being, creation, extension, corporeality, and with the several languages of assertion and doubt.

Throughout, the "I's" of the trilogy alternate in the roles of creator and created. They take on themselves the full responsibilities of birth, movement, persistence in space, and decline. *Molloy* presents the problem of creation in its vital statement. Both its titular hero and Moran go on "quest journeys," in search of each other, with these objectives: to find their causes, to unite as aspects of the same self. There is a typical Beckettian doubt concerning precise place, *status quo* and *terminus ad quem.* The characters also diminish, become less and less self-certain, gradually lose their wholeness of being, as they proceed toward each other. Both are creators, as each imagines or projects himself into relationships with others; both are also "machines" or "men-using-machines," the "Cartesian centaurs" of which Hugh Kenner speaks. The bicycle, the crutch, the stick, become spatial adjuncts of the body; the mind projects as the body diminishes. As are the other members of the trilogy, *Molloy* is a drama of cognition and creation, as opposed to the traditional representation of characters involved in plot. This change, as we have seen, had a long history before Beckett applied his special talents to it: Joyce's Bloom (and particularly Bloom-Stephen of the Circe episode) and his Earwicker ("Here Comes Everybody," "Haveth Childers Everywhere"), Proust's Marcel. Modern literature is abundantly supplied with instances of the epistemological quest.

Whereas *Murphy* and *Watt* may be considered Beckett's final exercises in shedding the Joycean influence, *Molloy* is pure and primary Beckett. The opening pages resort to elementary questions of origin and cause. "I began at the beginning" in "my mother's room," and the first question has to do with the biological versus the creative source of being. Beyond that, there is the question of going on, that "rumour rising at birth and even earlier, What shall I do? . . . And to follow?" Molloy speculates about another being, who is identified in part 2 as Moran, searching for and merging with Molloy. He peers through the haze of a dimly seen Antepurgatory, at "Belacqua, or Sordello, I forget." The mother is after all a trivial cause; Molloy seeks a father or a self's self. "But in spite of my soul's leap out to him, at the end of its elastic, I saw him only darkly, because of the dark and then because of the terrain, in the folds of which he disappeared from time to time, to re-emerge further on, but most of all I think because of other things calling me and towards which too one after the other my soul was straining, wildly" (13).

This passage may almost be taken for Beckett's primary text: the creature straining to see and to define his creator, at the same time straining toward "others," who are either creators or creatures; the mélange of relationships undecided and ill-defined; and at the heart of the quest the "I," who is, at least for a definable moment a person (that is, a possible soul with a physical parallel in material substance). Beyond this there is

the confusion of times, of "several different occasions," so that
the relationships are not even spatially secure: "And perhaps it
was A one day at one place, then C another at another, then a
third the rock and I, and so on for the other components, the
cows, the sky, the sea, the mountains" (17).

These are major concerns because Molloy was not "caused"
in birth, or cannot believe he was. His mother had had him
when she was very young, so that they are now both old crones,
"sexless, unrelated" (21). His relationship with her is comical,
indifferent: "I know she did all she could not to have me"
(23), and she'd jostled him during the prenatal months and
thus "spoiled the only endurable, just endurable, period of my
enormous history" (23). But he rejects the mother not because
he resents her but because his is an epistemological not a
biological question; the matter of the "spermarium" is, after
all, simple and minor. The fact is that she had not succeeded in
getting him unstuck and he was therefore destined for "less
compassionate sewers" (23). Setting aside the womb as cause,
Molloy turns to the less obvious and more bewildering issue of
creation as artifact as opposed to accident. The fact is that he
does exist, that he does have a body; the issue is not that, but
has to do with self-definition, a question of the imaginative
extension of matter in and through and beyond space.

Something of Watt adheres in Molloy. He speculates upon
possibilities; he imposes language upon them. But, unlike
Watt, he comes back to the fact of Molloy lying in the ditch,
eating grass. As his physical members deteriorate (they do in
all Beckett heroes, noticeably and painfully), Molloy turns to
"machines." The crutch is an extension of the leg, or a
substitute leg; and the motion crutches give the man becomes a
"rapture," a "series of little flights, skimming the ground. You
take off, you land, through the thronging sound in wind and
limb, who have to fasten one foot to the ground before they
dare lift up the other." (86) Motion begets motion; the paths
described by the crutches go beyond definable places and
immensely expand Molloy's world. But he is not sure if he

carries himself or the world carries him (88) . In any case, his
powers of this kind are bound to diminish, for they depend
upon a corruptible body, whose members will diminish and
may disappear altogether. Death is a condition Molloy finds it
hard to accept, "a condition I have never been able to conceive
to my satisfaction" (91) .

He has recourse to both Murphy's and Watt's devices for
circumventing it: trying first, in a sea voyage, to transcend
bodily limits; then, in an obsessive rational concern over the
relationship of pebbles to pockets, to force existence into a
language and logic of trivial choices: "And sitting on the shore,
before the sea, the sixteen stones spread out before my eyes, I
gazed at them in anger and perplexity" (95) . But the stones
are themselves forms, and their disposition in his pockets is a
challenging symmetry. Molloy would think ideally of "sixteen
pockets, symmetrically disposed, each one with its stone. . . .
This would have freed me from all anxiety, not only within
each cycle taken separately, but also for the sum of all cycles,
though they went on forever. . . . And it was above all
inelegant in this, to my mind, that the uneven distribution was
painful to me, bodily" (99) .

This question of symmetry, balance, and "elegance" is of the
essence in Molloy's development. As a body he is not
distinguished; in relation to his mother he bores himself and
she him; beyond these are the questions of his having been
more substantially created, by himself or some other, or that
some other and he have mutually obliged. If this last, then the
qualities of the mind become the saving grace, and the matter
of cycles, choices, languages, decisions, is preeminent.

Above all in Molloy's journey, there is the question of
physical pain. He disintegrates before our eyes, having at first a
bicycle which magnificently extends his power of motion; then,
crutches, whose assistance in motion temporarily give him an
exhilarating, almost a metaphysical strength. But they too
depend on relatively sound members, or at least members of
which they may be accessories. When they are gone, they leave

the agony and monotony of painful crawling, like a secular, a reduced, motion along the stations of the cross. "But I am human, I fancy, and my progress suffered, from this state of affairs, and from the slow and painful progress it had always been, whatever may have been said to the contrary, was changed, saving your presence, to a veritable calvary, with no limit to its stations and no hope of crucifixion" (105) .

Pain is an inheritance of the body, and cannot be explained away, and was not by Descartes. For Molloy, the two kinds of pain are the "monotonous" and the "variable," and both of these (though the second is the more "heroic") lead to skepticism, most of all to the fear that God does not exist, or that if He does the fact is of little consequence, or that in any case He "will not come." The strategy of life reduces itself to a "going on" and a "waiting"; and Beckett moves further and further from a justification of the worth of either. Molloy convinces himself that he must go on, though he cannot say why. "But it is forbidden to give up and even to stop an instant. So I wait, jogging along, for the bell to say, Molloy, one last effort, it's the end. That's how I reason, with the help of images little suited to my situation. And I can't shake off the feeling, I don't know why, that the day will come for me to say what is left of all I had" (110) .

Both Molloy and Moran begin in a state of comparative soundness (they both bear testimony to existence) , then proceed toward self-disintegration, as they move toward each other and toward mutual identity. Edith Kern speaks of Moran as the creator of both Watt and Murphy, though Molloy is "a part of him," not just a creature but inseparably identified with Moran.[4] They are not "separate phases" of a greater creation, but bear the same burdens and suffer the same painful deterioration of body and spirit. If a difference may be cited, it is that Moran is more conspicuously the creative imaginer, the

4. "Moran-Molloy: The Hero as Author," *Perspective* 11 (Autumn 1959) : 185.

"fabulous artificer," Molloy more given to meeting emergencies by improvisation.

Jacques Moran begins in full and arbitrary command of his faculties. This is simply to say that he is more confident of the rational life than he should be and is subsequently punished by declining further than Molloy because he has a longer way to go. "I had a methodical mind and never set out on a mission without prolonged reflection as to the best way of setting out. It was the first problem to solve, at the outset of each enquiry" (134). This firmness has in it nevertheless the seed of doubt, and Moran's confidence is "beset by enemies" that are in themselves products of his imagination. The rationalist mind, of which Moran is one of Beckett's more interesting specimens, suppresses doubts, or ignores their causes, but they remain nevertheless and return to haunt and damage him.

He begins in the full Cartesian confidence, subsides, finds that he can pierce "the outer turmoil's veil"; going out, "I drown in the spray of phenomena" (151). But his real crisis is Molloy, as pain was Descartes'. In a sense Moran is a symbolic compensation for Descartes' errors of omission. He applies "principles" to the question of Molloy and his pain: there are five Molloys, he says, the fifth "that out of Youdi"; the other four are "He that inhabited me, my caricature of same, Gaber's and the man of flesh and blood somewhere awaiting me" (157). That is, there are five creative acts whose products are Molloy; each of the creators is part of a scheme of creation, at least at first responsibly initiated by Moran. But this is to substitute rationalization for reality: "how far [were] these five Molloys . . . constant and how far subject to variation" (158).

Moran is both creator and creature, artist and experiencing object, assailant and victim. He is, above all, as human creature, subject to the same physical deterioration as Molloy. When he lies ill in the wood, his leg paining him, he suffers exactly the same diminution of powers. He experiences visions of an "intruder" self, which at once is Molloy and "vaguely resembled my own" (206).

When he returns to his home, in pain and barely able to move at all, the metamorphosis is complete. "Certain questions of a theological nature preoccupied me strangely. As for example. . . . 4. How much longer are we to hang about waiting for the antechrist? . . . 7. Does nature observe the sabbath? . . . 13. What was God doing with himself before the creation? 14. Might not the beatific vision become a source of boredom, in the long run? . . . 16. What if the mass for the dead were read over the living?" (228–29).

The notes, from which the above questions are taken, are a parody set of principles, directed against the rational order of statements and answers to questions found in Descartes. In the end, all has become doubt. Moran, on crutches now, is on the way to becoming Moran-Molloy: "My knee is no better. It is no worse either. I have crutches now. I shall go faster, all will go faster. There will be happy days. I shall learn" (240). *Molloy* ends in ambiguities, as it began in them: "Then I went back into the house and wrote, It is midnight. The rain is beating on the windows. It was not midnight. It was not raining" (241).

As *Molloy* ends in suffering, pain, and doubt, *Malone Dies* opens in the expectation of death: "I shall soon be quite dead at last in spite of all. . . . I could die to-day, if I wished, merely by making a little effort, if I could wish, if I could make an effort. But it is just as well to let myself die, quietly, without rushing things" (1). Malone is ostensibly an expression of Dostoevsky's underground man, but he is a passive figure, not in any way in rebellion against the world or using himself to flout the realms of conventional sense or reason. Nor is he Kafka's spirit brooding over legalistic intricacies of his moral obligation or in the self-hateful condition of Gregor Samsa. Malone simply "lies dying"; "I shall die tepid, without enthusiasm," he says (1).

As such a man, Malone moves out from the first novel of the trilogy, an extension of the predicaments of Molloy-Moran. The trilogy is, quite simply and superficially stated, a portrayal of the loss of self. It begins with the impact of pain (and loss of

members) upon self-confidence; it proceeds to explore the
mind of a moribund; it ends upon the question of the total loss
of name and of naming, of being and creativity. It ends very
much as *Endgame* ends, were it considered a sequel of *Waiting
for Godot*.

The matter of dying in Beckett's work is basically a question
of self-inventory: Who is it that is dying? How may he identify
himself if he is to die? How may he die "significantly"? In
Malone's case, it is a matter of properties, of things with which
he, as a dying being, can be identified, if it is to be known that
it is he who has died and dying that has occurred to him. First
in the inventory is the room in which he has been left to die, "a
plain private room apparently, in what appears to be a plain
ordinary house" (5) . There are no mirrors, no Lisas or Sonias
to remind him of a commiserating Christ, no one to explore his
conscience with him or in spite of him. We have only a body
lying on a bed, a stick, a pencil, some paper; there is a sense of a
consciousness diminishing, but in this case, "the loss of
consciousness for me was never any great loss" (6) .

Malone suffers the customary Beckettian deprivation and has
recourse to the usual contrivances for struggling against it.
Since he has neither bicycle nor crutch, nor could use them if
he had, he cannot assert himself spatially. Aside from the very
useful stick and the indispensable pencil, he is reduced to
elementals: "What matters is to eat and excrete. Dish and pot,
dish and pot, these are the poles" (7) . Even so, he anticipates
the time when even these sustaining functions will cease:
"There is virtually nothing [my body] can do" (8) .

He has recourse to the mind. The mind always remains, in
Beckett's world, long after the body has ceased being
endurable. He will write his memoirs, create a succession of
beings to whom he can attach himself and thus be in a sense
responsible for an existence. The experiment is engaging but it
has its low moments: "What tedium," he says after an
especially uninspiring exercise (12) . Further, the creation
which is the memoir and the fact which is his moribund present
self are not always convincingly the same; the exercises in

recreation are interspersed by moments of isolation, "the old dark gathering, the solitude preparing, by which I know myself" (12) . "But I know what darkness is, it accumulates, thickens, then suddenly bursts and drowns everything" (13) . Even the act of creation is uncertain; the words "slip, slide, . . . perish"; they "run riot in my head, pursuing, flying, clashing, merging, endlessly" (22) .

Actually, the fact of existence is only palliated by the imagination. Malone has frequently to come back to elementary functions and sounds: pains that "seem new to me," the feel and sound of sucking. These impressions are all parodic versions of the *cogito:* I suck, therefore I am, and so forth; "The search for myself is ended" (23) . But it is more than a deterioration of the *res cogitans,* because unconsciousness threatens and when it occurs epistemological questions will vanish: "I was time, I devoured the world. Not now, any more. A man changes. As he gets on" (26) . In the end the only formula left will be *Malone meurt.* The process of dying itself has its generalizing effects: his life had been full of a buzzing of sounds, a spray of phenomena. Age generalizes them, into "one vast continuous buzzing. The volume of sound perceived remained no doubt the same, I had simply lost the faculty of decomposing it" (32) .

Meanwhile the other Malone egos are drawn out of his mind: Saposcat, Lambert the pig butcher, others. But they do not cohere and in any case the words he uses to define them produce "mortal tedium" (43) . He returns to this room and this place: perhaps it is, after all, already a tomb, "and this space which I take to be the street in reality no more than a wide trench or ditch with other vaults opening upon it." The question of his present state is prompted by the tedium of the memoirs and by the suspicion that this basement is after all a tomb, with "tiers of basements one on top of another" (45) .

But this decline of confidence alternates with moments of revival. Malone is sure there are other people in this house, and that life is going on. But is any of this real? It is just as likely that "in reality all that is perhaps nothing but my worms"

(45). For example, the room has no real light or color, except "in so far as this kind of grey incandescence may be called a color." He himself, he says, "emit[s] grey." (46–47) If his worst doubts are realized, he and his pencil are really engaged in a Poe-esque dialogue, an act in cerements and not a ceremony. In any case, the pencil has diminished so that it is now almost useless; very soon there won't be enough of it to hold (48).

These speculations lead naturally to the doubt that he had in fact been born. However he may answer that question, "I shall go on doing as I have always done, not knowing what it is I do, nor who I am, nor where I am, nor if I am" (52). Beyond the tedium, the doubt, the painful sense of moribundity, there is that resolve (it dominates, as an "affirmative note," Beckett's stories and plays) ; but it must constantly be renewed and checked. Its natural ally is the figure of Macmann, third creature-surrogate of Malone. Macmann, while he stands in the same relationship to Malone as the others, is an assertion beyond being merely an invention. Like Malone in aging, he is nevertheless alive and standing straight, and in love with another creature, Moll, a "little old woman, immoderately ill-favoured of both face and body" (85). She wears for earrings two long ivory crucifixes, which "swayed wildly at the least movement of her head" (86). They are the thieves; "Christ is in my mouth," a "long yellow canine bared to the roots and carved, with the drill probably, to represent the celebrated sacrifice" (93). Christ as creator has been reduced to occupying a cave, an opening, an orifice, from which life or its blasphemous facsimile emerges or should emerge. Molly Bloom also associates love with crucifixes; and Molly will sometime become Moll, one-toothed and offering love *in extremis*.

> *To the lifelong promised land*
> *Of the nearest cemetery*
> *With his Sucky hand in hand*
> *Love it is at last leads Hairy.* [92]

Both Moll and Macmann are, nevertheless, last-breath exercises of Malone's imagination. The boredom and the exhaustion its efforts create will now lead to last gasps: "To be dead, before her, on her, with her, and turn, dead on dead, about poor mankind, and never have to die any more, from among the living" (93) . Yet, he urges, "Try and go on" (107) . And he does, until spasms of dying and fitful creation alternate in his last moments.

> never there he will never
>
> never anything
>
> there
>
> any more [120]

Malone dies, without a comma or a period to spare. His creative energy has sputtered and died; the pencil is gone, the stick lost, and he is himself no more than expendable and corrupt body. In its alternation of creative and dying gasps, *Malone Dies* is paradigmatic of the "absolute absence of Absolutes" in Beckett's work. His struggle to find and then to maintain identity is limited from the beginning to the possibilities of a desperately inquiring mind and the diminishing potencies of a dying animal.

The trilogy appropriately concludes with a book called *The Unnamable.* "Unquestioning. I, say I. Unbelieving" (3) . *The Unnamable* is the extreme form of the "un-novel"; facts established in paragraph one of the traditional novel are here still in doubt at the end. Vivian Mercier has said concerning this question, "The Unnamable's interior monologue may go on to infinity, for all we know. If it were to, we might describe this novel as a curve having one of its axes as an asymptote. In other words, as y (the length of the novel) approached infinity, x (the content of the novel) would approach nearer and nearer to zero. Content zero, length infinity—these are the mathematical limits of the novel." [5]

5. "The Mathematical Limit," *Nation* 188 (14 February 1959) : 145.

Together with this provocative idea of the anti-novel's extension to an infinity of noncontent, there is the fact of the babble itself; it is like the meaningful nonsense of the talking clown, and it bears a philosophical resemblance to the silent-picture antics of Buster Keaton, occasionally of Charlie Chaplin. Hugh Kenner speaks of it as "an anxious audible dumb-show . . . immaculate solipsism compelled to talk, talk, talk, and fertile in despairing explanations for its own garrulity." [6] In this sense, *The Unnamable* is a lineal descendant of *Watt,* as an epistemological comedy. The gravely serious import of it, however, lies in the belief that—assuming nothing else to be certain—to talk is the only guarantee of identity. The talk is itself loaded with the contradictions which a rudderless self-assertion promotes. In *The Unnamable* the self reaches, not its logical conclusion, but as Kenner says, "the centre of the solitary world" (22).

The determination of Molloy to "go on" at all costs, Malone's decision to persist, Moran's pushing his inquiry beyond the conventional setting in which he begins—these are all contained and negated (they exist in a shell of their opposites) in the Unnamable's spew of meditation. The questions are real enough, and terribly important: Who am I, how do I relate to other objects, and do these objects exist outside me or are they a product of my mind, if I have a mind, if I am I? They are not answered; negation almost catches up to assertion in this final novel. "The thing to avoid, I don't know why, is the spirit of System."

The Unnamable cannot be placed or defined. He is any and all of Beckett's *M*'s and *W*'s, and the negation of any and all of them. For example, Malone "passes before me at doubtless regular intervals, unless it is I who pass before him." But perhaps it is Molloy, who is wearing Malone's hat? (5). But could Molloy be here, without my knowledge? (6).

Then, as to the Where am I? This place: what is it and how

6. "The Beckett Landscape," *Spectrum* 2 (Winter 1958) : 9.

big is it? "I like to think I occupy the centre, but nothing is less certain" (8) . The basic figure of Beckett's work is the circle, or fraction thereof. Watt speculates upon a painting as depicting the circle in search of its center; Gogo and Didi of *Waiting for Godot* describe circles, with hats, words, repetitions of scenes; Molloy, with crutches and oars; the single actor of *Act without Words* I moves ever toward and away from a circle of light, which continues to deceive him until he refuses to allow it; Krapp circles back again and again to a certain point in his "last tape." The Unnamable is preoccupied with circles, almost to the exclusion of all else. "In a sense I would be better off at the circumference, since my eyes are always fixed in the same direction. But I am certainly not at the circumference" (8–9) . Perhaps the most provocative circular motion in Beckett's fiction is that described by Mahood's crutches, which make irregular loops around the earth. "And my course is not helicoidal, I got that wrong too, but a succession of irregular loops, now sharp and short as in the waltz, now of a parabolic sweep that embraces entire boglands, now between the two, somewhere or other, and invariably unpredictable in direction, that is to say determined by the panic of the moment" (54) .

But Mahood is no longer capable of such movement, but only of rest, sitting within a jar outside a third-rate chophouse, cared for by its mistress, who comes once a week to move him and clean his residence. "Stuck like a sheaf of flowers in a deep jar, its neck flush with my mouth, on the side of a quiet street near the shambles, I am at rest at last" (55) . Even in a state of rest, Mahood is a congeries of spheres, placed neatly in still another; his head, "covered with pustules and bluebottles," alone emerges from the jar; the rest of him, without thighs, legs, or feet (which have apparently just gangrened or rusted off) is an irregular loop within another (56) . Within this roly-poly there exists a mind which is similarly spheroidically or spirally preoccupied with the questions and negations that are the novel's substance.

But then, the Unnamable is not strictly Mahood, nor is he

any of the others; negation follows quickly on the heels of creation. His final naming is to be of Worm: "It will be my name too, when the time comes" (69). But he should like some evidence that he has existed, before he becomes Worm, "such as a kick in the arse, for example, or a kiss, the nature of the attention is of little importance, provided I cannot be suspected of being its author" (77). The desire is in the line—the last of the line—of the desires in Beckett's heroes to be recognized; one is reminded of Murphy's disquisition on the eternal Kick and the absence of the eternal Caress, though even a Kick from the great unknown is evidence of existence. But the Unnamable has succumbed to the "blooming buzzing confusion," the "spray of phenomena," and cannot discriminate among them, or himself from them.

In these terms, he can only spell out the rudiments of creation: "One alone, then others. One alone turned towards the all-impotent, all-nescient, that haunts him, then others" (82). Is he the "one alone"? Has he created the others? It comes down to the absolute necessity for dying as an end-term of being born and living: If this is *not* a process of which you can be aware as participant and observer in one, "the thing stays where it is, nothing changes, within it, outside it, apparently, apparently" (116). The great scandal is not having any identity, and the Unnamable ends in a frenzy of disgust over this failure: "To have no identity, it's a scandal, I assure you, look at this photograph, what, you see nothing, true for you, no matter, here, look at this death's-head, you'll see, you'll be all right, it won't last long, here, look, here's the record, insults to policemen, indecent exposure, sins against holy ghost . . ." (125–26).

This and the passage that follows are an elaborate parody of official patterns of self-identification, of naming and numbering. The Unnamable, in not being able to answer any of the questions, testifies to his own anonymity and to the falsehoods of official procedure (rather like scenes in Kafka's *The Trial* and Ionesco's *The Killer*). The badges of identification, like the cunning of the Heideggerian "they" in Nathalie Sarraute's novels, are a cover for a vast anonymity and nondescriptness. What "they" want him to be isn't enough: "I must understand, I'm doing my best, I can't understand" (138). Strangely, but perhaps more surely than is at first apparent, the Unnamable concludes in an hysteria of can't and must and will. "I can't go on in any case. But I must go on. So I'll go on. Air, air, I'll seek air, air in time, the air of time, and in space, in my head, that's how I'll go on" (148).

The rhythms of contradiction and suasion continue to the end, which is not an end but a continuation, a process whose echoes ring in time and space. If he had some task, say to fill two vessels, or maybe four or a hundred, "to be emptied, the uneven to be filled, . . . in a certain way, a certain order." This is the "meaningful gesture," to correspond to the act of Emmett Kelly and his dustpan. There is the fable of the man "coming and going among his casks, trying to stop his hand from trembling, dropping his thimble, listening to it bouncing and rolling on the floor, scraping round for it with his foot, going down on his knees, going down on his belly, crawling" and so on: the man depending on the thimble which is himself or at least the act of himself (156).

The novel and the trilogy end in that kind of ambiguous resolve, the comic-pathetic insistence on being as against the unbeing of E. E. Cummings's "mostarians." "Where I am, I don't know, I'll never know, in the silence you don't know, you must go on, I can't go on, I'll go on" (179).

These hesitations, ambiguities, irresolutions are the mess and mixture of existence and identity with which the trilogy closes. With the exception of *Endgame,* where even the suggestion of them is rare indeed, and *Texts for Nothing,* where almost everything but the voices has disappeared, the theme continues in the rest of Beckett's work. They are skillfully and brilliantly dramatized as the acts of "waiting" in his most famous play.

Robbe-Grillet as a Critic of Samuel Beckett

Bruce Morrissette

Two critical articles by Robbe-Grillet allow us to measure both the development of a coherent view of Samuel Beckett's theater and the evolution of certain literary theories for which Robbe-Grillet found illustrations and supporting evidence in Beckett, as well as other implications running somewhat contrary to Robbe-Grilletian principles.

The first text appeared in *Critique* of February 1953, entitled "Samuel Beckett, auteur dramatique." The second article, which remained unpublished in French for a number of years, was written in 1957, published in Italian translation by Renato Barilli in *Una via per il romanzo futuro* in 1961, and finally included in *Pour un nouveau roman* (1963) under the title "Samuel Beckett, ou la présence sur la scène." This second essay, which contains a modified version of the first, with additions and cuts, appears in the Richard Howard translation, *For a New Novel* (1965),[1] as "Samuel Beckett, or Presence on the Stage." Robbe-Grillet introduced into the earlier piece, based chiefly on a discussion of *Waiting for Godot,* an important idea missing from the original version and added to it a close study of *Endgame.* The final text emphasizes the continuity of certain basic aspects of Beckett's work, in which the critic finds important parallels for his own

Bruce Morrissette is Professor of French Literature and Chairman of the Department of Romance Languages and Literatures at the University of Chicago.

1. All quotations in English from the 1957 version of Robbe-Grillet's text are from *For a New Novel,* trans. Richard Howard (New York: Grove Press, 1965), pp. 111–25. Since that essay is so brief, individual page numbers will not be indicated. Translations of the 1953 text, in that year's February issue of *Critique,* are my own.

theories and brings out the appearance of a certain
signification or meaning which Robbe-Grillet would reject as
dangerous. These various ideas are typical of Robbe-Grillet's
assertions in the numerous literary manifestos which have
bolstered his role as the chief spokesman for the so-called, and
sometimes self-styled, school of the New Novel in France.

What interpretation of Beckett does Robbe-Grillet offer in
1953, and what new contributions to the study of Beckett's
literary doctrines, viewed as complementary to his own, does
Robbe-Grillet make in 1957? A mixture of commentary and
quotation will best serve to show the evolution of
Robbe-Grillet's ideas on Beckett, and to demonstrate the
metaphysical implications that may be drawn, according to a
famous statement of Sartre, from any literary technique.

The piece "Samuel Beckett, auteur dramatique" of 1953
begins with a succinct, almost laconic summary of *Waiting for
Godot*. The little action contained in the play is presented in
schematic form. One small change occurs in this résumé in the
1957 text. In the 1953 account of act 1, Robbe-Grillet does not
mention the first appearance of the little boy, but he refers
back to it later: "A young boy, *who had already come in at the
end of the first act,* comes back bringing the same message . . ."
(my italics). In the 1957 text, however, we find inserted in the
account of act 1:

And no one is surprised when a young boy arrives (Didi,
moreover, thinks he has already seen him the day before) bringing
this message: "Mr. Godot won't come this evening but surely
tomorrow."

This insertion, obviously, not only reinforces the idea of cycles
and perpetual recurrences in the play, but also permits the
author to avoid the awkwardness of the belated reference to
this event and to write at that point instead, "The same little
boy returns, bearing the same message. . . ."

After emphasizing the extraordinarily potent attraction of
this play "made out of nothingness," but which "holds

together, without an empty space," Robbe-Grillet in 1953
devoted to the stage performance itself a number of
observations that he eliminated later in the 1957 study. He
commented on the modest, almost minute size of Roger Blin's
theater, the current changes in intellectual and critical climate
(which made of this play, which would have caused a scandal
in the Parisian theater of twenty years earlier, "the most banal,
the least audacious expression imaginable" of human misery) ,
the parallel success of Ionesco's early plays, and the like. Along
with these passages, Robbe-Grillet omits in 1957 the last
paragraphs of the first essay, which deal sarcastically with
several radio performances of *Waiting for Godot* as well as
other projects threatening to degrade the play. Obviously, by
1957 most of the controversial aspects of Beckett had subsided,
and the author could now turn his attention exclusively to the
analysis of the work under discussion, in a search for literary
affiliations.

The remaining portions of the 1953 piece remain valid in
1957 and continue to fit Robbe-Grillet's conception of Beckett's
work. In the new study he again itemizes and discards as
accessory the various critical interpretations current then, as
now, among the critics: the root-word *God* concealed in *Godot,*
Godot as the "earthly ideal of a better social order," Pozzo as
the dictator or the exploiter "who keeps thought enslaved,"
Godot as Death or as Silence, and Godot as "that inaccessible
self" that Beckett pursues in all his works. After this inventory
of rejected views, Robbe-Grillet develops what remains: the
"less than nothing," the "regression beyond nothing," whose
stages are identified. "What little had been given to us from the
start—and which seemed to be nothing—is soon corrupted
before our eyes, degraded further, like Pozzo who returns
deprived of sight, dragged on by Lucky deprived of speech."
In this general disintegration, the climax occurs when the four
characters, having all fallen to the ground upon each other,
create a formless mass from which Didi's voice emerges, saying
"We are men!"

Nothing, continues Robbe-Grillet, escapes the destructive force of this *regression:* neither speech—torn to pieces in the burlesque rhetoric of Pozzo's monologue on the twilight—nor thought, which is undermined and destroyed by a whole series of paralogical and absurd reasonings (parallels which Robbe-Grillet recognizes in Lewis Carroll and Alfred Jarry) as well as by such passages as the "explanations" given by Didi when Gogo asks why Lucky does not put down his suitcases, or the great monologue of Lucky "thinking"—where logic not only mocks itself, but proves in addition that the only "honest logic" that can be applied nowadays to serious problems merely succeeds in causing a still further regression of that feeble if not ridiculous support of contemporary man, his *thinking* intelligence.

In repeating so much of his original essay of 1953, Robbe-Grillet obviously wished, in retouching the style and varying somewhat the order of presentation of ideas, to inject into the earlier development one important idea, not named in 1953, of which he had recently, in 1957, become the spokesman, and which he desired to illustrate on the basis of the older text. This idea was the existentialist conception of the *être-là* or thereness that Robbe-Grillet calls *presence*. This idea, inherited directly from Sartre (especially from the key passages of *Nausea* concerned with the café *banquette* and the chestnut-tree root), and previously associated almost exclusively with *objects,* is extended by Robbe-Grillet first to include *gestures* (thus rendering them, in Roland Barthes' term, "objectal"), then to include *characters* themselves.

One can retrace the origin and development of this idea of thereness or presence in other writings of Robbe-Grillet. Only six months after the appearance of the first Beckett article, Robbe-Grillet issued a study of Joë Bosquet describing surrealist attempts to capture the *"être-là des objets"* or thereness of *things* through new techniques of writing and the use of a new *language* (see *Critique,* October 1953). Later, following the "Quarrel of *Le Voyeur"* (thus promoted by the

Editions de Minuit in a brochure of that title in 1955) ,
Robbe-Grillet brought out a series of articles in *L'Express*
entitled "Literature Today," which, together with an
important review of Nathalie Sarraute's *Age of Suspicion* and
his first full-scale literary manifesto, "A Future for Fiction,"
expressed a coherent literary doctrine then termed "Realism of
Presence." [2]

This "new realism" is to emerge principally from what
Robbe-Grillet calls "the essential factor that will determine the
new *reality* of the world: things will henceforth be
characterized by their *presence,* or what may be termed their
power, and their method, of *being there.*" And after things
come gestures and characters themselves: not only "gestures
and objects will be *there,*" but also "the future hero . . . will be
there," indifferent to all the "multiple possible interpretations"
that criticism may devise. In the case of Nathalie Sarraute, the
chief fault in her idea of "subconversation" is its failure to
recognize and admit the "solid presence" of *words* themselves,
when uttered.

To bring in and apply this idea of *presence* to the early study
of Beckett, Robbe-Grillet first composed a new first page to
precede his remarks on *Waiting for Godot,* wherein he
announced and defined the theme. He then proceeded to insert
the term and idea by means of references worked into the old
text to reinforce the notion, ending with a new concluding
portion which in turn served to link the first essay, thus revised,
to the new section on *Endgame* which completes his
demonstration of the *thereness* or presence of Beckett's world
and its characters implied by his new title, "Samuel Beckett, or
Presence on the Stage." The newly-written beginning reads as
follows:

2. From the title, "Un Réalisme de la présence," of one of the articles
in the series, "La Littérature d'aujourd'hui," *L'Express* (October 1955–
February 1956) . The review of *L'Ere du soupçon* appeared in *Critique*
(August–September 1956) ; the manifesto, "Une Voie pour le roman fu-
tur," appeared in the *Nouvelle Revue Française* (July 1956) .

The human condition, Heidegger says, is *to be there*. Probably it is the theater, more than any other mode of representing reality, which reproduces this situation most naturally. The dramatic character *is on stage,* that is his primary quality: he is *there*.

Samuel Beckett's encounter with this requirement afforded a priori, an exceptional interest: at last we would see Beckett's man, we would see *Man*. For the novelist, by carrying his explorations ever farther, managed only to reduce more on every page our possibilities of apprehending him.

Murphy, Molloy, Malone, Mahood, Worm—the hero of Beckett's narratives deteriorates from book to book, and faster and faster. Feeble, but still capable of traveling on a bicycle, he rapidly loses the use of his limbs, one after the other; no longer able even to drag himself along, he then finds himself imprisoned in a room, in which his senses gradually abandon him. The room, shrinking, is soon reduced to a simple jar in which a rotting and obviously mute trunk ultimately falls apart altogether. At the end there remains no more than this: "the shape of an egg and the consistency of glue." But this shape and this consistency are themselves immediately denied by one absurd sartorial detail: the character wears garters, which is especially impossible for an egg. We are therefore once again put on our guard: man—man is not yet *that*.

Thus all these creatures which have paraded past us served only to deceive us; they occupied the sentences of the novel in place of the ineffable being who still refuses to appear there, the man incapable of recuperating his own existence, the one who never manages to be present.

But now we are in the theater. And the curtain goes up. . . .

The various reinforcements of the theme of presence inserted into the revised text that follows this new beginning are designed to bring out aspects of *Godot* already mentioned in 1953, but whose earlier commentary seemed to require further development in line with the new concept. For example, where the author had first written simply, "From beginning to end, the audience *follows;* it may lose countenance sometimes, but it is *affected*," he now deepens his original idea by leading into the new principle of presence: "it may lose countenance sometimes, but remains somehow compelled by these two beings, who do nothing, who say virtually nothing, who have no other quality than to be present." In a similar vein, here is a new remark cut into the old text:

As for Gogo and Didi, they refuse even more stubbornly any other signification than the most banal, the most immediate one: they are men. And their situation is summed up in this simple observation, beyond which it does not seem possible to advance: they are *there*, they are on the stage.

Finally, in a new concluding section to his study of *Godot*, Robbe-Grillet summarized the "metaphysics of presence" that he found in the play, relating it then to that other basic existentialist notion, *freedom*, freedom which extends to everything *except* the possibility of escaping from presence itself. Note again that Robbe-Grillet applies this idea not only, as with Sartre, to things, but also to dramatic characters and their actions, to the "personage on the stage." For the dramatic character is found, normally, in a situation where conventions of stage acting usually prevent us from believing in true presence, since everything on the stage is by definition a game of artificial illusions, a *trompe-l'oeil* of roles already memorized and rehearsed. The power of Beckett's theater comes through especially in its seeming to escape from this artificial determinism of the conventional stage, in its appearance before us as an "open" or completely *free* theater. All the "accessories of the play," writes Robbe-Grillet, may well deteriorate, may be reduced to less than nothing,

But the two tramps remain intact, unchanged. Hence we are certain, this time, that they are not mere marionettes whose role is confined to concealing the absence of the protagonist. It is not this Godot they are supposed to be waiting for *who has "to be,"* but they, Didi and Gogo.
We grasp at once, as we watch them, this major function of theatrical representation: to show of what the fact of *being there* consists. For it is this, precisely, which we had not yet seen on a stage, or in any case which we had not seen so clearly, with so few concessions. The dramatic character, in most cases, merely *plays a role*, like the people around us who evade their own existence. In

Beckett's play, on the contrary, everything happens as if the two tramps were on stage *without having a role.*

They *are there;* they must explain themselves. But they do not seem to have a text prepared beforehand and scrupulously learned by heart, to support them. They must invent. They are free.

Of course, this freedom is without any use: just as they have nothing to recite, they have nothing to *invent* either; and their conversation, which no plot sustains, is reduced to ridiculous fragments: stock responses, puns, more or less abortive phony arguments. They try a little bit of everything, at random. The only thing they are not free to do is to leave, to cease *being there:* they must remain because they are waiting for Godot. They are there in the first act, from the beginning to the end, and when the curtain falls it does so, despite the announcement of their departure, on two men who continue waiting. They are still there in the second act, which brings nothing new; and again, despite the announcement of their departure, they remain on stage when the curtain falls. They will still be there the next day, the day after that, and so on . . . *tomorrow and tomorrow and tomorrow . . . from day to day . . .* alone on stage, standing there, futile, without past or future, irremediably present.

From this we see that Beckett's first play constituted for Robbe-Grillet the perfect demonstration of that opaque, stubborn, persistent presence which the new literary personage or character assumes in confronting his predecessors, such as they are found in novels of psychological analysis, the theater of ideas, and in all "explanatory" literature.

Armed with this binary system of explication of Beckett's works, Robbe-Grillet will now apply the two principles of regression and presence (of which the latter, needless to say, is considered the most interesting, since it reflects an important aspect of his own theories) to the study of *Endgame.* This second section again starts with a résumé of the play under examination, but in this case, instead of presenting an almost over-simplified account, devoid of commentary, as he had done for *Waiting for Godot,* Robbe-Grillet mixes with the summary of the second play elements of ideological analysis: references to freedom, choice, regression toward a minimum state of being, and the like. The following excerpts will show the different tone of this text:

> But then man himself, who is there before our eyes, ends by disintegrating in his turn. The curtain rises on a new play: *Endgame,* an "old endgame lost of old," specifies Hamm, the protagonist.
> No more than his predecessors, Didi and Gogo, has Hamm the possibility of leaving to go elsewhere. But the reason for this has become tragically physical: he is paralyzed, sitting in an armchair in the middle of the stage. . . .
> In relation to the two tramps, Hamm has therefore lost that ridiculous freedom they still possessed. . . . As a matter of fact, he appears to us somehow imprisoned in his retreat; if he has no desire to emerge from it, he now does not have the means to do so either. This is a notable difference: the question for man is no longer one of affirming a position, but of suffering a fate.
> And yet, within his prison, he still performs a parody of choice: he interrupts his "turn" at once, he insists on being pushed to the center, the exact center of the stage. . . .
> . . . There is nothing left for Clov to do but leave . . . but, hat on his head and bag in hand . . . Clov remains there, near the open door, his eyes fixed on Hamm, who veils his face with a bloody handkerchief, as the curtain falls.

An initial analysis yields thus, in *Endgame,* throughout and even in its last scene, the "essential theme of presence." For:

> everything that is, *is here,* offstage there is only nothingness, nonbeing. . . .
> Similarly, everything is present in time as it is in space. To this ineluctable *here* corresponds an eternal *now.* . . . And the conjunction of space and time merely affords, with regards to a possible third character, this certitude: "If he exists he'll die there or he'll come here."

Thus the universe, deprived of its "elsewhere" as well as of its past, and with no exit other than death, excludes any idea of progress as well as any *meaning* whatsoever. The critic quotes Hamm's remark, uttered when he is struck by a sudden doubt: "We're not beginning to . . . to . . . mean something?"—and Clov's sardonic reassurance: "Mean something! You and I, mean something! (*Brief laugh.*) Ah, that's a good one!"

On reaching this point in his demonstration, Robbe-Grillet introduces certain ideas which he will not fully develop for another year, and which will form an important base of thought in the well-known article "Nature, Humanism, Tragedy," that appeared in the *Nouvelle Revue Française* (October 1958). These ideas concern the danger, in the creation of a literature of *non-meaning*, that the novel or play involved may be "recuperated" into a system of meaning by virtue of its "tragic development." Robbe-Grillet appears to detect, in Beckett's theater, a tendency toward such a recuperation, a proof of the extreme difficulty of protecting works of non-meaning from contamination, of keeping them intact and pure in their existential presence. Compare the following extract from the *Nouvelle Revue Française* article with the ensuing passage from the text on Beckett:

Tragedy may be defined, here, as an attempt to "recover" [*récupérer*] the distance which exists between man and things as a new value; it would then be a test, an ordeal in which victory would consist in being vanquished. Tragedy therefore appears as the last invention of humanism to permit nothing to escape. . . . It is a trap, and a falsification.

Here, perhaps, is the origin of this notion (or at least its first written form in Robbe-Grillet's works), suggested, apparently, by the new examination of Beckett's theater undertaken by Robbe-Grillet at the time of *Endgame:*

But this waiting for death, this physical misery which grows worse, . . . all this gradual rot of the present constitutes, in spite of everything, a future.

Whence the fear of "meaning something" is perfectly justified: by this accepted consciousness of a tragic development, the world has thereby recovered [*récupéré*] its whole signification.

And in parallel, before such a threat (this future simultaneously terrible and fatal), one can say that the present is no longer anything, that it disappears, conjured away in its turn, lost in the general collapse. "No more pain-killer. . . ." "No more biscuit. . . ." "No more bicycle. . . ." "No more nature. . . ." *There is no more present,* Clov could finally announce, in the same gloomy and triumphant voice.

And the fact that Hamm talks of "moments for nothing, now as always," that he repeats many times "Something is taking its course," proves in the final analysis, Robbe-Grillet argues, that Hamm himself acknowledges the *non-existence of his own presence,* of his being-there, which becomes then merely an illusion: "I was never there. Clov! . . . I was never there. . . . Absent, always. It all happened without me. . . ."

Once more, then, declares Robbe-Grillet, the "fatal trajectory" of all Beckett's characters, in his novels as well as in his plays, including Gogo and Didi, Pozzo and Lucky, Hamm and Clov, Murphy, Molloy, Malone, Mahood, and Worm, has occurred. The complete meaning of this will not be made clear until the writing of "Nature, Humanism, Tragedy." From today's vantage point, it is apparent that Robbe-Grillet was expressing at the end of his article a certain disappointment with Beckett. Without going to the full extent of denouncing the apparent recuperation of meaning in *Endgame,* through a sort of tragic assimilation, Robbe-Grillet contented himself with emphasizing, in somewhat ambiguous fashion, perhaps, Beckett's own *destruction* of that "presence on the stage" which in the earlier portions of the article he had singled out as the essential value of *Waiting for Godot:*

> The stage, privileged site of *presence,* has not resisted the contagion for long. The progress of the disease has occurred at the same rate as in the narratives. After having believed for a moment that we had grasped the real man, we are then obliged to confess our mistake. Didi was only an illusion, that is doubtless what gave him that dancing gait, swaying from one leg to another, that slightly clownlike costume. . . . He, too, was only the creature of a dream, falling back into the realm of dreams and fiction.
>
> "I was never there," Hamm says, and in the face of this admission nothing else counts, for it is impossible to understand it other than in its most general form: *No one was ever there.*
>
> And if, after *Godot* and *Endgame,* there now comes a third play, it will probably be *The Unnamable* again, third panel of the

trilogy of novels. Hamm already enables us to imagine its tone, by the novel he makes up as he goes along, creating sham situations and manipulating phantoms of characters into action. Since he is not there himself, there is nothing left for him now but to tell himself stories, to operate marionettes, in his place, to help pass the time. . . . Unless Samuel Beckett is reserving new surprises for us. . . .

In conclusion it can be stated that the evolution of Robbe-Grillet's theory and doctrine allowed him to state, in 1957, much more clearly than in 1953, both Samuel Beckett's contribution to the destruction of signification and the potentially "dangerous" tendency exhibited in such plays as *Waiting for Godot* and *Endgame* toward a sort of tragic recuperation of meaning implied by the acceptance of a retreat from presence and *being-there,* suggestive of a kind of return to the "old myths of depth." Without going so far as to argue that Beckett himself was trying to reintroduce signification into his works (which, after all, may fairly be viewed as *denunciations* of a "tragified" universe) , Robbe-Grillet appeared regretfully to discover that Beckett's work *could* give rise to certain implications or conclusions that went counter to the principles that Robbe-Grillet was currently developing and putting forward more and more urgently as a basis for the New Novel. In 1957, the rigorously phenomenological stage of these doctrines, founded on the central idea of a "realism of presence," and a totally meaningless, neutral *being-there,* determined and limited Robbe-Grillet's appreciation of Beckett's plays.

If, as Roland Barthes has proposed in his preface to my book *Les Romans de Robbe-Grillet,*[3] there has been a gradual emergence of an idea of this author as "integrated, or to put it better, reconciled with the traditional aims of the novel," if, beyond Robbe-Grillet's doctrine of non-signification we may discern more and more clearly a Robbe-Grillet whose works possess a "meaning," one may see in this situation a certain

3. Paris: Editions de Minuit, 1963.

parallel to Robbe-Grillet's own discovery in Beckett's works, around 1957, the possibility of a certain signification contaminating the purity of what had seemed to be only meaningless presence. Will Robbe-Grillet come to accept not only Beckett's "meaning," but also his own?

It seems doubtful, in any case, that Robbe-Grillet, the author of "Samuel Beckett, or Presence on the Stage," will again seek in Beckett's works parallels or reinforcements of his own doctrines. Unless Robbe-Grillet is reserving "new surprises" for us. . . .

The Strange World of Beckett's "grands articulés"

Germaine Brée

translated by
Margaret Guiton

*I, with my mad presumption of throwing
a little light on something.*

Beckett

Few contemporary novelists are as reticent on the subject of their art as Samuel Beckett. Few—for the past five or six years and especially in the United States—have aroused so much discussion. This is partly because *Waiting for Godot* and *Endgame* brought Beckett an almost worldwide public, partly because, in the United States, the numerous studies of Joyce's works prepared a small group of readers for the unfamiliar novels of his compatriot and friend.

In one of his rare press interviews Beckett made a somewhat surprising statement, perhaps for the benefit of his commentators.[1] He never, he declared, reads philosophers and does not understand them. The key to his novels must be sought in his own sensibility. It is here, and here alone, that his characters, in some mysterious manner, are born. And yet the fact remains that Descartes is the narrator of *Whoroscope;* that Democritus and Schopenhauer appear in the poems of *Echo's Bones;* that the Pythagoreans and Geulincx, quoted in *Murphy* and the respective favorites of Neary and Murphy, have never ceased to haunt his world; [2] that his early studies of Joyce

Germaine Brée is Vilas Professor of French and Permanent Member of the Institute for Research in the Humanities at the University of Wisconsin, Madison.

1. Gabriel d'Aubarède, *Nouvelles Littéraires* (16 February 1961).
2. Hugh Kenner in *Samuel Beckett: A Critical Study* (New York: Grove Press, 1961); Frederick J. Hoffman in *Samuel Beckett: The Language of Self* (Carbondale: Southern Illinois University Press, 1962); Samuel Mintz in "Beckett's *Murphy:* A Cartesian Novel," *Perspective* 11 (Autumn 1959): 156–59; and Jacqueline Hoefer in "Watt," *Perspective* 11 (Autumn 1959): 166–82 have all shown the extent to which Beckett's work demands of the reader a solid philosophic background. Professor Julius Weinberg of the University of Wisconsin has shown me a very pertinent

(1929) and Proust (1931) reveal a considerable facility for methodical, abstract discussions; and finally that, from a certain point of view, Beckett's work has an affinity with that of the most metaphysical of French critics, Maurice Blanchot.

Indeed Samuel Beckett's fictional world, especially *Watt,* contains a quasi-Rabelaisian parody of all the rhetorical and logical devices that have permitted Western man, like Beckett's Ubu-esque creation, the "man-pot" Mahood, to hold a "partially waterproof tarpaulin" over his skull. Describing, reasoning, discussing, examining—Beckett's characters never tire of these activities, though no two of them proceed in exactly the same way. They share our "deplorable mania" not only for "when something happens wanting to know what" but furthermore for wanting, like Watt, to know why. Beckett is thus something of a contemporary Faust who, through the agency of his characters, indiscriminately, and with ferocious humor, undermines all our past and present attempts to give reality an intelligible structure, to "think out" our human situation.

We can thus readily understand that Beckett should find philosophy unintelligible—as regards its proposed aims, not its intellectual procedures. These he tirelessly ridicules. Not without reason did he invent Macmann, that character Malone talks to himself about, who, while believing that "he had done as any man of good will would have done in his place and with very much the same results, in spite of his lack of experience," nonetheless acknowledges that, in gardening, he is "incapable of weeding a bed of pansies or marigolds and [of] leaving one standing" (72). Beckett's verbal clowning produces a similar devastation, as do certain Jarry-like inventions which allow him to reduce our relations with the physical world to the

----

parody of Leibnitz in *Watt* (132–35). Mr Endon, the mad chess player with the vacant eye, in *Murphy,* Mr Knott, Watt's master, who creates an infinite number of starving dogs in order to dispose of his left-overs, and other persistent "Godots" emphasize this particular aspect of Beckett's work.

status of a simple diagram: two pots for nourishment and evacuation; a bag of canned foods; a pebble or, in prosperous times, sixteen pebbles to suck; and so forth.

Like Joyce, perhaps still more than Joyce, Beckett seems marked by the scholasticism of his philosophy classes at Trinity College. We can find many traces of it in his imaginary world. Descartes and Geulincx are perhaps given an important role in his early novels because they broke with the great intellectual tradition which from Plato to Thomas Aquinas, via Aristotle, conceived creation as a moving hierarchy of creatures oriented toward a perfect and definitive form, a final cause, God. Descartes thus unintentionally prepared the way for Beckett's "great articulates"—creatures whose special articulation, in body, thought or speech, even though sadly defective, makes them forget that they are really "frightened vagabonds," willy-nilly dragging aimlessly along, dying by degrees, while words and images spin round and round inside their bony white skulls. Skulls, jars, rooms, or other habitations, and the monotonous surrounding "country" form the two inseparable and rhythmically alternating settings for the adventures of Beckett's great articulates: beings who travel, or rather wander, toward some illusory "home" or "refuge," telling each other their adventures, while their dual disarticulation proceeds insidiously, "by direct route."

Beckett's characters seem to parody the pre-Copernican theory that all incomplete and abortive forms move toward that which perfects them by completing them. They are strangely intent on travel if only in spirit, even when bedridden or "in jars," or on relating their travels; they seek one another and form unstable couples when, for a few brief moments, one seems to appear in order to complete the other: Celia and Murphy; Watt and Sam; Molloy and Moran; Malone and Macmann; Mahood and Worm; Pim and Bem—to name a few. Identified with each in turn, yet each time reemerging, modified by the contact, just as the different characters emerge from one another, there always finally remains he who is known only by his voice, a voice which, as a matter of fact, is not his own, the nameless one who is "alone here, the first and last" and nonetheless is never there, the animator of this verbal cosmos and source of its Logos, like the God of Genesis.

Murphy, tied to his rocking-chair by seven scarfs, attempting to attain perfect repose through an increasingly frenetic rocking can hardly fail to remind us, however vaguely, of certain Thomistic categories: that, for example, of celestial beings halfway between God and terrestrial beings who, since they are endowed with essential forms, know no other kind of movement than that of movement in repose. Murphy's ignominious fall, hindside foremost—which does not in the least discourage Murphy himself—is but the first of a whole series of falls precipitating Beckett's characters, one after the other, into any and every muddy ditch. Beckett thus brings out both the pathos and absurdity of our mental postures by grossly simplifying them and turning them into concrete situations which his characters act out physically: Pim (whose identity merges with that of the narrator of *How It Is*), his shoulders firmly encircled by an arm whose hand plunges into his bag, crawling in the mud with a can opener, his main educational tool, between his buttocks, is the latest, and strangest, of Beckett's fantastic inventions.

It is significant that Beckett should devote so much space to descriptions of his characters' physical bearing—their gaits and means of locomotion, from bicycling to crawling.[3] Strange to us, though completely natural to them, these are both comic and puzzling: Murphy, as perceived by Celia, standing motionless in the middle of a London thoroughfare, staring up at the sky; Watt's curious gyrating movement; Molloy perched on his bicycle with his crutches and game leg; the absurd, Ubu-esque structure formed by the Morans, father and son, as they proceed, on their single bicycle, along the roads that will not lead to Molloy; and finally, "the trip by direct route" "in

3. See Kenner, "The Cartesian Centaur," in *Samuel Beckett: A Critical Study.*

darkness mud" of the voiceless protagonist of *How It Is,* doing
the "right leg right arm push pull flat on your stomach silent
curses left leg left arm push pull flat on your stomach silent
curses fifteen meters stop waddle." A Beckett character's means
of locomotion is a piece of factual evidence, a *donnée* such as
might be discerned by an inhuman eye observing the successive
variations each infinitesimal character brings to the
continuous, irresistible movement carrying it along into the
interior of an unchanging countryside.

Beckett's cosmos retains a few traces of the medieval sky, "a
world up there" occasionally glimpsed "in the blue," far from
the mud and excrements. Although the episodes in *Murphy* are
located, with Joycean precision, in London and Beckett's early
environment near Dublin, where *Watt* also begins and ends,
the scenes of the succeeding novels become progressively vague.
Hill, swamp, shore, sea, forest, open country, city are
eventually reduced to a single flat stretch of mud. This too,
however, is related to medieval metaphysics: the universe of
concentric zones, the symbolism of the circle and the center, of
the elements and seasons, of light and movement. Beckett's
man, like medieval man, is "molded from all the kingdoms."
"There somewhere man is too," Moran solemnly remarks as he
reflects on his mission to find Molloy, a "vast conglomerate of
all of nature's kingdoms, as lonely and as bound" (*Molloy,*
151). When Beckett's characters refer to birth, wombs,
expulsion, copulation, excrements—Beckett seems particularly
obsessed with fecal matter and urine [4]—in short, to human
existence, the situations and images have Freudian overtones.
But, after *Watt,* Beckett's characters evolve in a setting which

---

4. Despite a few grotesque descriptions of copulation and some allusions
to masturbation, Beckett does not give much prominence to sexual
functions, the genital organs of his protagonists being for the most part
in pitiable condition. On the other hand, Beckett himself seems to have
become aware of the often pointless monotony of his recurring scatological
jokes and allusions: the protagonist of *The Unnamable* at one point
decides to eliminate them.

is, on the whole, more in the tradition of Dante or of Milton; [5] we sense a familiar metaphysical vision beyond the imaginary structure.

This world, with its primeval slime, its expulsions, falls, and painful progressions, its halts and temporary refuges, its play of light and shade, its creatures sinking into or emerging from the mud, is now and then strikingly reminiscent of Dante's *Divine Comedy*—particularly, perhaps, as seen through Gustave Doré's illustrations. "Nights without Night" and "Days without Day," to borrow Michel Leiris's title—everything unfolds in the "imperfect shade" and "doubtful light" of an engraving, each character evolving in what Malone calls "my personal light," or else in that indirect lunar light in which this dim world is sometimes rather gently bathed.

Dante, to be sure, as many critics have pointed out, made a deep impression on Beckett's imagination. The lazy Belacqua, whom Dante places in the indecisive zone of Antepurgatory, is one of his special favorites, as also, though to a lesser extent, Sordello, his companion—the poet who at first is silent.[6] And Beckett, as he constructs his "mental country," occasionally alludes to Dante. The narrator of *The Unnamable*, "stuck like a sheaf of flowers in a deep jar, its neck flush with my mouth" (55), his head held up by an iron collar; the narrator of *How It Is,* crawling on his stomach with his face in the mud; the crippled Moran, painfully proceeding through a forest during an entire winter; Macmann, lying under the open sky during a violent rain storm—how Dante-like these situations and places are! They recall the glacial rain in the third circle of the inferno; the forest of suicides in the seventh; and, persistently, the memory of Malebolge's domain, the

5. In "From an Abandoned Work" performed over the BBC on 14 December 1957, the elderly protagonist and narrator, like Krapp, dictates his autobiography, seeing himself again as a young man studying Milton's cosmology with his father.
6. Belacqua is the protagonist of Beckett's first stories, *More Pricks Than Kicks* (London: Chatto & Windus, 1934) ; he reappears, directly or indirectly, in all the novels, and is mentioned again in *How It Is.*

eighth circle, where the perjurors, or falsifiers in words, drag themselves through the mud throughout eternity.

All Beckett's characters, including Murphy, are victimized by words, and all, beginning with Watt, must contend with that voice, "qua-qua," presiding over the birth of characters and scenery which accompanies the reader as faithfully as Virgil accompanied Dante. Unlike Virgil, however, it has a wide range of tones, according to whether or not it asks, or answers, all the questions.

These characters are "entrusted with missions" and inhabited by voices. At the beginning of *Molloy* a vaguely defined character, who is seated on a protuberance in the shadow of a rock, is ordered to go and find his mother—a mission that is imposed on him, an obligation he cannot evade. Later another more clearly defined character named Moran receives another order, from somewhere else, to set out in search of Molloy. Both will afterwards be obliged to make a report on their adventures. The narrator of *The Unnamable* is surrounded by numerous emissaries who force him to speak and who must be "satisfied." The entire adventure of the voiceless character in *How It Is* consists in obliging another person, Pim, to emit a few words, by "extorting" his voice from him. Malone seems to have chosen freely to write, but it is a form of defence against an "old debtor." And Watt, one of the "old members" of the gang and the first victim of the word, loses the faculty of common speech at Mr Knott's house; he nonetheless continues to repeat exactly the same broken phrases, in increasingly complex combinations, for the benefit of another character, Sam, who then interprets them.

These missions and obligations are apparently futile since none of the designated envoys reaches his goal. Watt begins his visit at Mr Knott's, the other characters begin their stories, calmly and reasonably, intent only on accurately observing and reporting existing events; but they gradually find themselves impelled into difficult zones where other voices mingle with their own, where other characters appear before them, so that

Pim-Bem of *How It Is,* himself apparently a derivative of Mahood's abortive Worm, thinks for a moment that perhaps a "not one of us" exists whose "anonymous voice" is heard in the blurred but nonetheless communicable words extracted from, murmured by, the infinite series of Bem, Pim, Bom that he glimpses moving very slowly in closed ranks from west to east. In the same way, after *Watt,* one, then several omnipresent narrators, all using the first person, emerge from the omniscient narrator of the traditional novel form. They meet, converse, collide, sometimes in the same sentence, and replace each other without warning. The same device was already used by Laforgue; with Beckett it is of more than purely literary significance: the passage from the author's "I" to that of a character creates a third, and unknown, "I." To close in on the language of everyday discourse, to track it down and find—and never find—a voice which is one's own, is the task of a poet or a metaphysician.

Speech is the animating principle of Beckett's comedy which, as such, is very far removed from that of Dante. Unlike Dante's tortured victims, Beckett's characters discuss their miserable and repugnant situation very calmly; they find it not only tolerable but, on the whole, fairly good and, primarily concerned over the possibility of eviction, accept its inevitable deterioration in good spirit. When it comes to describing this situation, enumerating its advantages, discussing its resources, effecting certain improvements, hanging on, they could hardly be excelled. Inventing "begging boards" adapted to the almsgiver's psychology; fixing up a row boat so that it is waterproof on top with a hole in the bottom for immersion purposes; finding the best way to suck sixteen stones one after the other in perfect order; finding the perfect solution to the difficult problem of locomotion if you happen to have two stiff legs of unequal length; making the continually deferred inventory of one's possessions—Beckett's characters undertake these "little diversions" with happy zeal. They throw themselves into the game *à mots perdus* as it were, sometimes enjoying it for several pages at a time. Beckett's fantasy and humor are here strangely mingled both with ferocity and with compassion.

If, however, these characters are commanded to tell a story or relate their own adventures, panic inevitably ensues. Molloy, Moran, Mahood, and others assume voices and forms as best they may, appear and disappear without ever being completely born; they die piecemeal, departing this life feet first as all must do, but without ever ceasing to disappear; meanwhile "the other," the nameless narrator who, after *Watt,* always begins the story in the first person, speaks on and on. This is the "I" heard in *The Unnamable* before Mahood appears with his complement, Worm—that recalcitrant larva who lends an ear even though he refuses to be born:

This voice that speaks, knowing that it lies, indifferent to what it says, too old perhaps and too abased ever to succeed in saying the words that would be its last, knowing itself useless and its uselessness in vain, not listening to itself but to the silence that it breaks. . . . It is not mine, I have none, I have no voice and must speak, that is all I know. . . . [26]

A sort of anguish hovers over the human comedy, the drama of a creation continually menaced by abortion, an unsuccessful enterprise, situated somewhere between darkness and light, which must always be re-begun. Beckett himself advanced the theory in his essay on Bram van Velde.[7]

Beckett's fiction, committed to failure, thus apparently stems from a very personal experience: this onerous obligation to speak—an activity of vital importance, inspired by a force that comes from "elsewhere," and frightens him because it threatens to plunge him down into the eighth circle of hell with the falsifiers in words—he who would have been so well satisfied with Belacqua's rock. In order to name "the unnamable," say "the unspeakable," he must resort to the "jokes," "fairy tales,"

7. See the third dialogue in Samuel Beckett, "Three Dialogues," *Samuel Beckett: A Collection of Critical Essays,* ed. Martin Esslin (Englewood Cliffs, N.J.: Prentice-Hall, 1965) .

and "lies" that will enable these specters to make their way toward light. At the same time Beckett is also faced with the cruel necessity of destroying his fable in order to protect himself, as best he can, against the possibility of being alienated (depredated, expropriated, dispossessed, dislodged, displaced) by "the other" that he has created. He is thus obliged to flout the forms emerging from his story by every possible means. He must annihilate everything susceptible of being annihilated; everything, in other words, that is part of himself. Beckett is not inclined to "upholster" the truth. He does not wish to add anything to reality, he does not wish to transform anything. This is why he has so little patience with those who attempt to reduce his "fables" to a system of clear ideas. As the narrator of *The Unnamable* remarks, with somewhat exaggerated eloquence: "Perhaps I shall be obliged, in order not to peter out, to invent another fairy-tale, yet another, with heads, trunks, arms, legs, and all that follows, let loose in the changeless round of imperfect shadow and dubious light" (27). The "others" who "pass by" the narrator are thus able, by dispossessing him, to "pass for" him, abandoning him, nameless, before an empty, "immeasurable" stretch of time which—sand, mud, water or whatever—insidiously suffocates him. These confrontations of narrator and character; the substitutions, during the course of the story, of one protagonist for another; the emergence, from nothingness, of one or several characters—sometimes an infinite series of new and *sans imprévu* "representatives," "agents," "surrogates," or "avatars" of "the unnamable"—these all give rise to considerable confusion, agitation, and also anguish. At such times Beckett's style begins to pant, take on incantatory overtones, produce a sense of uneasiness, while, both in contrast and in defiance, countering and neutralizing the incantation, irony, parody, and occasionally coarseness intervene, and the author begins to multiply his admonitions to himself: That's enough, no, not that; something went wrong here. During the whole course of the story the narrator comments on its developments: "Well,

well, I wasn't expecting that"; "This will all have to be
rewritten in the pluperfect"; "Now that we know where we're
heading, let's go"; "What a bore"; "I'm fed up with all this
make believe." He also occasionally addresses the reader: "I'm
using the present tense, it's so easy to use the present tense
when you're dealing with past events. It's the mythological
present, don't pay any attention to it." It is up to us to decide
which of the various "I"s is presently speaking, to keep up with
the various verbal tricks and traps which often fit into existing
patterns of rhetoric. Beckett here turns Joyce's devices to his
own ends: puns, subtly dislocated quotations of prose or poetry,
unexplained allusions, unfamiliar words taken from the
technical language of philosophy, medicine, or natural history.
In this respect he is nearer to Queneau than to any other
contemporary writer. Since Beckett is extremely learned, no
existing lexicon or encyclopedia would be adequate for those
seeking a precise definition of every term or explanation of
each allusion. These are all undoubtedly procedures
characteristic of the epic form—negative, as it were anti-heroic,
epics unfolding in an "immeasurable time"; "badly" told,
taken up over and over again by the voice that animates the
characters—characters vaguely aware that they are yet once
again about to make gestures they have already made several
times before. The evolving presence in Beckett's world is not so
much the scenery and characters, "conveniences" that can
easily be renewed, as the quality and behavior of this voice.
Beckett sometimes indulges in surprisingly facile effects, lingers
over puerile jokes; the voice idles along, fading into an
interminable plashing sound; the same ironic dialogue
monotonously recurs; the reader yawns. But the writer never
abandons his hand-to-hand combat with language, his
unceasing struggle to subject it to an "unnamable" truth
resuscitated by this very combat and by-passed as soon as it is
named, his own past-present.

   Beckett's often brutal descriptive realism, which links him
with the expressionists, should not obscure the specifically

"fabulous" character of his novels. *Murphy,* despite the strangeness of its hero, is, from this point of view, still close to the familiar adventure story genre, solidly anchored in everyday reality. But beginning with *Watt* and the visit to Mr Knott, the strange and monstrous depths of Beckett's universe increasingly tend to absorb the characters who are part of himself. One is reminded of Odilon Redon's disturbing creatures; of the bizarre, although innocent, monsters Dubuffet seems to mold out of mud; or of Michaux's "properties." Vivian Mercier, who is also Irish, considers Beckett's combination of the grotesque and the macabre a form of Irish humor that is also found in native legends and fairy tales.[8] Beckett's characters remind him of "sheela-na-gig"—figurines with bald heads, emaciated bodies, crooked legs, and enormous mouths and genitals. According to Mercier they reflect primitive man's anguished reaction to the process of sexual reproduction, a form of death, and expulsion from the maternal womb, a prefiguration of his expulsion from life. It would indeed appear that Beckett's characters stand, as it were, between himself and the "murmur" of a voice situated in nothingness, forming a sort of barricade against dread.

The stories told are, moreover, strikingly similar, unfolding according to a cyclical epic pattern, frequently pointed out by Beckett, which becomes increasingly simplified: voyage, quest or encounter, combat, separation, return; sometimes, especially in the early novels, the patterns are complicated by secondary episodes, pauses in sheltered spots and love affairs in deceptive refuges, for example—that are "seen" retrospectively and seem to parody certain types of fiction. The characters, no less than the stories that they tell, have a certain air of family resemblance, and a whole network of reminiscences— encounters, objects, words—are carried over from one novel to the next. Everyone wears the clownlike Beckett uniform, or what remains thereof: for the hats, long, stiff coats, odd

8. "Samuel Beckett and the Sheela-na-gig," *Kenyon Review* 23 (Spring 1961) : 299.

shoes, and ill-fitting, cast-off garments of the "human envelope"
may vanish one after the other; there still remains the long
white hair, dirty and matted, the accumulated filth of centuries.
As a matter of fact we soon begin to realize that, from
Murphy to *How It Is,* it is doubtless the same adventurer that
goes his way and gives birth, from book to book, to the
unpredictable and inevitable book that follows.
Beckett thus follows his own adventure on the trail of "that
little creature in numerous disguises" who haunts him. Each
stopping place along the way appears to be the last but always
turns out to be "next to last" or the "penultimate." He too, like
his own characters, must set out again, proceeding from west to
east, against all natural forces and the underlying order of the
cosmos. His own adventure thus rejoins that long, monotonous
human enterprise that is based on written language, as old as
man himself and never finished. And so the annihilation of
Samuel Beckett proceeds along its course.

It is, to be sure, a long way from *Murphy* to *How It Is.*
Beckett's fictional output falls naturally into three groups
separated by two "pauses." The early short stories and novels
that were originally written in English, *More Pricks Than
Kicks, Murphy,* and *Watt,* are told "objectively" by an
omniscient narrator. In the trilogy, *Molloy, Malone Dies* and
The Unnamable, Beckett uses the first person narrative form
he had already tried in his short stories, but adapts this
well-worn instrument to complex new forms, based on spoken
language, that are flexible, ambiguous, and disconcerting.
With *Texts for Nothing* Beckett, undermining the existing
structure of both plot and syntax, had already started moving
toward the unfamiliar yet entirely intelligible form of *How It
Is.* Beckett seems to be attempting, in every domain of his work,
to reduce speech to an underlying pattern that is nonetheless
easily grasped. From now on, with a systematic use of ellipses,
he eliminates everything that the reader himself is able to
supply.

This novel, we are informed at the outset, is divided into

three parts: the encounter of the protagonist and narrator with his likeness Pim, "how it was, how it is," "before, during and afterwards"—one of the frequently recurring leitmotifs. It is written in a prose devoid of punctuation and capital letters which is arranged in approximately equal blocks of words separated and accented by blank spaces; two long pauses emphasize the triple division, a typographical arrangement that does not seem unusual today. The label novel is perhaps the only surprising aspect of this work; had Beckett called it a prose poem it would not have surprised anyone. The story is not really based, as has been said, on a single long sentence. Rather it develops like a musical composition. The recurring blanks produce a series of falling cadences, which gives the rhythm; the syntax, drastically simplified but nonetheless unimpeachable, gives the story its impetus and movement. Each group of words gathers together various motifs— ritualistic, incantatory themes that recur more and more frequently and through which the strange passion and happiness of Pim-Bem unfolds: their meeting "in the mud, the dark- ness"; the ferocious education for snatching a "cruelly extorted" voice from Pim; Pim's departure; the ensuing meditation "in the mud, the darkness" which gives rise to a faint hope. Is there perhaps a "not one of us" who feels concern for "all of us" and whose fragmented voice vibrates in "all of us," giving authenticity to human speech? The interchangeable Pim-Bem-Bom would thus find dignity as "the theater of a word rediscovered in the darkness, the mud." But the howl of despair and anguish in the face of death ultimately remains unanswered. No more of the "visitors" or "pictures" that entertained Malone and Mahood and passed before the eyes ("not the blue eyes, the other ones") of the traveller with the sack at the beginning of the story. With *How It Is* Beckett seems to have emptied his imaginary world of all that is not essential to a fundamental image of man's fate, arriving at a sort of diagram of his own intimate drama: a dumb mortal committed to physical disintegration, headed for death, but who is at the same time possessed by a voice, "not his own," which he is unable to annihilate. *How It Is* is hardly any longer a novel; it is rather a fable, channeled into a very carefully controlled form. Nothing, this time, has been "left to chance." The words stream along fluently and easily, evoking everything that is no more once it has been; everything that is imperfect and committed to nothingness from the outset—images, memories, feelings, thoughts. They extricate everything that gets stuck in the mud during the slow slipping down toward death which constitutes Beckett's time: hair, buttocks, can opener, incongruous as they may seem—just as Pim's education, situation and song may seem incongruous—here find their significance in a very natural way. This unity of incongruities is an exact image of the intimate contradiction which the novel illustrates without resolving. At the same time, however, nothing here throws any light on the nature of a future novel, if such there is to be, by Samuel Beckett, or the means he would use to impose once more a form and limits on "the Unnamable" that dwells within him. Amid the "qua-qua" of the rumor of words that splashes around and within him, what word (his-own-and-not-his-own) will he now extort from himself?

Black Humor: The Pockets of Lemuel Gulliver and Samuel Beckett

Edith Kern

In his *Anthologie de l'Humour Noir,* Breton referred to the eighteenth-century Irishman Swift as the veritable initiator of this aspect of literature. It was his *Anthologie,* Breton tells us in a later edition, that since its publication in 1939 had established in France the term *humour noir* in its current meaning, namely, as the equivalent of German *Galgenhumor* (humor in the face of the gallows, or in a broader sense, in the face of adversity). To define the term, Breton had adopted from Freud a somewhat coarse example. He had referred to the episode, told by Freud, of a man condemned to death who, as he was being led to the gallows on a Monday, observed that this was a bad way to begin a week. Had Beckett been known at the time Breton published his first edition of the *Anthologie* in 1939, or at the time of the second in 1947, or had Breton added more authors and material to his last edition in 1966, Beckett most likely would have found a place in this collection. For one can easily spot in the twentieth-century Irishman's work moments similar in mood to the Freudian episode and of as black a humor as that of Swift. In Beckett's *Waiting for Godot,* for instance, Estragon and Vladimir want to hang themselves, but find that the only tree available in their universe is too weak to support both their bodies. Indeed, no one has been more felicitous in illustrating black humor than Winnie in Beckett's *Happy Days,* as she asks the rhetorical question: "How can one better magnify the Almighty than by sniggering with him at his little jokes, particularly the poorer ones?" and

Edith Kern is Professor of French and Comparative Literature at the University of Washington.

as she provides the answer: "Oh well, what does it matter, that
is what I always say, so long as one . . . you know . . . what is
the wonderful line . . . laughing wild . . . something
something laughing wild amid severest woe" (31).

Though Breton could not include Beckett in his *Anthologie,*
other critics have been well aware of certain affinities in the
humor of the eighteenth-century Swift and the twentieth-
century Beckett.[1] It seems to me that a juxtaposition of the two
writers spotlights basic similarities and at the same time gives
us some insight into what sets them and their eras apart. On
the theory of *pars pro toto,* namely, that what is true for
one part of a work should be applicable to its entirety, I
have focused on their use of one small article, namely pockets,
which both writers use in significant ways. In the case of Swift,
pockets play an important part in the adventures of Lemuel
Gulliver, the protagonist of *Gulliver's Travels.* In the case of
Beckett, pockets are in one form or another present in his
entire work and to such an extent that a psychiatrist might well
be intrigued by this phenomenon. It must be stated, however,
that our concern here is not a psychoanalysis of the author, but
rather the role which such pockets play in the realm of the
author's humor.

One usually remembers with glee the scene in *Gulliver's
Travels* where he tells about his arrival in the land of the
Lilliputians and—frightening monster that he appears to
be—has to submit to a minute search of his person by the
country's officers. "I took up the two officers in my hands," he
reports, "put them first into my coat-pockets, and then into
every other pocket about me, except my two fobs, and another
secret pocket which I had no mind should be searched, wherein
I had some little necessaries that were of no consequence to any

1. Notably John Fletcher, "Samuel Beckett et Jonathan Swift: Vers une
étude comparée," *Littératures* (Annales publiées par la Faculté des Lettres
de Toulouse), 10 (1962): 81–117.

but myself. In one of my fobs there was a silver watch, and in the other a small quantity of gold in a purse." [2]

The gaiety and hilarious abandon which seems to permeate Swift's narration at this point should not make us oblivious to its full significance. For the pattern used here is almost a parody of that of the hero in world literature who descends into unknown depths, encounters marvelous adventures, and returns to tell about them. Thus—to name but a few—Dante descended into the Inferno; Don Quixote into the cave of Montesinos where he had a grotesque apparition of his beloved Dulcinea; and Goethe's Faust into the realm of the Mothers which revealed to him the mainsprings of creation. The officers of the Emperor of Lilliput descend into mere pockets, the dimensions of their experience matching their own puny nature. But their report, too, is replete with wonders. Their account does not touch on man's fate. It concerns neither great events nor magic, nor philosophic insights. They encounter neither men in torment nor enchanted princesses. But the things and engines they see are as miraculous to them as the appearance of his Dulcinea to Don Quixote. Thus their report, though couched in soberly bureaucratic language—as befits the occasion and the dignity of these officers—reveals their sensation of mystery and admiration. By means of their report and the objects they bring to light, an entire age seems to emerge from the pockets of Lemuel Gulliver, as an entire Combray was to emerge from Marcel's "tasse de thé": an age based on reason which began with the seventeenth century and even today is not altogether extinct.

They had found what they considered to be a huge silver chest with a cover of the same metal and filled with a sort of dust that set them both "sneezing for several times together." They came upon what seemed to them a pile of large white sheets bundled together and covered in part with mysterious black figures that they surmised to be writing. In the depth of

2. Jonathan Swift, *Gulliver's Travels,* ed. J. F. Ross (New York and Toronto: Holt, Rinehart and Winston, 1956), p. 18.

one pocket there was to be seen a large black "engine, from the back of which there extended twenty long poles," which made them conjecture that the Man-Mountain used it to comb his hair. Other dangerous-looking engines they identified as weapons. And then "there were two pockets," the report reads,

which we could not enter: these he called his fobs; they were two large slits cut into the top of his middle cover, but squeezed close by the pressure of his belly. Out of the right fob hung a great silver chain, with a wonderful kind of engine at the bottom. We directed him to draw out whatever was fastened to that chain; which appeared to be a globe, half silver, and half of some transparent metal: for on the transparent side we saw certain strange figures circularly drawn, and thought we could touch them, till we found our fingers stopped with that lucid substance. He put his engine to our ears, which made an incessant noise like that of a water-mill. And we conjecture it is either some unknown animal, or the god that he worships; but we are more inclined to the latter opinion, because he assures us (if we understood him right, for he expressed himself very imperfectly) that he seldom did anything without consulting it. He called it his oracle, and said it pointed out the time for every action of his life.[3]

Surely, if Clefren Frelock and Marsi Frelock, the two officers who made the descent and wrote the report, had not been able to back up their strange tales by exhibiting the objects in question, they would have aroused total disbelief in their Lilliputian hearers—of the kind encountered by Don Quixote who had to chide Sancho for his ignorance in worldly matters which made him unable to grasp anything that could be grasped only with difficulty.

The world of wonders which Clefren and Marsi Frelock conjured up for the Lilliputians, on emerging from Lemuel Gulliver's pockets, was a world of seventeenth- and eighteenth-century luxuries and inventions, known though still novel to those dwelling in the England of Swift. "The silver chest" could be recognized as a snuffbox—the inhaling of snuff having spread in England during the seventeenth century and

3. Swift, p. 20.

become almost universal in the eighteenth century. In Spanish and French plays of the seventeenth century, including Molière's *Dom Juan,* references can be found to this growing habit. The pocket comb, whose ostentatious use by the French marquis had been held up to ridicule by Molière, must still have been a comparative novelty in Swift's day. The mysterious globe with its incessant noise is obviously a descendant of the Nuremberg egg, the prototype of all portable watches. Already in the seventeenth century, people had started to carry these cumbersome eggs in their pockets, but further inventions made them more manageable and finally blazed the trail for their present-day glory. Previous ages had measured time by means of water clocks, sundials, or pendulum clocks. Town-dwellers and villagers alike listened for the sound of the bells of churches and monasteries in order to tell the time of the day. An hour did not arbitrarily consist of sixty minutes but was longer during the summer and shorter during the winter, to permit the division of the day into twelve even parts. It was not until the advent of the portable watch and its wide-spread use that people began to come under the spell of Chronos and to worship him.

It is interesting to realize that Gulliver's pockets contained, besides the symbol of Chronos, those of Mammon and Mars. Gulliver carried, of course, that formidable engine, the fire pistol—duly admired and dreaded by the Lilliputians. He showed as much concern for his gold pieces as for his precious watch—thus reflecting the ever-growing money-consciousness of the age. Again, it seems to be the seventeenth century whose literature gives evidence of a growing awareness of the value of money. Amidst the marvelous adventures in the Cave of Montesinos Don Quixote suddenly came to realize that even enchanted princesses need money. For Dulcinea's maid approached him with tears in her eyes, begging him to lend her mistress six piasters against the security of an almost unused petticoat. In a number of Molière's comedies young lovers as well as old Sganarelles are quite concerned with money. And it seems to be particularly in eighteenth-century fiction, for instance, in Voltaire's *Candide,* the spiritual offspring of *Gulliver's Travels,* that money-consciousness most blatantly asserts itself, reflecting the mood of the age.

By having us look at the world of Gulliver's pockets through the startled eyes of the Lilliputians, Swift makes us see it as if for the first time, and in ironic distortion at that. The result is humor, which, as the book progresses, becomes bleaker and blacker. It is just as interesting, therefore, to note what he omits from this satire as what he includes. Concealed from the Lilliputians are those little necessaries that Gulliver considered "of no consequence to any but myself." This attitude apparently reflects Swift's own reaction and that of his age to exclude from writings matters of too private a concern. But Lemuel Gulliver also refuses to surrender to the Emperor of Lilliput the two most cherished implements which his pockets contain and which are to be of the greatest importance in the development of the story: his reading glasses and his "perspective" or telescope. Reading glasses, although already known in some form to the Middle Ages, did not become popular until the advent of the printed book and were not used widely until the seventeenth century. The telescope, having been invented in Holland by the beginning of the seventeenth century, must still have been considered a rare and treasured possession in the early eighteenth century. Gulliver's own reverential attitude toward these instruments is never diminished by the incredulity or ignorance of the Lilliputians. When he exposes snuff, comb, watch, pistols, and money to their ridicule, Swift half-humorously, half-seriously distances himself from the social and scientific extravagance of his age and satirizes what was usually known as "progress." But not so in the case of the glasses and the telescope. It was clearly his intention to exclude all satire from inventions of such import that are likely to improve man's sight and insight.

The things that come out of Lemuel Gulliver's pockets belong to a well-ordered, rational, human world. There is among them no personal souvenir of a romantic nature, and none of the clutter of natural objects that might collect in the pockets of a small boy. All are selected with discrimination and intelligence. They reveal Swift's respect for useful inventions and discoveries. In the eyes of Gulliver, tobacco, comb, watch, glasses, telescope, and money—all serve practical purposes. All serve man—as does the entire universe in the eyes of the eighteenth century. There is no waste, no superfluity, no absurdity—except as these objects are perceived through the uninitiated eyes of the Lilliputians. It is only through their presence that Swift makes us notice that all is not well in the best of all possible worlds and that man's idolizing of Chronos and Mars is absurd. Yet even these absurdities seem to be of such a nature that they are capable of being remedied by the sheer application of intelligence, moderation, and human reason. The world of Lemuel Gulliver's pockets is akin to the world of Descartes, who conceived of man as both an intelligence and an imperfect machine. Man, Gulliver's world seems to imply, has enough ingenuity to improve his imperfect sight with the help of implements and engines. His absurdity is but the result of faulty reasoning which can be corrected. It is not unreasonable, therefore, to hope that man can be cured and his world improved so that even Lilliputians can understand and approve of it.

If Swift's humor then provides us with a satire of and an insight into the spirit of the eighteenth century by revealing to us the content of Gulliver's pockets, Beckett's humor displays before us a great number of characters provided with or even contained in pockets and redolent of the spirit of our age as well as timelessly pointing beyond it.

In his novel *Watt*, one's first impression is of sheer exuberant playfulness when the protagonist tries to obtain a key which his colleague Erskine keeps in his pocket. Watt seems to savor the phonetic and verbal gymnastics and the inherent illogicality of his account:

For the pocket in which Erskine kept this key was not the kind of pocket that Watt could pick. For it was no ordinary pocket, no, but a secret one, sewn on to the front of Erskine's underhose. If the pocket in which Erskine kept this key had been an ordinary pocket, such as a coat pocket, or a trouser's pocket, or even a waistcoat pocket, then Watt, by picking the pocket when Erskine was not looking, might have obtained possession of the key for long enough to record its impression in wax, or plaster, or putty, or butter. Then when he had recorded the impression he could have put the key back in the same pocket as the pocket from which he had taken it, having first taken care to wipe it clean, with a damp cloth. But to pick a pocket sewn on to the front of a man's underhose, even when the man was looking the other way, without arousing suspicion, was not, Watt knew, in his power.

Now if Erskine had been a lady. . . . But there, Erskine was not a lady. [127]

If a world reveals itself here it is at first one of slapstick comedy. But we see grotesque significance in the fact that a key greatly desired by Watt and which would open the door to a room he greatly desires to enter is so completely pocketed and is as utterly unobtainable as Kafka's Castle.

Pockets are used in a similar spirit of apparent playfulness by the author-hero of *Molloy* when he ponders at great length about how he can distribute sixteen pebbles over four pockets so as to be sure that he can suck in turn each pebble at regular intervals. The easiest way to solve the problem, he decides, would be either to decrease the number of stones or increase the number of pockets. But that would be a cowardly way out. A better solution comes to him at last, like a sudden illumination. He must sacrifice what he calls the principle of "trim." Once he is no longer concerned with a true balance and equal distribution, he realizes that "All (all!) that was necessary was to put for example, to begin with, six stones in the right pocket of my greatcoat, or supply-pocket, five in the right pocket of my trousers, and five in the left pocket of my trousers, that makes the lot, twice five ten plus six sixteen, for none remained, in the left pocket of my greatcoat, which for the time being remained empty, empty of stones that is, for its usual contents remained, as well as occasional objects. For where do you think I hid my vegetable knife, my silver, my horn and the other things that I have not yet named, perhaps shall never name" (96–97) . Molloy then proceeds to describe in great detail his system of distribution and sucking, his "series of sucks and transfers." Again, what seemed to be sheer exuberant playfulness acquires depressing overtones. For Molloy argues with a seriousness and scholarly precision which reduce *ad absurdum* all logic, all systems, and all endeavors to prove anything at all. The sixteen stones and their distribution over four pockets come to serve as a foil for Beckett's concept of the surd and the absurd which seem to hold sway in his entire work.

It is perhaps because Beckett's protagonists are so often on the go, and carry all their belongings with them, that their pockets and bags are given so much attention in almost every one of his works. The protagonist of *Watt,* for example, as if to emphasize the futility and emptiness of his existence and to symbolize homeless man clinging to useless possessions, usually carries about two small bags. They are preferable to one large bag, he tells us, and he would have preferred to carry none at all. Those bags are three-fourths empty. One of them is carried by Watt as if it were a club, the other as if it were a sandbag. What they contain Watt never divulges, for what counts is that they are cumbersome and yet difficult to abandon; self-imposed yet insignificant—like most of man's burdens. In *Waiting for Godot,* Lucky almost collapses under the weight of a heavy suitcase each time he appears on stage. He seems unable even to put down his load and seems doomed to carry it for eternity.

There are other Beckett characters with pockets full of such futile objects as pieces of string, carrots, and turnips. Among them are Vladimir and Estragon of *Waiting for Godot.* The protagonists of the unpublished novel *Mercier et Camier* ransack the pockets of their only possession, a raincoat, before abandoning it, and find there "a whole life":

Punched tickets of all kinds . . . burnt matches, on the edges of bits of newspaper obliterated notes of irrevocable appointments, the

classic final tenth of a pointless pencil, several creased sheets of toilet paper, some condoms of doubtful impermeability, and dust. A whole life.
Nothing we need? said Mercier.
I say, a whole life, said Camier.

In *How It Is,* one of Beckett's latest novels, the protagonist crawling naked through the mud clutches a sack which is tied around his neck with a cord. It contains cans of tuna which he opens by means of a can opener and whose content he consumes from time to time listlessly. In its sadism and its humor, which is as black as the mud, this novel seems to stress the sack as container even more than its content. The fact that the word *sack* belongs to the few basic words of the Indo-European vocabulary which have maintained themselves in almost unchanged form in all its tongues attests to its fundamental significance. Being capable of an infinite number of sexual and basic biological connotations, the word occurs in innumerable metaphoric and proverbial expressions and can be associated with gestation, birth, and burial. Not only the protagonist is naked here, but his entire world has been reduced and stripped to its essentials.

One does not need a Lilliputian point of view to see reflected in such pockets filled with strings, burnt matches, and dust, such sacks carried by naked protagonists crawling in the mud the reflection of a universe which is far removed from that of Swift. In the black humor of Beckett neither reason nor the inventions of man's fertile mind finds expression. Man seems no longer the master of a universe which he can bend to his desires and from which he can extract useful tools—as long as he adheres to reason. His life is but dust. The objects which surround him encumber him, rather than help him by their purposefulness. If he introduces objects in his writing, Beckett, unlike some contemporary French novelists who have "taken the side of things," reveals a world where "things are in the saddle and ride mankind." This is, above all, the impression conveyed by Winnie, the protagonist of his play *Happy Days.*

Winnie passes her day, "another heavenly day," in an arid
plain and under a scorching sun, as she pulls from her bodice
and a large black bag beside her an array of unassorted
articles: toothbrush, toothpaste, reading glasses, lipstick,
mirror, nailfile, a medicine bottle, a silly little hat with a
feather, and even a music box which plays a sentimental tune.
Her meticulous adherence to a specific ritual determining the
order in which she extracts these objects from bodice or bag,
the care she takes to make herself beautiful, and her anxious
concern to make these activities last out the day, make one
waver between pathos and laughter. Winnie's vanity and
adherence to decorum become ludicrous in view of her
strangely stationary and totally isolated existence, and we
inadvertently join in her "sniggering" and her "laughing wild
amid severest woe."

How well the world that emerges from Winnie's bag reflects
the spirit of our time is inadvertently illustrated by a recently
popular American song. It is entitled "She Can't Find Her
Keys," and it evokes a situation of slapstick comedy. A boy
takes his girl home and waits while she cannot find her keys. It
is teasingly left to our imagination to decide whether the girl's
inability to find these keys is due to absent-mindedness,
innocent confusion, or womanly wiles, as with each additional
verse she extracts from her pocketbook an ever-growing heap of
objects: lipstick, powder, bubblegum, bobbypins, curlers,
tweezers, cold cream, candy bars, nail files, schoolbooks,
gumdrops, glasses, magazines, hairspray, and jellybeans, and
the long inventory finally ends, in absurd exuberance, with
"TV-set, electric fan, and ashcan." The objects which come to
light from the girl's pocketbook are almost identical with those
contained in Winnie's bag and bodice. Their clutter makes us
see the boy and girl of the song lost in a totally man-made but
chaotic world dominated by objects which are superfluous and
which so encumber man with their clutter that he becomes
their slave rather than their master.

But Winnie's world gains a deeper significance because she

herself is in a pocket as it were. For she is buried in a mound of earth, at first to her waist and then to her neck. Alone in that deserted plain and in her pocket-like mound, Winnie seems almost a stage rendering of Heidegger's concept of *Dasein,* that is, of human existence. She seems to be that *lumen naturale* that sheds the light of human understanding upon the universe of which man is part, bestowing individuality and temporality on that-which-is-there. Without her presence, the plain wherein she is situated, the clouds in the sky would be the same but would remain undifferentiated. Winnie seems, however, helplessly "thrown," in the Heideggerian sense, into time, place and human-ness, while surrounded by the implements which belong to the everyday existence of man. But she also evokes Kierkegaard's "knight of infinite resignation" as she indulges in the humdrum occupations of Everyman (or Everywoman in her case) and does so with what would seem an inner freedom, the result of her awareness of the absurdity and paradox of existence. She seems to be inspired by the Kierkegaardian belief that the conception of an eternal happiness transforms the individual's entire existence and "is a process of dying away from the immediate." [4] For while she busies herself with the numerous things that are all about her in bag and bodice, her mind desires to be free—even of her body which is imprisoned in the large pocket of the earth. She can call the day a happy day and yet long for the moment "when flesh melts at so many degrees and the night of the moon has so many hundred hours" and when she "would simply float up into the blue."

Yet even the human mind is envisioned by Beckett as something like a pocket, something similar to a sphere or a sack. The protagonist of *Murphy* describes his mind as a chamber with three zones: light, half-light, and dark. In the first two zones:

4. Søren Kierkegaard, "Concluding Unscientific Postscript," *A Kierkegaard Anthology,* ed. Robert Bretall (New York: Modern Library, 1966), p. 240.

Murphy felt sovereign and free, in the one to requite himself, in the other to move as he pleased from one unparalleled beatitude to another. . . . [But] the third, the dark, was a flux of forms, a perpetual coming together and falling asunder of forms. . . . neither elements nor states, nothing but forms becoming and crumbling into the fragments of a new becoming, without love or hate or any intelligible principle of change. Here there was nothing but commotion and the pure forms of commotion. Here he was not free but a mote in the dark of absolute freedom. He did not move, he was a point in the ceaseless unconditioned generation and passing away of line.

Matrix of surds. . . .

Thus as his body set him free more and more in his mind, he took to spending . . . more and more [time] in the dark, in the will-lessness, a mote in its absolute freedom. [112–13]

As he lapsed in body he felt himself coming alive in mind, set free to move among its treasures. [111]

The room where Molloy, turned writer, arrives after his wanderings, "his mother's room" or womb, resembles this dimly lighted limbo. And similar limbos are inhabited by Malone and the Unnamable: enclosures that are limp and shapeless, permeated by a grayish light—sacks. They evoke the image of the Baudelairean "gouffre interdit à nos sondes," to which Beckett refers in his essay on Proust and wherein he sees "stored the essence of ourselves, the best of our many selves and their concretions that simplicists call the world." This was the source, Beckett claimed, from which "Proust hoisted his world," using "involuntary memory" as his "diver." For Beckett, then, the writer's experience consists above all of descent, and his task is to report of the treasures he has found in that bottomless sack filled with pure forms and commotion.

It is obvious that, unlike that of his literary Irish ancestor, Beckett's *humour noir* no longer implies a belief in man's ultimate salvation to be reached through the use of reason and ingenuity. What is contained in the pockets of his protagonists progressively defies order and purpose. It bespeaks, on the contrary, a universe both adrift and encumbered with meaningless objects, a universe which has lost the conviction that machines are perfect and that man may strive for perfection with their help. In this world, machines—whether human bodies or bicycles—decay and remain as sheer memories. It is as impersonal as the world of Lemuel Gulliver. Not because man is considered here above all a social being but because his individuality is but ephemeral in the perpetual coming together and falling asunder of forms. Thus what man carries in his pockets, bags, or sacks becomes less and less meaningful and is discarded until from the pockets of earth and body there emerges man's mind replete with treasures which no Lilliputian but only the writer can extract and present to our disbelieving and wondering eyes.

Beckettian Paradox: Who Is Telling the Truth?

Raymond Federman

I cannot be silent. About myself I need know
nothing. Here all is clear. No, all is not clear.
But the discourse must go on.
So one invents obscurities. Rhetoric.

The Unnamable

The world of Samuel Beckett is full of paradoxes—deliberate contradictions which negate every possibility of movement, knowledge, rationality, understanding, and coherence on the part of the creatures that inhabit that curious world. Yet, the more these creatures are immobilized, dehumanized, the more they find themselves sequestrated into fictional and verbal impasses, the more freedom they seem to gain to extricate themselves. Quite often, they counteract the fiction (the "hypothetical imperatives" as Molloy says) imposed upon them by a fictional paradox of their own.

Thus most statements made by the voice (or the many voices) speaking in Beckett's fiction—whether that of the author disguised as an ironic (or unreliable) narrator,[1] or that of the narrator-hero (certainly unreliable) seemingly responsible for his own fictitious existence—lead to flagrant contradictions. "Here all is clear. No, all is not clear" (*The Unnamable*, 7).

The often quoted closing statement of *Molloy* is another striking example:

Then I went back into the house and wrote, It is midnight.
The rain is beating on the windows. It was not midnight.
It was not raining. [241]

Of course, no one is to argue that whoever makes this statement is free to write, "It is midnight. The rain is beating on the windows," even if actually it is not midnight, and it is not

Raymond Federman is Professor of French at the State University of New York at Buffalo.
1. The expression "unreliable narrator" is used here in the same sense which Wayne C. Booth gives it in *The Rhetoric of Fiction* (Chicago: University of Chicago Press, 1961) ; see pp. 339–74.

raining. The paradoxical effect of this statement is, in fact, destroyed if one recognizes that it is formulated on two different levels of rhetoric. The affirmative part of the statement (in the present tense) corresponds to a fiction invented before our eyes by the narrator-hero ("I went back into the house and *wrote* . . . ," he specifies), whereas the negative part of the statement (in the past tense) merely points to a reality which may or may not be true and, therefore, does not necessarily relate to what is being written by Moran in "the report" he claims he has been told to write. Fiction, in other words, need not agree with reality, especially when it is explicitly presented as sub-fiction—counterfeit inventions of the characters themselves. Since the author never speaks in his own name in the narration, however, the reader is under the impression that what is stated omnisciently is reality. Thus the statement, "It was not midnight. It was not raining," produces the effect of being real, of being the truth, even though it is a fictitious illusion, and what becomes clearly questionable, clearly unreliable, is the sub-fiction written by Moran: "It is midnight. The rain is beating on the windows."

Maurice Lecuyer, in a penetrating essay entitled "Réalité et imagination dans *Le Grand Meaulnes* et *Le Voyeur*," deals with that specific problem of modalities in the narrative process, and he states in regard to the various levels on which a narrator can function that if "he describes conditions and actions in the present, whereas in reality he is sitting in front of a sheet of paper, pen in hand, in the process of composing that description, is this not the sign of a non-reality? Described in the past, the scene reveals itself under its true identity: one knows it to be only a representation of a souvenir; described in the present, it does not appear, however, reconstituted, or relived, but truly experienced in an interior manner. It is no longer a representation which rises from the memory, but a phantasm born of the imagination." [2] This is apparently the

2. *Rice University Studies* 51 (Spring 1965) : 9 (my translation of Mr. Lecuyer's French) .

situation in *Molloy,* or for that matter in most of Beckett's
fiction. The paradox results, however, from the fact that there
is a confusion between representation (events told in the past)
and invention (events told in the present).

Beckett's creatures have a prodigious talent for forgetting,
even their own names. "My inability to absorb, my genius for
forgetting, are more than they reckoned with. Dear
incomprehension, it's thanks to you I'll be myself, in the end,"
says the Unnamable (51). Therefore, since fiction
(traditionally) is based on remembered realities and
experiences (transformed of course by the process of
imagination), every statement made by the Beckettian voice is
likely to be invented rather than remembered.

When Molloy is forced, by public authority (not by a
hypothetical imperative this time, but by a policeman who
wants to arrest him) to name himself, he cries out with
deliberate effrontery:

And suddenly I remembered my name, Molloy. My name is Molloy,
I cried, all of a sudden, now I remember. Nothing compelled me to
give this information, but I gave it, hoping to please I suppose. [29]

Molloy is quite obviously inventing a name for himself, making
of himself "a phantasm" of his own imagination rather than
giving of himself "a representation which rises from the
memory."

Moran's report, similarly, is (or will be) fraudulent—just as
Molloy's self-nomination is fraudulent—because it is
postulated against the background of a narration which
purports to pass for reality, but which actually is invented, and
therefore unreliable. What creates the paradox here is that this
narration (the whole second part of the novel—Moran's oral
description of his search for Molloy) opens (in the present
tense) with the same statement Moran uses when he begins to
write his report:

It is midnight. The rain is beating on the windows. I am calm. All
is sleeping. Nevertheless I get up and go to my desk. . . . My report

will be long. Perhaps I shall not finish it. My name is Moran, Jacques. . . . I remember the day I received the order to see about Molloy. It was a Sunday in summer. [125]

Moran then relates (in the past tense) his adventures as he *set out* in search of Molloy until the day he *went back* into the house to write his report. He gives us only the first two sentences of his report (in the present) which, supposedly, will relate what he experienced (in the past) from the moment he received "the order to see about Molloy" to the day he sits down to write his report. But what has happened in the course of his narration is that the affirmative statement about the night and the rain beating on the windows has passed from one level of fiction to another—from the level of pseudo-reality (remembered events) to the level of sub-fiction (invented events). Consequently, the negative part of the statement that closes the novel ("It was not midnight. It was not raining.") is not only in direct contradiction with what is being written by Moran, but also with the whole second part of the novel, and by extension, since the second part of the novel is postulated against the background of Molloy's own counterfeit fiction, the entire narrative becomes a paradox.[3] In other words, not only Moran negates his own fiction, but also Molloy does when he tells us:

And when I say I said, etc., all I mean is that I knew confusedly things were so, without knowing exactly what it was all about. And every time I say, I said this, or I said that, or speak of a voice saying,

3. It has been argued that the second part of the novel should have preceded Molloy's fiction, and that Beckett's reversing of the order of the narration is purely gratuitous. If that were so, the paradoxical effect, essential to Beckett's fiction, would be destroyed. Edith Kern in her essay, "Moran-Molloy: The Hero as Author," *Perspective* 11 (Autumn 1959), points out, quite correctly, that "a reversal of the order in which the novel's parts are presented reveals, indeed, that the work would lose in artistic appeal what it would gain in clarity through such reorganization. If Moran's account of his adventures were to precede that of Molloy, the reader would be deprived of the element of suspense and the artistic challenge to pierce the mystery that shrouds their relationship, and with it the novel's meaning" (189).

far away inside me, Molloy, and then a fine phrase more or less clear
and simple, or find myself compelled to attribute to others
intelligible words, or hear my own voice uttering to others more or
less articulate sounds, I am merely complying with the convention
that demands you either lie or hold your peace. For what really
happened was quite different. [118–19]

Molloy is definitely speaking here of the confusion that exists
between actuality (the present) and the pseudo-reality (the
past) created by the conscious writer. It would indeed be
preferable for Molloy (and similarly for Moran) not to try to
relate what he thinks happened, for as he well knows "what
really happened was quite different." But since Molloy, like all
the other Beckettian creatures that are given the delusory
power to talk for themselves, cannot "hold his peace" and must
go on talking, we can assume that what he is telling us is a lie.
Thus when he says "I said, etc.," speaking of the past in the
present, he is merely inventing a fiction even though he claims
"I quote from memory" (119). In fact, earlier in his narrative,
Molloy makes it quite clear that his predicament as
narrator-hero (narrator/narrated) forces him to deal in
contradictions: "Not to want to say, not to know what you
want to say, not to be able to say what you think you want to
say, and never to stop saying, or hardly ever, that is the thing to
keep in mind, even in the heat of composition" (36).

The whole fiction of *The Unnamable* is based on the same
obligation to speak, to go on speaking ("you must go on, I can't
go on, I'll go on"), even if it means inventing, getting more
and more caught up in the liar's paradox. Early in the novel
the Unnamable states: "Past happiness in any case has clean
gone from my memory, assuming it was ever there" (6–7).
Therefore, since he "cannot be silent," he too invents
"obscurities. Rhetoric" (7). But the Unnamable, whose
"genius for forgetting" is explicitly noted, is much more of a
deliberate inventor, much more of a liar than his predecessors.
As such, he is able to create for himself not only a hypothetical
beginning, but he even attributes to himself a memory:

I remember the first sound heard in this place, I have often heard it since. For I am obliged to assign a beginning to my residence here, if only for the sake of clarity. Hell itself, although eternal, dates from the revolt of Lucifer. It is therefore permissible, in the light of this distant analogy, to think of myself as being here forever, but not as having been here forever. This will greatly help me in my relation. Memory notably, which I did not think myself entitled to draw upon, will have its word to say, if necessary.[4] [9–10]

On this fraudulent basis, he can also negate his own self, his own fiction, any time he wishes by simply speaking about nothing: "Would it not be better if I were simply to keep on saying babababa, for example . . ." (28).

The muttering creature of *How It Is* goes even further in negating his own inventions. Although he insists throughout the narrative that he is quoting from memory "past moments old dreams back again or fresh like those that pass or things things always and memories" (7), the opening statement of the novel (set on the dual basis of the past and the present) reveals the ambiguity of his fiction: "*how it was* I quote before Pim with Pim after Pim *how it is* three parts I say it as I hear it" (7; my italics). In his case, however, the negation of fiction is much more flagrant, much more deliberate, but at the same time much more paradoxical. He ends his verbal contortions in utter confusion over the possibility of deciding whether or not he has told us anything reliable in what he calls the "last version" of his life. His only certainty is that he is totally submerged in darkness and that he is lying face down in the mud. That is the actuality of his predicament—fiction on the first level. But he cannot understand how he has managed to give us the record of his verbal progression—fiction on the second level. His last resort, therefore, is to negate the

4. The French text (Paris: Editions de Minuit, 1953) is even more explicit in revealing that the narrator-hero is inventing his own fiction: "Car je dois supposer un commencement à mon séjour ici, ne serait-ce que pour *la commodité du récit*. . . . Voilà qui va singulièrement *faciliter mon exposé*" (16–17; my italics).

hypothesis on which his babblings ("this unqualifiable murmur") was postulated:

all these calculations yes explanations yes the whole story from beginning to end yes completely false yes

that wasn't how it was no not at all no how then no answer how was it then no answer HOW WAS IT screams good

there was something yes but nothing of all that no all balls from start to finish yes this voice quaqua yes all balls yes only one voice here yes mine yes when the panting stops yes [144–45]

One could quote endlessly passages from the novels and plays of Beckett which negate one another as they are brought together: statements which end into verbal impasses from which the speaker extricates himself by formulating other statements that contradict what he has just said. Most readers of fiction object to seeing taken away with one hand that which they have been given with the other, but unless they can accept this "anti-fictional" aspect of Beckett's fiction they will continue to deal with it as a paradox. Undoubtedly, it is this kind of uncertainty, this backtracking ambiguity which gives Beckett's fiction its paradoxical aspect, as though it were constantly on the brink of crumbling into nonsense, into self-negation. Only if one accepts the interplay between two levels of rhetoric can one gain an understanding of the Beckettian paradox. In other words, when reading Beckett, one must constantly guard against imposing on the fiction one's own notions of order, truth, plausibility, and reality.

Beckett, of course, did not invent fictional ambiguity. He merely exploits it to its utmost degree of confusion, and, as he himself said:

The confusion is not my invention. We cannot listen to a conversation for five minutes without being acutely aware of the confusion. It is all around us and our only chance now is to let it in. The only chance of renovation is to open our eyes and see the mess.[5]

5. As quoted by Tom F. Driver in "Beckett by the Madeleine," *Columbia University Forum* 4 (Summer 1961) : 22.

This admonition reveals to what extent Beckett is willing to allow confusion to enter into his work, and at the same time it warns us that we should be ready to accept confusion in whatever form it may take: contradictions, negations, paradoxes. It is only when we attempt to reconcile the contradictory aspects of the Beckettian dialectic on the basis of our preconceived notions of fiction that the paradox is created. Too often, we are guilty of reading paradoxes into Beckett's fiction because we cannot accept that which destroys itself as it creates itself—that which is contrary to common sense, or that which points to itself, even though ironically, as paradoxical. And yet, the primary meaning of a paradox is, as defined by the most basic dictionary: "a tenet contrary to received opinion; . . . an assertion or sentiment seemingly contradictory, or opposed to common sense, *but that yet may be true in fact.*" [6] This definition can indeed apply to the whole Beckett canon, and more specifically to the narrator-hero's ambivalent role as a recipient of fiction and a dispatcher of fiction, as a creature that is both, as the Unnamable says of himself, "the teller and the told."

Moran, for instance, experiences on the one hand his quest for Molloy, and on the other he writes (or will write) a report about it. Supposedly these two will coincide. Moreover, even though Moran is launched on the traces of Molloy, who remains untraceable, the relationship between their two narratives becomes a perfect correspondence, a perfect superimposition, in spite of the many contradictions one can read in the novel. Ludovic Janvier explains this contradictory aspect of the narrative discourse by saying:

In *Molloy,* for example, where everything is duplication, the essential of the "dialogue"—and it is at the same time the dynamics of this story—lies in the commerce that Molloy entertains with himself, writing himself, telling himself, commenting himself just as Moran, the other pole, the other narrator of the novel writes

6. *Webster's New Collegiate Dictionary* (6th ed.), s.v. "paradox"; my italics.

himself, tells himself, comments himself. . . . Moran is the
Moran-of-Molloy as consciousness is consciousness-of-something.[7]

There is a further complication, however, a further confusion
in the Beckettian paradox (particularly as exploited in
Molloy) that prevents us from accepting it readily on the terms
of our own received opinion. The paradox, like the metaphor,
brings together two normally exclusive elements; but whereas
the metaphor reconciles what may be two incongruous objects
or two incompatible concepts by placing them on the same
level of comprehension, on the same level of rhetoric, the
paradox, on the contrary, creates a split between the two
elements it brings together, whereby one negates the other.
Very often, in Beckett's fiction, this split occurs (as exemplified
by the closing statement of *Molloy*) on two different levels of
rhetoric. And as such even the paradox itself is undermined,
negated, not only within a single statement, but in the whole of
fiction. Thus while there is a seemingly perfect duplication of
events between the two parts of *Molloy,* and it appears that
Moran becomes Molloy in the end, there is also a perfect
negation of one part by the other, just as there is a total
negation of Moran by Molloy and vice versa. Molloy's fiction
negates Moran's report because it is unreliable, unconfirmed
one might say (Moran never finds Molloy) , and Moran's
fiction negates Molloy's adventures because it is invented.
Therefore, when Moran reveals at the end of his futile quest
that he "had not been able to go to him, and grow to be a
friend, and like a father to me," and he adds that,
consequently, Molloy has not been able to "help me do what I
had to do" (222) , he is flagrantly admitting the failure of his
quest, the negation of his fiction.

But in fact, what is negated here is not fiction itself, but a
traditional concept of fiction, the concept of storytelling.
Neither Moran, nor Molloy, nor the Unnamable, nor any of

7. "Samuel Beckett: La plaie et le couteau," *Le Monde,* 17 January
1968, p. iv (my translation of Mr. Janvier's French) .

the other narrator-heroes, has been able to tell a coherent story about himself or about his invented playmates. This is undoubtedly the most crucial if not the most original aspect of Beckett's creative process: his fiction no longer relates a story (past realities reshaped by the process of imagination into an artistic form), but it simply reflects upon itself, upon its own chaotic verbal progress, that is to say upon its own (defective) substance—language. When the anonymous narrator-hero of "The Calmative" states: "All I say cancels out, I'll have said nothing" (*Stories and Texts for Nothing*, 28), or when the Unnamable affirms: "To tell the truth, let us be honest at least, it is some considerable time now since I last knew what I was talking about" (49), they, like all the other Beckettian voices, are merely reflecting on the language of their fiction, and not on the fiction itself. The *Texts for Nothing*, as ambiguous as the title may be, are not stories about nothing, they are reflections, meditations on language, on the nothingness of their language. They are stories without stories whose only substance is the discourse of which they are made. Or as the voice in "Text eight" says: "It's an unbroken flow of words and tears. With no pause for reflection. . . . it's for ever the same murmur, flowing unbroken, like a single endless word and therefore meaningless, for it's the end gives the meaning to words" (111).

In this respect, Beckett's fiction separates itself from the traditional narrative, and even from such an experiment in "anti-fiction" as *Les Faux-Monnayeurs* of André Gide which is primarily a reflection on fiction by fiction rather than a reflection on fiction by its own language. Or as Claude-Edmonde Magny said of Gide's novel, it is "le roman du romanesque." [8] Beckett's fiction, on the contrary, could be called "le roman du langage."

André Gide based his whole concept of fictional counterfeitness on the premise that fiction cannot pass for

8. *Histoire du roman français depuis 1918* (Paris: Editions du Seuil, 1950), p. 251.

reality, and in *Les Faux-Monnayeurs* (one of the great paradoxes of the French novel) ,[9] he deliberately toys with his narration to force the reader to distinguish fictional events from what may appear to be real events. He does so not only in *Le Journal des Faux-Monnayeurs,* which functions as a critical mirror for the novel, not only by his interventions in the novel, but also by the introduction into the narrative of a writer-protagonist, Edouard, who seemingly assumes responsibility for shaping the various elements of the fiction. Gide can then pretend to give away his authorial control in order to criticize and even contradict the course which his novel is taking: "Events fell out badly," he tells us.[10] And elsewhere, referring to his characters as though they had a life of their own independent of his creative authority, Gide deplores:

People . . . [who] are cut out of a cloth which has no thickness. . . . No past weighs upon them—no constraint; they have neither laws, nor masters, nor scruples; by their freedom and spontaneity, they make the novelist's despair; he can get nothing from them but worthless reactions.[11]

The same could indeed be said of Beckett's creatures—"libres et spontanés, ils font le désespoir du romancier." In that sense, Beckett's fiction functions in a way similar to that of Gide. His narrator-heroes seem to create themselves and their own fictional environment, "sans scrupules" and with total disregard for their creator's responsibility toward the narrative.

The essential difference, however, is that Gide makes of authorial interventions the subject of his novel, whereas Beckett tends to disappear behind his creations thereby making

9. In closing her brilliant analysis of Gide's novel, Claude-Edmonde Magny states in *Histoire du roman:* "On comprend alors l'apparent paradoxe qu'offrait ce roman doué d'un sens réel, mais informulable en termes intellectuels, fût-ce par l' auteur" (278) .
10. *The Counterfeiters,* trans. Dorothy Bussy (New York: The Modern Library, 1927) , p. 204; the French can be found in *Romans* (Paris: Gallimard, Edition de la Pléiade, 1958) , p. 1110.
11. *Counterfeiters,* p. 204; *Romans,* p. 1110.

of them free agents of "speechlessness." Gide's attitude is that of the self-conscious author who "injects a functionless reflexivity" into his work to undermine the traditional concept of storytelling,[12] but no one is "fooled" by his disabused attitude, even when he says: "Passavant, Lady Griffith, tous ces gens m'ennuient; que viennent-ils faire ici?" Beckett, on the contrary, is subtly hidden in the voice of his protagonists to the extent that they are capable of speaking against their "irresponsible" creator, accusing him of trying to impose upon them not only a story when there is no story to tell, but also words when words are meaningless:

> He thinks words fail him, he thinks because words fail him he's on his way to my speechlessness, to being speechless with my speechlessness, he would like it to be my fault that words fail him, of course words fail him. He tells his story every five minutes, saying it is not his, there's cleverness for you. He would like it to be my fault that he has no story, of course he has no story, that's no reason for trying to foist one on me. [*Stories and Texts*, 91–92]

This curious reversal of roles, whereby the voice of fiction speaks against itself, is possible because having no longer a story to tell ("of course he has no story") through his characters, the author simply allows his storyless creations to define themselves on the basis of their own substance—words, empty words, until there will be nothing more to say, for "even the words desert you, it's as bad as that" (*Stories and Texts*, 70) .

As such, Beckett's fiction becomes a denunciation of the illusory aspect of fiction—stories which pretend to pass for reality. But the truth is that fiction is not reality, it is simply a language which tells its own story, its own true story. Beckett's *speaking words* are telling the truth about themselves: they are telling us that they are words: "Words, mine was never more than that, than this pell-mell babel of silence and words"

12. Albert Cook, *The Meaning of Fiction* (Detroit: Wayne State University Press, 1960) , p. 35. Mr. Cook goes on to say, "in *Les Faux-Monnayeurs* Gide injects a functionless reflexivity that mars what is otherwise his best novel."

(*Stories and Texts,* 104) . This shift from a language that tells *a* story to a language that tells *its* own story ("I say it as I hear it," that is "how it is") reveals how Beckett's fiction has passed from one level of rhetoric to another, and as a result how the Beckettian paradox—a paradox created by the dual level of storytelling—has itself been negated.

Olga Bernal, in a recent article in *Le Monde,* opens an entirely new vista into Beckett's creative process when she states: "For Beckett's Molloy, the condition of the object was to be without a name, and inversely. If the literature of the past described reality (or believed it did) , that of today realizes that what it describes is not reality, but the very language of which it is captive as soon as it begins to speak. And no doubt, this is the first time in the history of literature that language no longer situates itself opposite the world but opposite itself." [13] This declaration emphasizes the revolutionary stance which contemporary fiction is taking in relation to traditional fiction. If Olga Bernal's claim is true, however, it applies only to a certain portion of Beckett's creation—those major works which follow the contradictory closing statement of *Molloy.* Everything that precedes that statement (*More Pricks Than Kicks, Murphy, Watt,* the unpublished *Mercier et Camier,* and *Les Nouvelles*) led inevitably to this moment of flagrant contradiction, to this confrontation of fiction by its own language.

All the fiction that precedes the moment when Moran goes back into the house to write his report is set on a dual level of storytelling. In all these works, a narrator, more or less self-conscious, more or less present and active in the story, reveals by his interventions (as Gide does in *Les Faux-Monnayeurs*) the fraudulence of fiction on the basis of a split between two levels of narration. Only in *Watt* and in *Molloy* does the narrator succeed in becoming a counterpart for the protagonist of the novel (Sam-Watt, Moran-Molloy)

13. "L'Oubli des noms," *Le Monde,* 17 January 1968, p. v (my translation of Miss Bernal's French) .

thus creating the Beckettian paradox. In the other early novels and stories, the narrator is merely a distant witness of the fiction, but not an active participant. Therefore, even though the narrator in *More Pricks Than Kicks* tells us of his relationship with Belacqua Shuah, "We were Pylades and Orestes for a period, flattened down to something very genteel," [14] and the narrator in *Mercier et Camier* claims: "Le voyage de Mercier et Camier, je peux le raconter, si je veux, car j'étais avec eux, tout le temps," [15] in fact these stories are not told by narrators, but are omnisciently controlled by the self-conscious author.

Starting with *Malone Dies*, pseudo-reality and sub-fiction unify into a single level of rhetoric as author, narrator, and narrator-hero converge into one voice. Thus from a narrative that describes experiences as though they had been lived in the past, the fiction beyond *Molloy* relates experiences lived in the present, or rather in a kind of present-future condition. Ludovic Janvier explains this shift from present-past to present-future when he writes: "Moran and Molloy, from the perspective of their oral present looked toward the days of wandering they lived until then. The narration was that present-past indicating what had been. Moran and Molloy told their beginnings. Malone, on the contrary, wants to indicate that which he has not yet lived. He looks toward that near future in which his present allows itself to be drawn: Malone dies. The present of his narration nourishes itself on the coming future of this moribund who speaks. It is turned entirely toward what will be. Malone tells his end." [16] In other words, Malone has reached that condition to which all his predecessors were aspiring. He has become the writer locked in a room, sitting in front of a sheet of paper, pencil in hand,

14. (London: Chatto & Windus, 1934), pp. 44–45.
15. *Mercier et Camier*, p. 1 of a typescript of the original unpublished manuscript (courtesy of Samuel Beckett).
16. *Pour Samuel Beckett* (Paris: Editions de Minuit, 1966), p. 64 (my translation).

describing the present of his future condition, describing the language of his fiction.

Although Moran claims to be a writer, the scribe of Molloy's fiction which he writes (or will write) according to the instructions he received, he only gives us the first two sentences of his report. Moran is only halfway between the teller and the told. He remains controlled by the "hypothetical imperatives" which govern all of Beckett's fiction prior to *Malone Dies*. Moran does not fulfill his mission. Undoubtedly, it is because he and Molloy, like all the others who precede them, are still physically, socially, and realistically in movement (even though they gradually suffer disintegration and dehumanization) that they cannot achieve the solipsist condition of Malone. Nevertheless, the question remains about the credibility of their fiction. Who is telling the truth? Is Moran telling the truth about the lie of his and of Molloy's fiction? Or is Malone lying about his fictional truth? We are again caught in the vicious circles of the liar's paradox. For if Molloy, Moran, and their predecessors are telling the truth it is about a lie (the lie of fiction), and if Malone and his successors are lying, it is about the truth of their condition (verbal authenticity). Beyond this one will never know, or rather one can only hope, as does the voice in the *Texts for Nothing*: "And yet I have high hopes, I give you my word, high hopes, that one day I may tell a story, hear a story, yet another, with men, kinds of men as in the days when I played all regardless or nearly, worked and played" (105).

Adventures of the First Person

Robert Champigny

*"So, for this new year, you is reesolving
to be a new man?" "Yep, mebbe with
blue eyes, keen blue eyes, and a bicycle."*

W. Kelly, *The Incompleat Pogo*

Descartes' methodical doubt does not extend to Being itself: as a matter of fact, one may doubt that a certain thing, or kind of thing, exists, but not that there is something rather than nothing. Furthermore, Descartes does not question the meaningfulness of language, at least not of the language which is used in the *Meditations:* the existence of what is denoted is doubted, but not the existence of what denotes. Thus, meaning, or the act of meaning, would appear to be the first being, or kind of being, implicitly asserted through the Cartesian doubt: in Husserl's terminology, intentionality; in Descartes' words, thinking.

Instead of this, Descartes concludes the opening moves of the *Meditations* by positing a self defined as a "thinking thing." Thinking is not asserted in itself, but as the attribute of a person, or spirit. Thanks to the apparently innocent use of the first person in the presentation of the problem, thanks also to the fleeting apparition of the "evil genius" (deceiver and deceived are personified entities), the device of personification has passed unnoticed. Not so in Beckett's *The Unnamable.*

This monologue starts with the following questions: "Where now? Who now? When now?" The second question suggests an attempt to place and compose a person, or character. But the stress on the word *now* threatens this project from the start: especially the question "When now?" *Now* is a term which serves to set the present moment in a temporal field. The answer to the odd question "When now?" would have to be something like this: "Now is when the word *now,* or an

Robert Champigny is Research Professor of French at Indiana University.

equivalent, is uttered." The question reminds us that temporality rests on temporalization. Language may or may not temporalize. Likewise, persons depend on personification. Language may or may not personify. This is what the second question "Who now?" suggests. It incites us not to take the device of personification for granted. For it depends on temporalization.

"Where now? Who now? When now? Without asking myself. I, say I. Without thinking it. Questions, hypotheses, call them that. Keep going, going on, call that going, call that on." [1] The introduction of the first person pronoun complicates matters. Suppose that personification works, that we forget the creation of persons in favor of the persons created. We should still have to decide to what entity, and to what kind of entity, the pronoun *I* refers. We are dealing with a monologue, not with a conversation. Will the *I* manage to be identified with one of the persons posited in the temporal field? Or will it remain on another plane, which would not admit of the category of the person? "Without thinking it" would, in this case, mean: "Without turning the *I* into a person." On the other hand, can the personal form "I think" be reduced, without loss, to an impersonal form such as "There is thinking"? This is suggested by the use of infinitives (more striking in the French original: *demander, dire, appeler, aller*).

But such phrases as "without asking myself" and "without thinking it" may well have the effect of a preterition: pushing aside attracts the attention to what is pushed aside. As a matter of fact, instead of being eliminated, the first person will keep haunting the monologue as a kind of question mark. Time and again, the monologue will attempt to graft the pronoun on a person, or character. If the question "I. Who might that be?"

---

1. I have intentionally departed from Samuel Beckett's own translation, which reads "unquestioning" instead of "without asking myself" and "unbelieving" instead of "without thinking it." I have decided to remain closer to Beckett's original, "sans me le demander" and "sans le penser," to prove certain points in the discussion that follows.

(68) could be answered satisfactorily, if the personification could "take," the monologue would apparently have reached its objective, or at least an objective.

But preteritions may also attract the attention to the language which is used. And this effect is obtained even more clearly by metalinguistic interventions: "Questions, hypotheses, call them that," "call that going, call that on." The three questions with which the text starts indicate the direction of the search. But the sentence "Questions, hypotheses, call them that" focuses the attention on the indicating itself: we look at the pointing finger, rather than toward what it might indicate. Whereas the text of Descartes avoided letting the attention dwell on stylistic devices, the text of Beckett brings them into light. Before going into more detail, let us sum up the consequences.

As the monologue proceeds, a *we,* a *they,* a *you,* a *he,* will crop up, and they will be grammatically connected with the *I.* The monologue will then start composing a tableau, a scene, circumstances, a setting, in the manner (duly caricatured) of a novel, or biography. But a paralyzing reflection will set in, an equivalent to "Call that going, call that on." Suppose that a person, *he* or *I,* appears to be placed in a biographical setting. We come upon a formula such as "I lied," or "I am inventing." We are thus tempted to shift to a fictional perspective. Can the first person find its dwelling in a fictional character? It seems to favor a character whose name begins with *M* (because of *me, myself?*). But another character in *M* emerges: the first person tries on this new identity in passing. Then, apparently disgusted, it turns toward a character in *W* (because of *we?*). These divagations of the first person, this caricature of a device common in modern novels (shift in pronoun to go with the point of view), do not allow whatever verbal game is in progress to remain in clutch as it were. At times, weariness and exasperation appear to set in: "enough of this cursed first person" (77). Yet the monologue goes on. Personification slips in again. A new character game begins.

In fact, the monologue goes around in circles. Rather than with a meditation, we are dealing with a rumination. There are returns in Descartes' text; but their purpose is to check and corroborate, in the manner of a scientist, or of a conjurer. In *The Unnamable,* on the contrary, going back is designed to erase: words are killed with words, which in turn need words to kill them. Since, however, there has to be a last word, it will be: "I'll go on." This is also the forced ending of Sartre's *No Exit.* The characters in this play go on trying to justify themselves with words in their hellish eternity. In *The Unnamable,* the *I* keeps trying to personify itself with its here and now. Or it pretends.

In ordinary speech, *I, here,* and *now* are objectified as an individual among individuals, as a place among places, as a moment among moments. But they have to objectify themselves: these three words refer to the subjective root of objectification. To use a mathematical metaphor: here is the zero place, now the zero moment, I the zero individual. One might say that *The Unnamable* plays on the resonances of these phrases.

The plan of the analysis which follows, the distinctions which I shall draw between semantic perspectives, bear no relation to the progress of Beckett's monologue. For it does not progress; and it does not distinguish between perspectives. Its only method, if it can be called a method, is in the mystic tradition; it illustrates the *via negativa:* "affirmations and negations invalidated as uttered, or sooner or later" (3). Everything is presented on one plane, flattened, sometimes muddled to the point of frenzy:

what are you seeking, who is seeking, seeking who you are, supreme aberration, where you are, what you're doing, what you've done to them, what they've done to you [always, or rather: still], prattling along, where are the others, who is talking, not I, where am I, where is the place where I've always been, where are the others, it's they are talking. . . . [138]

Let us first consider the attempt to place the first person in a biographical field. This involves situating the body as a spatial thing: "It is well to establish the position of the body from the outset" (22). The monologue describes a posture; it even provides a torrent of tears, probably in order better to outline the skin. Trouble arises when the attention turns to clothes: "Am I clothed? I have often asked myself this question, then suddenly started talking about Malone's hat, or Molloy's greatcoat, or Murphy's suit" (23). The question about clothing, which would normally bear on something accidental, appears to become essential in this case. Parodying Descartes, one might ask: "Am I a clothed thing?" In other words: "What constitutes my spatiality? Where does it begin?"

There is also the matter of the eyes. Tears objectify them; yet they go on seeing. And what is seen can be considered part of the seeing: "I'm the air, the walls, the walled-in one, everything yields, opens, ebbs, flows, like flakes, I'm all these flakes" (139). The subjective body resists reification. It is a diversity of unstable prehensions, the playground and battleground of self and not-self. Phenomena are more or less mine and not mine, according to circumstances.

Let us turn toward temporal location. The first person should refer to a world-line. Memory provides a past, but not everything which is to be included in a *curriculum vitae:* when and where I was born is based on hearsay evidence. The monologue goes further. It undermines the positing of a past, by presenting it as a stylistic convention: "I am obliged to assume a beginning to my residence here, if only for the sake of [the] clarity [of the story]" (9–10). If what is remembered cannot be posited apart from the act of remembering, memory cannot be distinguished from imagination: "I invented my memories" (152). Of course, one might point out that such a statement implicitly recognizes the difference between past and present, and between truth and falsehood: "Invention" is asserted and it is asserted in the past. But, in this monologue, there are no privileged utterances. A statement like "I lied" enjoys no special status: is it to be considered true, false, or neither? The monologue illustrates in its own way the Paradox of the Liar.

It is in relation to other persons that I can, not only reify, but personify, myself. The others fashion a certain objective person; they teach the child to recognize himself as this person, to answer "I" when he is told "you." They try to "saddle me with [the] lifetime [of a human being]" (59). This is a recurring motif in the monologue: it would be convenient and restful if the others took complete charge of this person whom they insist on defining and judging. One would have only to repeat what they say, substituting "I" for "you." But they want a commitment: they want one to identify what one feels to be with this objective person. The monologue points out the ontological gap between these two notions of the self: "Do they believe I believe it is I who am speaking? That's theirs too. To make me believe I have an ego all my own, and can speak of it, as they of theirs" (81). To the extent that the objective self is not assumed, the socio-historical field is not cognitive; it is esthetic. It becomes a fictional field and the persons in it become characters. Needless to say, the monologue provides no firm basis for a distinction between cognitive and fictional perspective.

Let us, then, adopt a fictional perspective. Stylistically, the first person can be used to refer to one of the characters; thus it may find a dwelling in a fictional field. But it is to be noted that, in this case, the first person is deprived of its here and now: to choose a certain moment of the fictional process as present is arbitrary.

The monologue shows only half-hearted attempts at characterization. A story gets started, picturesque details are provided (a legless character in a jar: so as better to be fixed?). Then the narration goes adrift, peters out. Another story emerges, reaches its crest, breaks down. A female character is

named Marguerite on page 74, Madeleine on page 75,
assuming that there is only one. There are shifts in tenses, from
the past, to the present, to the future.
On which character is the first person to be grafted?
"Nothing doing without proper names. I therefore baptise him
Worm. It was high time. Worm. . . . It will be my name too,
when the time comes, when I needn't be called Mahood any
more" (69). In this fluid and chaotic fictional field, the
characters cannot achieve a clear and distinct identity; and the
first person cannot be anchored:

That was always the way. Just at the moment when the world is
assembled at last, and it begins to dawn on me how I can leave it,
all fades and disappears. I shall never see this place again, where my
jar stands on its pedestal, with its garland of many-coloured
lanterns, and me inside it, I could not cling to it. [65]

The discrepancy between subjectivity and objective person
which we had noted has become the discrepancy between
subjectivity and objective character. Characters are more freely
composed, they can be more accommodating, but the here and
now has to be forsaken. This would explain why the first
person cannot be passed on to a character, as well as the failure
of characterization itself: its arbitrariness and gratuitousness
are emphasized in the monologue.

What is created does not manage to gain its autonomy from
the act of creating. We are thus thrown back on a psychological
perspective, a perspective in which inchoate characters, or
persons, would-be attitudes and ego-images, act in an inner kind
of drama. In any case, when a reader is said to "identify" with a
fictional character, that is the sort of thing which is meant.
Likewise, "Madame Bovary, c'est moi" does not mean that
Flaubert believed he had been, was, or would be married to a
fictional character named Charles Bovary.
A psychological model eliminates the problem of deciding
which character is to be labeled "I." Each mental attitude is a
self, is one of my selves: "For if I am Mahood, I am Worm too"

(70). But these two vaguely personified images do not exhaust possibilities: "is one to postulate a tertius gaudens, . . . I . . . at last?" (71). If two attitudes are objectified, a third one is needed to posit them as ego-images, as two of *my* selves. A spectator is needed. And in order to posit this spectator and recognize him as one of my selves, another spectator is needed, and so on ad infinitum. In this psychological perspective, it appears that the monologue has got caught in the trap of the Third Man argument, as applied to consciousness: "I knew it, there might be a hundred of us and still we'd lack the hundred and first, we'll always be short of me" (72).

Still another possibility: the first person might refer to the voice which speaks, to the act of speaking or writing the monologue. In everyday speech, the first person pronoun designates the person who is speaking, or is quoted. The failure of personification would still leave us with the act of speaking as a firm reference. The first person could then be said to designate a dramatic character in a one-character play not to be performed, so that the character might remain disembodied: a spirit.

But the reference provided by the act of speaking, or writing, proves no more satisfactory than the others. Time and again, it is implicitly adopted: "I shall never be silent" (4) ; "I'll go on" (17). But the text also questions the pertinence of calling *mine* the act of speaking as well as what is spoken of:

I'm all these words, all these strangers, this dust of words, with no ground for their settling, no sky for their dispersing, coming together to say, fleeing one another to say, that I am they, all of them, those that merge, those that part, those that never meet, and nothing else, yes, something else, that I'm something quite different, a quite different thing, a wordless thing in an empty place. . . . [139]

The metalinguistic aspect of the monologue helps give the impression that the words, in particular the first person pronoun, are quoted as much as assumed, mentioned as much as used. Think also of the experience of hearing oneself speak on a recording device: the voice is recognized as "mine" in the sense that it was not the voice of someone else that was recorded. But is it felt to be mine? In *The Unnamable*, between the intention and the performance of speaking, or writing, there seems to intervene a kind of alienation: mediumnic ("the others") , and mechanical.

The various kinds of identification which have been considered (body, socio-historical person, fictional character, inner attitudes, disembodied spirit) can be said to have failed because subjectivity cannot be absorbed by an object of thought. It could also be said that the failure is due to the discrepancy between two logical categories: individual and quality. Each type of identification was an attempt at individuation. And the first person cannot designate an individual to the extent that it is understood to refer to a quality of experience: self, or selfhood, or selfness, as opposed to not-self.

Indeed, a reference to a qualitative kind of self has to be postulated to account for common ways of using the first person pronoun. For, if selfhood were construed as an individual, the various kinds of identification that have been sketched would be impossible: either the self would be an individual other than all the individuals which may be tried on to see if they fit, or it would be one of these individuals and one only. If the self as quality were forsaken, there would be no difference between "I am raising my arm" and "my arm is rising." And if a reduction to a socio-historical individual could be achieved, "identification" with another person, or with a fictional character, would be impossible. The self as quality allows for individuation, while disallowing reduction.

But, when it is assumed, not merely quoted, the first person pronoun refers neither to a quality by itself, nor to an individual by itself: it expresses an individuation of the self, an individuation which can but remain incomplete because logically wrong: a quality cannot be turned into an individual, or a set of individuals. Thus could one account for the adventures of the first person in *The Unnamable*. The purpose appears to be to graft the first person on an individual, not in order to get rid of the self as quality, but rather to dissociate and liberate it verbally: "I . . . , no one" (163). The variety of attempted identifications, their ludicrous aspect, their repeated failures, serve to point out the impossibility of a reduction.

On the other hand, however, the dogged use of the pronoun undermines the attempt at a liberation through words, since the pronoun expresses the project of individuating the self. Thus, when the monologue suggests the desire to "be let loose, alone, in the unthinkable unspeakable, where I have not ceased to be, where they will not let me be" (66), the use of the pronoun makes one conceive of an individual, as opposed to other individuals ("they," "the others"), rather than of a quality, as opposed to another quality: self and not-self.

On the whole, the language of *The Unnamable* belongs to the dramatic sphere (hence my labeling it a monologue). Could a verbal dissociation of the self from the category of individuality have been better achieved through another kind of language? My analytic commentary would seem to have named the "unnamable," by the simple device of substituting nouns for a pronoun. But conceptualizing is not naming, at least not the kind of naming for which the monologue perversely pretends to be casting about: "individuation of the self" does not name the phenomenon as it occurs *hic et nunc*.

One might think also of poetic language: it would allow one to use the first person as a pronoun and yet point toward a quality rather than an individual. It would take into account the ways in which the self is individuated, in the first person or in others, by showing the phenomenon in reverse. But, again, could such a language be said to name? Poetry as such does not name things; it things names. It makes us aware that nothing can properly be named: strictly proper names could name only themselves.

Molloy or the Quest for Meaninglessness: A Global Interpretation

David Hayman

Few twentieth-century authors write so thoroughly for their time as does Samuel Beckett, whose strange and difficult books have proved a subject of lively controversy. But Beckett is not an isolated phenomenon. His misfit heroes trapped in an existential web, not of their own making, are counterparts of Kafka's faceless heroes in search of grace in a godless world; like Joyce's Leopold Bloom and Stephen Dedalus, they are aspects of every man in quest of function and fulfillment; like Proust's isolated hero, they tend to spin their world out of their own being, drawing upon the timeless matrix of their imaginations. But, while all these writers permit their characters to experience hope, Beckett depicts creatures for the most part as despairing, agonizing, and irreverent. The dimension which Beckett creates for and through his characters is paradoxically shapeless and circumscribed, each simple event having multiple ramifications. These, and other qualities in Beckett's works demand and defy elucidation.

Perhaps the appeal of Beckett's trilogy, *Molloy, Malone Dies* and *The Unnamable,* is best illustrated by Molloy's comments upon the little silver knife-rest which he has stolen from his hostess Lousse. This object is a banal one, a thing found on most French dinner tables, composed in this case of two X's joined by a rod upon which the diner rests his soiled knife. However, Molloy, knowing nothing of social behavior, finds in the knife-rest a source of endless speculation. After describing it to us at some length with evident relish, he concludes:

for a certain time I think it inspired me with a kind of veneration, for there was no doubt in my mind that it was not an object of

David Hayman is Professor of English and Comparative Literature at the University of Iowa.

129

virtu, but that it had a most specific function always to be hidden from me. I could therefore puzzle over it endlessly without the least risk. For to know nothing is nothing, not to want to know anything likewise, but to be beyond knowing anything, to know you are beyond knowing anything, that is when peace enters in, to the soul of the incurious seeker. [85–86]

Strikingly similar though far more complex is the nature of Beckett's novels whose content sparkles with possible meanings, almost unlimited in their ramifications. Like the knife-rest, the books are approximations of the infinite, an infinitude that is paradoxically and satisfyingly accessible.

Beckett's trilogy is for all its apparent formlessness a close-knit structural unit, though the novels are related to each other more through their form and direction than through any obvious system of interrelated characters or events. All of them are narrated in the first person. Each of them deals with a figure or figures whose condition is purged of the specific, that is, of those qualities which would detract from his universality or from his status as a metaphor for some aspect of human experience. The heroes of the trilogy are all artists, all writers and hence creators; yet they all exhibit a disgust for life to be matched only by the tenacity with which they hold on to it. All of them are models of the egocentric, but as the series progresses toward *The Unnamable* the narrators' worlds tighten and shrink. It is almost as if Beckett were examining layer by layer the mind of the artist and the sources of his inspiration. It follows that the Unnamable speaks from within the cave of the self in the voice of some obscene male sibyl. He spews upon the receptive page a steady stream of heavily-punctuated but almost disembodied thought.

In terms of our own experience this third novel is the monologue of a deaf mute who is at least partially blind and totally incapable of movement. Unfortunately for him, this seemingly hermetic existence is only semi-autonomous. Although his hopeless and joyless state is unalterable, he suffers in the shadow of vague fears. Only partially aware of the outside world, he feels compelled to reconstruct time and space. With his range of choice reduced to an almost absolute minimum, he persists in choosing and speculating. If the Unnamable has a body, he has no senses which would enable him to feel it. Nevertheless, he hears voices which assure him of his physical existence. In response to these he pours his being by turns into idealized creations of his fancy. In the past he has identified with the heroes of Beckett's other novels, Murphy, Watt, Molloy, and Malone; now he becomes or posits first a legless, armless individual named Mahood, a name which we might read Manhood, a creature who is finally installed in an outsize jug or funeral urn at the gate of a restaurant. Again he is Worm, a helpless, half-blind babe, tormented senselessly by the nameless minions of a nameless master. On one level of interpretation we see these two suffering creatures as projections of the psyche of a suffering god whom we must identify with the Unnamable himself. They are screens for the essential formlessness of the hero, shapes given to the half-formed doubts and the torment of the nameless and the inarticulate.

In this connection the reader familiar with the earlier novels *Murphy* and *Watt* will recall Murphy's favorite patient at the Magdalen Mental Mercyseat, Mr. Endon, the psychotic whose name and condition suggest his function. Mr. Endon is Murphy's ideal, the perfect closed system, impervious to outside influence. His successor, Watt's employer, the godlike Mr Knott, is in some ways even more so. Consciously or not, all of Beckett's characters are approaching this state. In the trilogy, Molloy is in quest of the womb, Moran is in quest of the Molloy in himself; the bedridden Malone writes out his days from the shelter of a sort of improvised room-womb. But the Unnamable's position is clearly the zenith. It is characteristic of Beckett's humor that this creature, situated on the brink of nirvana, yearns after the world of objects. In him the extremes meet. Paradise leans close to hell.

This brings us to a consideration of one of the unifying

devices of Beckett's trilogy, his systematic use of the three postmortal states explored in Dante's *Divine Comedy.* Although to Beckett's mind all mankind is in purgatory, each of the books in the trilogy contains ironically presented elements of all three of man's postmortal states. Furthermore, each of the three novels puts the ironic emphasis upon one of these states. *Molloy* is infernal, *Malone Dies* is purgatorial, and *The Unnamable* is paradisal. However, paradox is Beckett's stock in trade, and though *The Unnamable* as a novel depicts an ostensibly ideal state, the novel's central figure is in purgatory. Embodying as he does both the unmerited punishment of Worm and the equally unmerited rewards of Mahood, he is seen as forming a middle ground between heaven and hell.

In his article "Dante . . . Bruno. Vico . . . Joyce," Beckett defines hell as "the static lifelessness of unrelieved viciousness. Paradise the static lifelessness of unrelieved immaculation. Purgatory a flood of movement and vitality released by the conjunction of these two elements." [1]

Although the preceding passage was designed to explain Joyce's concept of existence, Beckett seems also to be defining his own view. We need not be surprised therefore that at each stage in his heroes' adventures apparent hell and apparent heaven give way to the only reality which man knows, that is, the constant purgatory of existence. It is this brutal irony which Beckett states in the following lines from the same article:

There is a continuous purgatorial process at work, in the sense that the vicious circle of humanity is being achieved. . . . On this earth that is Purgatory, Vice and Virtue—which you may take to mean any pair of large contrary human factors—must in turn be purged down to spirits of rebelliousness. Then the dominant crust of the Vicious or Virtuous sets, resistance is provided, the explosion duly takes place and the machine proceeds. And no more than this;

1. *Our Exagmination Round His Factification For Incamination Of Work In Progress* (New York: New Directions, 1939), p. 22.

neither prize nor penalty; simply a series of stimulants to enable the kitten to catch the tail. [22]

Thus the questing creatures, Beckett's tormented heroes, can, in spite of their apparent progress toward the pure state of bodilessness, do nothing more than accomplish the purgatorial spiral, moving ever inward—toward the immaculate and endless purgatory of *The Unnamable*. His latest full-length narrative, *How It Is,* deals finally with hell, portraying a nameless creature crawling endlessly through primeval muck and experiencing grotesquely sadistic pleasures with others of his kind. Figuratively the spiral has begun to unwind.

The second novel of the trilogy is *Malone Dies,* a first person account of his last hours, written by a dying invalid. The action is set in a room whose shape is known and whose contents are visible. The room however is in an undifferentiated location, that is, in an unknown building on an unknown street in an unknown town. Malone is mute and at least partially deaf; he cannot use his legs or lift his head, but he can write, feed himself, and manipulate the objects in his room with the aid of a long stick. His material needs are taken care of by an old woman who brings his soup and removes his chamber pot. However, about two thirds through the book the old woman stops coming and, losing his stick, Malone becomes more than ever a self-contained unit. Like the Unnamable, he indulges in the creation of other lives, hoping in this way to ease the torment of his last hours. Into this narrative of his present state is woven his daydream of the imaginary life of Sapo Saposcat, a name meaning knowledge of dung or of injury. This personage, a metaphor for mankind, is later renamed Macmann or son of man, that is, Christ. In the course of the tale he degenerates from a dilatory scholar to a friendless tramp to an inmate in an asylum or earthly paradise in which he finds only derisive joy and solace. His tale is a genially inverted parable of virtue and suffering, and he is not only a Jesus but also a Job. Like the narrator in *The Unnamable,* Malone as writer is a purgatorial battleground of evil and good; the two poles being represented by life or the tormented existence of Sapo-Macmann and death or the untold future into which the inert Malone sails.

In the larger cycle for the trilogy, *Malone Dies* is the purgatorial or medial novel. For Malone is, like Molloy, a namable being, a man aware of former existences and capable of apprehending and reporting his present condition. Like Molloy he is earthbound, conscious of his possessions and, though crippled, capable of ingestion and defecation. Unlike Molloy he tells not his own story but that of another; furthermore he divides his interest between the process of living and the process of dying. Symbolical of his transitional state is the fact that he eats during the first half of the book only, becoming increasingly detached as his narrative progresses. On the literal level of interpretation the reader is aware that this figure who has lost the use of his legs *may be* an extension of the semicripple Molloy, the latter being in his turn an extension of the somewhat less deteriorated Moran. At the end of *Malone Dies,* the hero may well be passing, not into death, but into the condition of the Unnamable.

The most complex of the novels in Beckett's French-Irish trilogy is *Molloy,* the bicyclical tale of two quest-heroes, active seekers after the nameless joys of salvation. The novel is sharply divided into two first-person narratives of equal length. The two wheels of the bicycle are connected by a messenger and steered by the divine will. The first tale concerns the adventures of Molloy, a crippled, amoral former tramp whose fear-ridden existence has led him finally to shelter, to an ironic rebirth out of the chaos of existence. For the condition toward which he has been unwittingly striving, the estate of his bedridden, incontinent, and now perhaps dead mother, represents both primal innocence and the ultimate inanity: the question mark at the end of the sentence of life. It is the sublimation of the self in a new sort of chaos. But Molloy is hardly ready for and perhaps not even capable of the final surrender: hence the apparent bliss of his present state is disturbed by his obsessive need to write down his restless past.

The second half of the novel is narrated by Molloy's opposite, the honest, lucid, highly moral, obsessively religious citizen Jacques Moran, who, in the line of his duty as special investigator or agent, has conducted an apparently fruitless search for Molloy whose existence and nature he intuits but does not understand. Moran's search has no end, for he makes no contact with his prey. But some sort of achievement is implied by the fact that he returns home in a condition of physical and moral reduction. The man of means and morals has become like Molloy a crippled, asocial, impecunious vagabond. He writes his report and prepares to depart for the unknown.

Moran is in fact exchanging one form of unawareness for another, the despair of the hunter for that of the hunted. Although within the range of the conceivable, his chances of reaching or of becoming Molloy are as slight as are Molloy's of reaching or becoming his mother; nevertheless, we may, as some critics have suggested, reverse the order of the narratives and see Moran as the youthful version of Molloy progressing toward age and death.[2] More plausibly, we may consider Molloy's mother, Molloy, Moran, and the too-often ignored Jacques Moran (Junior) as existing on separate shelves of being, realms which cannot coincide even intellectually except through the miracle of divine or intuitive intervention. Such intervention has undoubtedly awakened in Molloy an awareness of his mother and in Moran an awareness of Molloy. It will be noted that neither the mother nor Molloy is aware of the next higher shelf of existence, Molloy certainly knows nothing of Moran. My belief is that Molloy's mother, Molloy, Moran, and Moran's son all inhabit the same body; further, the events described in the two narratives are simultaneous and identical though viewed from different angles and differently

2. For a statement of this commonly-held position see Edith Kern's "Moran-Molloy: The Hero as Author," *Perspective* 11 (Autumn 1959) : 183–93.

ordered. Since the narrators are by their own admission untrustworthy to the point of absurdity, it seems probable that they are actually rationalizing the behavior of a posited third force (Youdi or Jacques Junior?) over whom they have progressively lost their power. It is by virtue of this third force that Molloy and Moran are able to interpenetrate, and their two accounts overlap in predictable but nevertheless striking ways. In order to clarify this and further interpretations I should like now to outline the plot of this, the first novel of the trilogy.

Both narratives are written in the first person by individuals who have lived through the events described. Both narrators record their experiences in a cynically blasé conversational tone. But Molloy, whose sense of time and place is rudimentary, mixes the imagined with the experienced, and the present with the past in a single paragraph of 117 pages. This paragraph follows a brief introduction in which the hero examines his present condition and position as a bedridden invalid in his mother's room and as a wage slave for an unnamed boss for whom he writes this tale. Molloy admits that he is unsure of the facts and that he is beginning at an arbitrarily set point in his tale. But it appears that in terms of calendar time, his narrative takes up a year, extending from mid-June to some time in the following spring.

His story, which concerns those events that have landed him in his mother's room and on the verge of belated extinction, begins with a description of himself watching one evening from a hillside vantage point outside his town as two men, A and C, pass each other on the road. After spending the night on the hill and descending in the morning on his crutches, he rides his bicycle into town. His manner of riding with one stiff leg brings him to the attention of the law, and he is taken from the city gate to the police station for questioning. Naturally, Molloy has no papers except bits of newspaper which he uses for hygienic purposes, but he finally manages to recall his name and the fact that his mother lives near the shambles. Upon his

release he once again rides out of town, spends the night in a
ditch and wakes next morning to the bleating of a herd of black
sheep being led by their shepherd and his dog perhaps to
pasture, perhaps to slaughter. That is, perhaps to paradise
perhaps to hell (or vice versa). Molloy returns to the town
where he inadvertently runs over and kills a dog named Teddy
and risks death at the hands of a mob. It is the dog's mistress,
Lousse, who saves the day by explaining that the animal "was
old, blind, deaf, crippled with rheumatism and perpetually
incontinent" (43). In short he was a canine Molloy, and she
had been on her way to have him put out of his misery. Lousse
then takes the murderer home with her and offers him shelter as
a Teddy-surrogate and a creature in need, though to quote our
hero: "There were no words for the want of need in which I
was perishing" (45).

Molloy spends some time in Lousse's house, confined to a
room and apparently in a comatose state; but when he comes to
himself, he protests so vehemently that he is freed and allowed
to spend the remainder of his time in the garden. Finally, his
bicycle having long since rusted, he escapes on crutches and,
after failing at suicide, leaves town in order to travel to the
seaside where he spends some time before once more feeling the
call of his mother. His most memorable occupation at the
seashore is the gathering and distributing in his pockets of
sixteen sucking stones. The account of how he finally succeeds
in guaranteeing the continuous circulation of these stones takes
up to ten pages of this sequence. Molloy's trip through the
forest is more eventful; for, during it, he loses what remains of
his powers and is finally reduced to a state of misery. Being
unable to progress in an upright position, he begins to crawl on
his belly like a snake:

The black slush of leaves slowed me down even more. But leaves or
no leaves I would have abandoned erect motion, that of man. And I
still remember the day when, flat on my face by way of rest, in
defiance of the rules, I suddenly cried, striking my brow, Christ,
there's crawling, I never thought of that. [120]

Formerly he has seen himself as a sort of second string Odysseus. Now he identifies at one remove with Christ:

> the slow and painful progress it had always been, whatever may have been said to the contrary, was changed, saving your presence, to a veritable calvary, with no limit to its stations and no hope of crucifixion, though I say it myself, and no Simon. . . . [105]

Early in his journey, however, this ironic Christ figure quite casually and very brutally murders a man who has accosted him. The calvary ends when the narrator crawls out of the forest within sight of town. It is spring and he is promised succour by an unidentified voice.

The second tale is written in a somewhat more conventional style by the meticulous special agent Moran. He is writing his report at the command of an unidentified voice but in fulfillment of his mission. His narrative, like that of Molloy, deals with the events of a single year. Sitting in his garden one summer Sunday, Moran is visited by the thirsty messenger Gaber, a character visible only to himself and his son Jacques. Through Gaber he receives a cryptic message from his boss Youdi. Moran and the boy are to go this day in search of Molloy. His orders are not precise, yet the narrator has little difficulty locating his quarry in his mind, and indeed, when he lies down on his bed during the afternoon, he manages to conjure up a precise vision, an epiphany far more realistic than anything which Molloy himself has given us. Both the details of the portrait and the circumstances surrounding the visitation call to mind Molloy's account of the tantrum he throws when he is locked up in one of Sophie's rooms.

> He had very little room. His time too was limited. He hastened incessantly on, as if in despair, towards extremely close objectives. Now, a prisoner, he hurled himself at I know not what narrow confines, and now, hunted, he sought refuge near the centre.
>
> He panted. He had only to rise up within me for me to be filled with panting.
>
> Even in open country he seemed to be crashing through jungle. He did not so much walk as charge. In spite of this he advanced but slowly. He swayed, to and fro, like a bear.

He rolled his head, uttering incomprehensible words.

He was massive and hulking, to the point of misshapenness. And, without being black, of a dark colour.

He was forever on the move. I had never seen him rest. Occasionally he stopped and glared furiously about him.

This was how he came to me, at long intervals. Then I was nothing but uproar, bulk, rage, suffocation, effort unceasing, frenzied and vain. Just the opposite of myself, in fact. It was a change. And when I saw him disappear, his whole body a vociferation, I was almost sorry. [154–55]

Moran has trouble setting about his work. First he has to fight a growing lack of self-discipline; then he must force his recalcitrant and ailing son into harness (this is the first time that the boy is accompanying him) ; finally he must be wary of the many unseen forces plotting against the success of his mission. He goes to lengths to prevent his aging and ambiguous cook, Martha, from knowing of their departure. He forces his son to leave behind his treasured stamp collection. He actually refuses to recall what little he knows of his instructions. To increase the cloak and dagger effect, they depart at night. Every detail is noted, every *i* is dotted in this narrative though nothing significant happens and the mission is a failure. The first part of the trip ends when our hero finds that his knee will no longer support him. He sends his son off alone to buy a bicycle in the town of Hole. While the boy is away he stays near their camp and fire. He has two visitors whose appearance echoes that of Molloy's A and C in that one of them carries a stick and the other wears an outlandish hat. The second of these visitors he murders under circumstances reminiscent of Molloy's act of violence. When his son returns after three days, the despotic father has himself carried on the bicycle as far as Bally-ba or Molloy country.

On the morning after their arrival the boy defects, leaving his father, with but little money and no bicycle, to suffer a fit of despair and inertia which ends when Gaber appears to him and delivers the laconic message from Youdi, "Jacques Moran, home, instanter." The journey home is harrowing but Moran finally arrives dressed in tatters and broken in mind and body at a deserted house and a ruined garden. Finding home no longer bearable, he writes his report to Youdi before departing, this time on crutches.

The tale which begins: "It is midnight. The rain is beating on the windows. I am calm. All is sleeping." (125) closes with the lines:

I lived in the garden. I have spoken of a voice telling me things. I was getting to know it better now, to understand what it wanted. It did not use the words that Moran had been taught when he was little and that he in his turn had taught to his little one. So that at first I did not know what it wanted. But in the end I understood this language. I understood it, I understand it, all wrong perhaps. That is not what matters. It told me to write the report. Does this mean I am freer now than I was? I do not know. I shall learn. Then I went back into the house and wrote, It is midnight. The rain is beating on the windows. It was not midnight. It was not raining. [241]

This novel has been described as an anti-novel in the tradition of Rabelais, Sterne, and Joyce and indeed we are aware that the form of the conventional novel is being satirized. But the term "anti-novel" is not descriptive. It would be more like Beckett to write an ante-novel and more appropriate to say that all of his books are what Northrop Frye calls Menippean Satires (a variety of sophisticated farce). At any rate in *Molloy* we are struck by the fact that nothing much is happening. Two vaguely insignificant quest heroes, two suffering clowns are decomposing: the one a noman, the other an everyman. Here is a deliberate reversal of pattern characteristic of Beckett's art. The quest hero is generally conceived of as going into the darkness to retrieve the light and achieve a meaningful existence. In *Molloy* shabby versions of the shining knight-errant achieve deeper darkness and meaninglessness.

Molloy's two parts are intimately linked, a complementary or an ironic couple contributing to a fascinating portrait of the universal man and an ingenious satire of his aspirations and accomplishments. Hence, it can be shown that every event and object described by Molloy is viewed from a different point of vision by Moran. But these relationships are screened by the paradox implicit in the identification of two such disparate creatures, by the displacement which events undergo in the mind of Molloy which knows neither time nor place and finally by the sublimation or distortion of Molloy-like ideas in the narrative of Moran. In one sense the reader is being willfully misled. Only after a second or third reading do we recognize the affinities beneath the contradictions: realizing, for example, that Molloy's vision of the black sheep and their shepherd at the beginning of his narrative is exactly contemporaneous with Moran's vision of them near the end of his tale, that their different reactions are consistent with their different and complementary roles as representatives of the extremes of chaos and order. Viewed in this light, the accounts dovetail in such a way as to cap the climax of a grotesque Abraham and Isaac parallel. Here is Moran-Abraham arriving with his son Jacques-Isaac in Molloy country, advancing toward the all-too-obviously good shepherd and his black sheep:

How I would love to dwell upon him. His dog loved him, his sheep did not fear him. Soon he would rise, feeling the falling dew. The fold was far, far, he would see from afar the light in his cot. Now I was in the midst of the sheep, they made a circle round me, their eyes converged on me. Perhaps I was the butcher come to make his choice. [217–18]

Molloy, in his account, unequivocally and in Old Testament terms identifies himself as the surrogate victim:

and the shepherd watching me sleep and under whose eyes I opened my eyes. Beside him a panting dog, watching me too, but less closely than his master, for from time to time he stopped watching me to gnaw at his flesh, furiously, where the ticks were in him I suppose. Did he take me for a black sheep entangled in the brambles and was he waiting for an order from his master to drag me out? [36]

We may on the one hand see Molloy expressing Moran's sublimated death wish; on the other hand Moran is preparing to butcher Molloy instead of his son. Further interpretations of these passages are of course possible, especially when we remember that Jacques Junior is carrying the knife.

The complementary identity of our two-in-one-hero and the nature of his bifocal vision are best illustrated, perhaps, by the two versions of the earthly paradise, the house-and-garden, a conventional security symbol which serves in these narratives to illuminate the position of the characters in relation to order and deepen the paradox of its rejection. Molloy's stay with Lousse takes up nearly 40 pages, falling precisely in the center of his 120-page narrative. His stay is divided roughly into two parts, the period spent in the house and the post-enclosure period during which he inhabits the garden. Moran describes two sojourns in his house and garden, the first lasting some eighteen hours but occupying almost 60 pages at the beginning of the 117-page narrative. The second, lasting through the spring, that is, a matter of months, but occupying only 4 pages at the end of his tale. I believe that the events described by Molloy represent a sublimation of what Moran experiences during these two periods.

Thanks mainly to his position in relation to the conventional time-space schema, and to his relative attachment to the material world, Moran gives more space to his treatment of this aspect than does the relatively detached Molloy. Moran's story deals with departure whereas Molloy's deals with his arrival. Furthermore, the as-yet imperfectly-severed Moran writes from the shelter of his house, while the as-yet imperfectly-acclimatized Molloy writes from his mother's bed.

Associated with Molloy's stay at Lousse's house are a number of objects and animals: fetishes, all of which have equal though opposite counterparts in Moran's paradise. For example, there is the dog Teddy which Molloy kills, helps bury, and with which he is identified by Lousse at the start of the episode. Moran feels drawn to and repelled by the neighbor's live pooch Zulu. Lousse's exotic parrot swears in two languages; his counterparts are Moran's prosaic chickens. There is also

Molloy's bicycle which rusts so badly during his stay that he leaves it behind him. After much calculation, Moran decides against taking his "autocycle" on his mission. Both gardens have wicket gates: Moran's is characteristically locked though he breaks the lock on his return; Lousse's gate is always open. Molloy and Moran both pay particular attention to their clothing: both have hats attached by strings though Molloy's is tied to his lapel and Moran's is fastened beneath his chin. More important perhaps are the two infinity symbols: the stolen knife-rest and Moran's beehive and the dance of the bees. Of the latter Moran says:

The dance was best to be observed among the bees returning to the hive, laden more or less with nectar, and it involved a great variety of figures and rhythms. . . . I was . . . stupefied by the complexity of this innumerable dance, involving doubtless other determinants of which I had not the slightest idea. And I said, with rapture, Here is something I can study all my life, and never understand. [231–32]

Associated with both of these terrestrial paradises are supernatural figures. Molloy's Lousse or Sophie Loy is best understood as a composite creature of allegory: the Gnostic and Neoplatonic personification of Wisdom—Sophia. Molloy, who finds her antipathetic, identifies her with the witch Circe who turned Odysseus' men into animals; thus he makes Lousse a symbol for both good and bad wisdom just as he himself is an emblem of man's highest and lowest qualities. Sophie's other name is Loy, or law in French, but Molloy, who hates constraint and order, prefers to call her Lousse, a name suggestive of light, louse, and freedom. Circe-Sophia is a curiously benevolent witch; the effects of her ministrations are strikingly similar to those which might be ascribed to the gift of Grace though she is accused of trying to poison Molloy with "moly." Sophie's human counterpart at Moran's is the sexually ambivalent cook Martha, a "fate who had run out of thread," who is accused of trying to poison Moran. She is the typical troublesome servant with inside knowledge of her master's affairs and a frustrated wish to control. Like Molloy's mother, she is absent when the wanderer returns home.

If Molloy is sheltered against his will in Lousse's garden and carried unawares to his mother's bed, Moran is driven from and to his own garden by Youdi through the offices of the messenger Gaber. If Molloy's goddess whom he associates with evil is apparently good, Moran's God (for Youdi is an anagram for Dieu or Yahweh) whom he thinks benevolent is apparently evil or at least whimsical and cruel. But here too there is ambivalence and self-perpetuating paradox: Youdi sends Moran on a fruitless mission and allows him to suffer pain and despair, but he is also sending him in quest of himself or of awareness; he is sending him toward some sort of paradise as well as toward some sort of doom. Like the Unnamable and Mr Knott and like the supreme authority postulated by Franz Kafka, Youdi is both ineffable and ignoble: the meeting place of extremes. Gaber, or the archangel Gabriel, partakes of the same paradoxes and by his presence in Moran's conscious world initiates some new ones. This pernicious angel of mercy furnishes on all levels the link between the two narrators. Significantly, after Moran ceases to see him, that is, shortly before Moran has begun to write, it is to Molloy that Gaber appears as taskmaster, to pick up and return his manuscript.

The only other figure related to the garden scene is Jacques Moran's son Jacques Moran, whose name according to his father "should cause no confusion." Like Jacques Moran Senior, and perhaps even more than he, the boy has no wish to leave the home, which for him is the garden of childhood, the pre-pubic paradise. Once he has left, however, the boy gradually assumes ascendency over his weakening father. Until finally, reaching maturity, he abandons Moran Senior and sets out on his own. Significantly, he is left in possession of the house and garden. This figure, who is hardly recognized by Molloy and barely sketched in by Moran, is, along with Gaber, one of the novel's unifying principals: the third member of an apparently infinite series of analogical trios. On the most literal level, however, he represents, first, hope in the future, being released energy, youth, and apparent freedom; second, despair, being doomed, as Moran indicates, to continue the cycle or spiral of existences. At any rate we may consider him to be the first term of the series concluding with the Unnamable. It is worth noting that only in terms of this sort of development at once temporal and psychic can we account for Jacques Junior's behavior and existence. The more commonly held belief in the inverted order of the narrative accounts neither for the role of the boy nor for the parallelism of the events, nor for the exact equivalence of the two narratives' lengths, nor for the obviously complementary vision of the two narrators. Furthermore, it implies a somewhat simple-minded gimmickry on the part of Beckett whose irony is more subtle. I would suggest that it should stand as a red-herring solution but that we would gain much by tracing the progression, not through Jacques to Moran to Molloy to Malone to the Unnamable but rather through Jacques to the tandem Molloy-Moran or better still through Jacques/Molloy-Moran.

Beckett, using the simplest of tools, a basic French or English vocabulary, a handful of allusions, some standard humorous devices, succeeds in evoking for each of his characters innumerable identities and for his book an interlace pattern as complex as those in the Irish book of Kells or as the Daedalian labyrinth.

I have already mentioned the Dantesque systems which help to give the trilogy its structural unity. In terms of these systems Molloy is, above all, hell. A novel of action as opposed to the novels of contemplation which follow, it treats, to use Beckett's words, "the static lifelessness of unrelieved viciousness." However, if we consider this novel in terms of its internal structure, we find that Molloy recumbent (a surrogate for his mother), as narrator of the first half, is released from the active life and therefore ostensibly in paradise. His image casts its rosy glow over the entire novel. Molloy active and questing is in purgatory, driven by "the flood of movement and vitality released by the conjunction of" the immaculate, or his mother, and the vicious, as represented by the world of Moran. Speaking of one of the men he has seen while perched on his hillock at the beginning of his tale, he remarks: "He . . . must have seen the rock in the shadow of which I crouched like Belacqua, or Sordello, I forget" (12) . The confusion of Dante's patriotic troubadour with his glorious sluggard is typical of Beckett, who has earlier used Belacqua's name for one of his characters (see *More Pricks Than Kicks*) . But both figures are in the *Purgatorio* and Molloy is appropriately on an eminence. If Molloy is in purgatory, it follows that Moran's state of complete involvement, his commitment to the material world, which is manifestly and comfortably evil, is in direct opposition to the recumbent and detached ideal and, hence, is predominantly infernal. It is therefore not surprising that he identifies with Sisyphus in the following passage:

> But I do not think even Sisyphus is required to scratch himself, or to groan, or to rejoice, as the fashion is now, always at the same appointed places. And it may even be they are not too particular about the route he takes provided it gets him to his destination safely and on time. [182]

In accordance with this interpretation, the movement of the book if thought of as being linear is backwards, from heaven to hell. In its turn each of the two tales represents a small postmortal cycle centering about the conventional utopian view of paradise as represented here by the house and garden. All of these statements may be modified if we alter our point of view. For example, we may say with equal justice that each of these positions is purgatorial or that there can be no movement from heaven, hell, or purgatory. For Beckett is applying as a principle and with telling effect the idea that opposites are equal, that extremes meet, and that all existence is "a kitten chasing its tail." This principle is drawn in part at least from the teaching of James Joyce's favorite philosopher-heretic,

Giordano Bruno, whose theories Beckett outlines in the following passage from his early Joyce article:

There is no difference, says Bruno between the smallest possible chord and the smallest possible arc, no difference between the infinite circle and the straight line. The maxima and minima of particular contraries are one and indifferent. Minimal heat equals minimal cold. Consequently transmutations are circular. The principle (minimum) of one contrary takes its movement from the principle (maximum) of another. Therefore not only do the minima coincide with the minima, the maxima with the maxima, but the minima with the maxima in the succession of transmutations. Maximal speed is a state of rest. The maximum of corruption and the minimum of generation are identical: in principle, corruption is generation. And all things are ultimately identified with God, the universal monad, Monad of monads. [6]

Beckett applies this view to every line, every identity, every concept, analogy, character, image, and book of his trilogy. Hence, the cycles within cycles that characterize its structure, the logical and valid contradictions evident everywhere, the improbable identifications. Hence the flux of movement in the brain of Beckett's readers. This is one reason why Molloy and Moran are one and opposite and why moments of madness and sadness for Moran are moments of peace and joy for Molloy and vice versa. It also explains why we may perceive impulses rising from the senseless dung and mold of Molloy's mother's couch to color the dreams of Moran and thus to bring to fruition the healthy powers of the adolescent Jacques Junior. It explains why Jacques's hopeless future is predicted by the presence of the other two characters, symbols and causes both of his decline and his rise; why from one angle Jacques Junior is the only real character in the trilogy, being the nominal possessor of the body in which the other aspects of his being are encased; and finally, why Molloy, the Morans (father and son), and Malone are all simply puppets motivated by the static mind of the Unnamable, that symbol of the dubious upper and lower reaches of existence. These seemingly endless permutations create the kaleidoscopic effects which are enriched and multiplied by seemingly endless analogical identities, which, like the coincidence of Jacques Junior's name, should, to paraphrase Moran, lead to no confusion.

We find, for example, parallels drawn from Plato, Descartes, Nietzsche, and Bergson; from Freud and Jung; from Christianity, Judaism, Hinduism and the sacred texts; from myth cycles and literature. Each of these contains along with its grain of truth a large pinch of the burlesque, both of which are complicated when the systems are brought into conjunction. Molloy may be seen as Christ (or one of the thieves), Descartes's mind as distinguished from matter, Bergson's creative imagination welling up from a time-free matrix, Plato's deathless soul, and we may say that these metaphors are at once apt and improper.

Principal among these analogies are those drawn from Freud, whom Moran quotes and paraphrases repeatedly in his narrative. Referring, for example, to the libido or the sum of the instinctual energies rising from a man's id, Moran muses, shortly after telling us that his boy deserted him:

And with regard to the Obidil [an anagram for libido], of whom I have refrained from speaking, until now, and whom I so longed to see face to face, all I can say with regard to him is this, that I never saw him, either face to face or darkly, perhaps there is no such person, that would not greatly surprise me. [222]

Obidil, or the sublimated pleasure impulse, does exist as Molloy, who consistently perceives reality through the screen of Moran's apprehensions, and who at one point says "deep down, and deep down is my dwelling, oh not deepest down, somewhere between the mud and the scum." According to Freud the id "is the dark, inaccessible part of our personality . . . we call it a chaos, a cauldron full of seething excitations. We picture it as being open at its end to somatic influences, and as there taking up into itself instinctual needs which find their psychical expression in it, but we cannot say in what substratum." [3]

3. *The Complete Introductory Lectures on Psychoanalysis,* ed. and trans. James Strachey (New York: W. W. Norton, 1966), p. 537.

Much (indeed, perhaps too much) can be made of this analogy, but for our purposes, it should suffice to state that Molloy's mother seems to be the id and that as such she is being replaced by her son who was formerly the libido; that Moran, who sees Molloy as inhabiting him, is by his attachment to conventions and his consciousness of time and place the superego or that part of the mind which keeps the id and libido in check and imposes order upon the conscious mind or ego, that is, upon Jacques Junior. It is by achieving the proper balance of Molloy (id or libido) and Moran (superego) that Jacques reaches his freedom and maturity. Other Freudian systems are simultaneously applicable: for example, there is the idea of the "pleasure principle" which Freud foils off against the "reality principle," deriving the first from the id and the second from the superego. When Moran, referring to his intention of taking his autocycle on his mission, says, "Thus was inscribed, on the threshold of the Molloy affair, the fatal pleasure principle," he identifies himself with the life instinct, showing, through the use of the word "fatal," both his antagonism toward the pleasure principle and his awareness of Freud's meaning. Moran's drama may be seen in this context as the gradual loss of identity to Molloy. This conflict he expresses as follows:

That a man like me, so meticulous and calm in the main, so patiently turned towards the outer world as towards the lesser evil, creature of his house, of his garden, of his few poor possessions, discharging faithfully and ably a revolting function, reining back his thoughts within the limits of the calculable so great is his horror of fancy, that a man so contrived, for I was a contrivance, should let himself be haunted and possessed by chimeras, this ought to have seemed strange to me and been a warning to have a care, in my own interest. [156]

A complementary development is evident in Molloy's final position as a tame and passive writer.

When we read *Molloy* we are first struck by the uproarious, the Rabelaisian verve of Molloy's monologue; the

exaggerations, the priggishness of Moran. We recognize
variations on the familiar figure of the clown and bum before
we see them as the metaphysical clown and the intellectual
bum whose humor tantalizes, distresses, and enlightens us.[4] In
passages like the following, the humor derives from the
inconsequential asides (marks of the clownish pedant) , the
abrupt transitions, and such unexpected words as "springing"
and "white-gloved." The situation itself and the behavior of
the characters are subordinated to the verbal gestures,
approximations of the art of the clown or the mime. Like the
clown, Molloy the narrator's timing is impeccable, his wit
precise and unadorned.

It ended in my understanding that my way of resting, my attitude
when at rest, astride my bicycle, my arms on the handlebars, my
head on my arms, was a violation of I don't know what, public
order, public decency. . . . Your papers, he said, I knew it a
moment later. Not at all, I said, not at all. Your papers! he cried.
Ah my papers. Now the only papers I carry with me are bits of
newspaper, to wipe myself, you understand, when I have a stool. Oh
I don't say I wipe myself every time I have a stool, no, but I like to
be in a position to do so, if I have to. Nothing strange about that, it
seems to me. In a panic I took this paper from my pocket and thrust
it under his nose. The weather was fine. We took the little side
streets, quiet, sunlit, I springing along between my crutches, he
pushing my bicycle, with the tips of his white-gloved fingers. [25–26]

4. This article was originally delivered as a paper in 1960, before
Beckett criticism had reached anything like its present pitch. It was first
published as part of an English department venture at the University
of Texas. In the meantime, important books by Hugh Kenner, Ruby Cohn,
John Fletcher, Ludovic Janvier, and Frederick Hoffman have added to
our store of insights, and Beckett's name has become a critical commonplace. Nevertheless, I have found it unprofitable to revise my conclusions
and have done little more for this reissue than increase the emphasis I
place on my view of the simultaneity of the events described in the two
narratives, a view which I feel is central to an understanding of the book's
rational basis. The account of Beckett's humor which follows is designed
to contribute to a balanced view of his achievement and method. It
cannot hope to compete with the complexity and coherence of Ruby
Cohn's study, which perhaps it supplements in some way.

Generally, we laugh at and not with the unconscious clown, Moran, who paradoxically resembles us and observes our modes of behavior far more than does Molloy. But we must not overlook the fact that the teller of the tale is not the quester but the product of the quest, a distanced and embittered self-mocker. In his discussion of local place names, for example, Moran's humor derives mainly from his dead pan use of unlikely terms (parodies, as one might guess, of Irish names) :

there exists with us no abstract and generic term for such territorial subdivisions. And to express them we have another system, of singular beauty and simplicity, which consists in saying Bally (since we are talking of Bally) when you mean Bally and Ballyba when you mean Bally plus its domains and Ballybaba when you mean the domains exclusive of Bally itself. I myself for example lived, and come to think of it still live, in Turdy, hub of Turdyba. And in the evening, when I went for a stroll, in the country outside Turdy, to get a breath of fresh air, it was the fresh air of Turdybaba that I got, and no other. [183]

Toward the end of Moran's tale we become aware of changes not only in the quester's situation but also in the narrator's humor. It is difficult to determine whether the following passage with its sardonic understatements and inversions, its deliberate blasphemy emanates from the superego or the id.

Certain questions of a theological nature preoccupied me strangely. As for example.
1. What value is to be attached to the theory that Eve sprang, not from Adam's rib, but from a tumour in the fat of his leg (arse?) ? . . .
3. Did Mary conceive through the ear, as Augustine and Adobard assert?
4. How much longer are we to hang about waiting for the antechrist?
5. Does it really matter which hand is employed to absterge the podex?
6. What is one to think of the Irish oath sworn by the natives with the right hand on the relics of the saints and the left on the virile member? . . .
14. Might not the beatific vision become a source of boredom, in the long run? . . .

And I recited the pretty quietist Pater, Our Father who art no more in heaven than on earth or in hell, I neither want nor desire that thy name be hallowed, thou knowest best what suits thee. Etc. The middle and the end are very pretty.

It was in this frivolous and charming world that I took refuge, when my cup ran over. [228–30]

The more we know about this novel, the more complex become both the humor and our reactions to it; for example, when we know that Lousse represents Wisdom and control and that Molloy is, among other things, the intellect as defined by Descartes and Freud's libido, then Molloy's inability to account for and adjust to Lousse's behavior becomes funny in a new way. Simultaneously, events take on graver implications, and we glimpse behind the protective screen of laughter our own embattled psyches. Molloy is no longer a bum, a clown, an incompetent unable to cope with a simple human situation. He is now also an aspect of our world doing his best against frightful odds. We are faced with a need to realign our sympathies and to redefine wisdom on several levels. An illustration of the manifold aspect of Beckett's humor is the following citation taken from Molloy's account of his first meeting with Lousse who has just saved him from the angry mob:

finally in his turn the constable too dispersed, the word is not too strong, grumbling and growling, followed by the last idlers who had given up all hope of my coming to a bad end. But he turned back and said, Remove that dog. Free at last to go I began to do so. But the lady, a Mrs Loy, I might as well say it now and be done with it, or Lousse, I forget, Christian name something like Sophie, held me back, by the tail of my coat, and said, assuming the words were the same when I heard them as when first spoken, Sir, I need you. And seeing I suppose from my expression, which frequently betrays me, that she had made herself understood, she must have said, If he understands that he can understand anything. . . . That is one of the many reasons why I avoid speaking as much as possible. For I always say either too much or too little, which is a terrible thing for a man with a passion for truth like mine. [44–45]

Once we have laughed at the usual gimmicks in the clown's repertoire, we realize that our laughter has disclosed absurdities which go beyond the usual foolishness and exaggeration of theatrical farce. Why does Lousse hold Molloy by the coattail? Why can't Molloy remember Lousse's name? Why is she Loy or Law in a different way or more than the policeman is? Why can't Molloy express himself more clearly when he writes so well? Why does Lousse claim to need him? Why does he feel he does not need her? Does he need her? What does he mean when he says he has a "passion for truth?" And finally, is not Molloy's remark about saying too much or too little evidence of a philosophical turn of mind?

A closer look at Beckett's comic devices will give us answers to some of these questions. First and most obvious is the inversion or explosion of a cliché, one of Molloy's favorite tricks as illustrated by his comment concerning the hostile mob "who had given up all hope of my coming to a *bad* end." This remark tickles our fancy by breaking the pattern of expectation; we have been trained to believe that the crowd should desire a good end for Molloy or at least that he should think the socially acceptable thought. If we grant Molloy humanity, which we do consistently in spite of the ironic sub-identities and the apparent absurdity of his behavior, we laugh first at the narrator's verbal trick, second at the nature of the mob's frustration, third at the despicable and undeserving object of its hatred. Finally, as we have been tricked into identifying with the mob, we laugh most uneasily at the fundamental truth conveyed by the renovated cliché and hence at our own sadistic tendencies. Of course the order of these events may be altered as may the extent of our reactions. Another sort of laughter is provoked by comic sequences like the following: "But he turned back and said, Remove that dog. Free at last to go I began to do so. But the lady . . . held me back by the tail of my coat." This is pure slapstick farce, depicting the conception and the frustration of a wish. However, Molloy suggests rather emphatically through the medium of juxtaposition that he has become a dog. Through this identification he sets off a chain of reactions at whose root is an almost inevitable empathy with the *cause* of our laughter, Molloy as narrator, who is also, by extension, the *object* of our laughter. By implication, we too have become dogs. A blow has been struck at our egos; we have been led to see ourselves as undesirables. Further consideration may permit us to muse upon the rightness of this identification.

To draw this material together, let us consider another source of Molloy's wit, his faulty powers of perception as expressed in the following: "But the lady . . . said, assuming the words were the same when I heard them as when first spoken, Sir, I need you." Molloy is then by his own oft-repeated admission an unreliable narrator and a poor witness; yet we persist in listening to him as though he tells the truth. We laugh at what we see to be some sort of clowning or exaggeration. We feel drawn into his little joke and become accomplices almost against our will, but we may also be amused because the remark coming in the midst of a factual narrative destroys our equilibrium. Ultimately, we must realize that he is, in fact, ignorant of the world and that he is fabricating his story using insights gained during Moran's (or the superego's) lapses. We may, for example, compare the preceding example with Moran's ambivalent reactions to the dog Zulu:

Sometimes, when I was in a good humour, I called, Zulu! Little Zulu! and he would come and talk to me, through the railings. But I had to be feeling gay. I don't like animals. It's a strange thing, I don't like men and I don't like animals. As for God, he is beginning to disgust me. Crouching down I would stroke his ears, through the railings, and utter wheedling words. He did not realize he disgusted me. He reared up on his hind legs and pressed his chest against the bars. Then I could see his little black penis ending in a thin wisp of wetted hair. He felt insecure, his hams trembled, his little paws fumbled for purchase, one after the other. I too wobbled, squatting on my heels. With my free hand I held on to the railings. Perhaps I disgusted him too. I found it hard to tear myself away from these vain thoughts. [144]

After humor, the aspect of this novel which will probably remain longest with the casual reader is its iconoclasm and satire. Beckett mocks just about everything from the concept of the divine to the idea of humanity, from our social institutions to our place names. Everywhere he applies the yardstick of the relative and the annihilating principle of Bruno's law of opposite equivalents. Thus God may well be the Unnamable and the concept of the free man is embodied in the absurdly enslaved Molloy, whereas Moran is the ultimate in civilization and God's servant. Security becomes detestable in Moran and pride ridiculous in Molloy. This satire is at once personal and universal; it is rendered timeless by the author's breadth of vision, but it is carefully worked into the fabric of the novel and subordinated to other aspects. A typical Beckett symbol serves many masters, operates on many levels, often achieving its satirical ends by indirection. For example, the heavy chain of keys carried by Moran on his journey is emblematic of the quester's materialism, his property, his security, his function, and perhaps even his virility. Connoting the "world" which Moran has built around his core of anxieties, the keys are foiled with the sucking stones that Molloy collects only to throw away. Like Moran himself, the keys have a story. Before leaving the house, the hero carefully locks everything in sight. After he places the heavy keys in his pocket, he walks with a decided list. Appropriately enough the keys fall to the ground during the murder scene, and later Moran must assume the posture of a snake to pick them up one by one. In this fashion he imitates the behavior of Molloy, who was obliged to crawl on his belly through the wood. Authority and moral control have degenerated by this point to the level of their symbols. Keys are useless without the house just as morality is meaningless without organized society. Finally, when Moran returns home, he finds that the keys will not open the wicket-gate and that he must break his way into his own garden. Like the ancient Egyptian who tried to take property beyond the grave, Moran has attempted to extend his security symbols and his concept of function to his inner world or beyond morality into an area where conventions (and keys) are inoperative.

Satire aims at the destruction of its object through analogy, the object being some aspect of our world or our behavior and preferably an aspect to which we believe ourselves to be fully committed. The keys are only one and not a terribly subtle example of Beckett's satirical metaphor. They furnish, however, a good example of how he enforces his satire, makes it hit its mark by means of echo metaphors, that is, by pairs of images, both of which, though somewhat wide of the mark, have as their focal point the reader's attitude. In this case the keys, which represent, for example, excessive dependence upon material props, are foiled against Molloy's sucking stones or parody possessions, inverted symbols of order. Molloy recognizes the valuelessness of these objects; Moran must be taught. The reader, while recognizing with Molloy the nature of the stones, and identifying with Molloy in this recognition, must nevertheless be faced with the fully elaborated equation before he sees that his is a double commitment: first to the concept of independence exemplified by Molloy and second to the involvement of Moran.

By affirming what Claude Mauriac has called our boundless poverty, by denying dimensions to the immeasurable, Beckett has for our edification and amusement thrown light upon the rich primal chaos residual in the forms of existence. I have said earlier that Beckett is controversial, that his novels are, like Molloy's knife-rest, symbols of infinity and sources of infinite speculation. *Molloy* may also be described as the unstable mean between the inexplicable object and the equally inexplicable organism, between Molloy's knife-rest and Moran's beehive with the "innumerable dance" of the bees.

Interpreting *Molloy*   John Fletcher

Of all Samuel Beckett's novels it is no doubt *Molloy,* written
about 1947 and published four years later, which raises the
most teasing critical questions. Written directly in French, it
was quite warmly received by critics in Paris, who tended,
however, to see in it "the end of a certain militant literature
thrown up by the Liberation," and even the end of all
literature—"twelve years after" its publication, Bernard
Pingaud did not hesitate to salute in the person of Samuel
Beckett the "last writer." [1] More recently, Ludovic Janvier has
come to grips with some of the problems of the novel and has
drawn particular attention to the homosexuality implicit in
Moran's attitude to his son Jacques and revealed most clearly
in the episode of the enema.[2] No other critic, so far as I am
aware, has attempted to explain the obscurities of the novel,
more especially the striking indications of an ambiguous
attitude toward the mother-figure. A few years ago I sketched
out an interpretation, based largely on the theories of Jung,
which saw in Molloy the antiself with which the self (Moran)
manages to be reconciled to the extent of *becoming* the antiself
Molloy in a painful synthesis which permits of a more genuine
and honest life than that abjured finally by Moran as a
frightening heresy.[3] Before I attempt to develop and expand

John Fletcher is Professor of Comparative Literature in the School of
European Studies at the University of East Anglia.
1. *"Molloy,* douze ans après," *Les Temps Modernes* 18 (January 1963):
1283–1300.
2. *Pour Samuel Beckett* (Paris: Editions de Minuit, 1966), pp. 278–79.
3. *The Novels of Samuel Beckett* (London: Chatto & Windus, 1964), p.
149.

these interpretations, however, it may be well to summarize the plot of this complex novel.

At the beginning of the first part, Molloy tells us that he is in his mother's room, having been brought there "perhaps in an ambulance, certainly a vehicle of some kind," since it was "last year" that he ceased to walk. Having taken his mother's place, he does not know what has become of her. He has now to write out his story for a man who comes to collect his pages once a week, and he describes, in a sort of vision, how his last journey began. He was on a hilltop, crouched in the shadow of a rock, from which he watched two men walk toward each other along a country road, meet, exchange a few words, and then go their separate ways; he calls them A and C. The man C has a cocked hat which Moran describes, when he sees it later in the story, as "quite extraordinary, in shape and colour . . . like none I had ever seen," and he carries a stout stick which Molloy later calls a club, when he thinks of the man again at the edge of the forest; and it is with this club in hand that C approaches Moran in the woods. After this important preliminary apparition Molloy declares that on waking he determined to go and see his mother. "I needed, before I could resolve to go and see that woman, reasons of an urgent nature," and the reasons that now impel him are connected with the need to establish "our relations on a less precarious footing." He fastens his crutches (without which, having a stiff leg, he is unable to walk) to the crossbar of his bicycle and sets out. On reaching the ramparts of his town he is arrested and later questioned by a sergeant at the police station for some obscure irregularity in his manner of resting on the bicycle. Released only late that afternoon, he goes to the country and some time afterward finds himself back in the town (he is no longer sure it is his mother's town) where he runs over a dog, whose owner, a woman called Lousse, protects him from the indignation of the bystanders and gives him lodging in her own home. He in some way replaces the dead animal in her affections and stays a "good while" with her, quite unable to leave, no doubt (he thinks) because she drugs his food. There he loses track of his bicycle, and eventually leaves without it, on crutches only, his initial concern to discover its whereabouts having changed to indifference. Molloy strongly hints that Lousse kept him for sexual reasons, but she makes no attempt to prevent his departure. After leaving her, he wanders around the town and contemplates settling in a blind alley; he even attempts unsuccessfully to commit suicide. Finally, leaving the town in some haste, he spends a while at the seaside, renewing the stock of sucking stones that keep him from feeling hungry. Soon, however, his mother's image begins again to harry him, and he moves inland through a forest, where his progress becomes slower and slower. A charcoal-burner, "sick with solitude probably," offers his unwanted affections to Molloy and is soundly belabored for his pains. No longer able to hobble, Molloy next takes to crawling, hears a voice saying "don't fret, Molloy, we're coming," and finally sinks into the bottom of a ditch at the very edge of the forest. It is from this ditch, evidently, that he is rescued in order to write his story in his mother's room, although he does not know what has become of her. Part 1 is thus circular, because the end refers to the beginning and vice versa.

The speaker in the second part gives his name as Jacques Moran and shows himself to be a meticulous individual, a practicing Catholic, a fairly affluent householder very proud of his property, and an employee of a mysterious agency (run by a man called Youdi) which has asked for the report we are to read. Moran's story begins one Sunday in summer when he is disturbed by Gaber, an agency messenger, who gives him urgent instructions to leave at once with his son, also called Jacques Moran, and look for a man whose name, says Gaber, is Molloy, but which to Moran sounds more like Mollose. In any case, the individual in question is "no stranger to" Moran, whose disquiet grows throughout the day: the affair, at first dismissed by Gaber as "nonsense," soon shows itself to be "no ordinary one" and begins to make Moran "anxious," then "confused," until finally he admits that he is "losing his head" and "floundering, I so sly as a rule." Having missed the last mass, he solicits private communion, which brings him no relief, and his lunch, eaten too late, lies heavily in his stomach. Painfully and laboriously, he prepares to set out. He feels for the first time a sharp pain in his knee, while he is giving an enema to his son.

We are informed that Moran's job requires that he track down certain individuals and then deal with them in accordance with particular instructions; sometimes he is asked for a report. In the case of Molloy, however, he is not sure what he should do with his quarry once he finds him, because he cannot remember what Gaber said on this point. He never finds out, for he has not been long on his journey before the pain strikes his knee again, paralyzing his leg. He sends his son to the nearest town to buy a bicycle so that they may proceed unhindered; the boy is away three days. During this period two important things happen to Moran. First, the man whom Molloy designated C, or someone very like him, approaches Moran in the woods and asks for a piece of bread. Complying with this request, Moran asks in return to be allowed to feel the weight of the man's stick, and the next day he breaks off a heavy stick like it for himself. He is poking his fire with this stick when a different man accosts him. This man, who bears a close resemblance to Moran himself, asks if the old man with the stick has passed by. Moran, "trembling all over," replies in the negative and orders his alter ego out of the way, but to no effect; so he clubs the man to death. "He no longer resembled me," adds Moran with evident relief, and his stiff leg, for a short while at least, bends normally again. Now that the self has been subjugated, reconciliation is possible with the antiself.

When his son returns with the bicycle, Moran says nothing about these events, and eventually, with the son riding and the father on the carrier, they reach Molloy's region. After a violent quarrel one night, Jacques abandons his father, and soon after, Gaber appears with an order for Moran to return home. Moran does so, assailed by growing decrepitude; he finds his house deserted, his bees dead, and his hens running wild. He determines to write his report and then leave again, to try to become free, to reject his manhood, and to live close to the earth. Thus this second part, in which the report is mentioned both at the beginning and at the end, is also circular.

It is obvious that such a story can be read on many levels. The most immediate is that of the detective novel. Moran is a kind of private detective who shadows Molloy, but then loses his vocation, abandons his assignment, and resigns his office. *Molloy* would thus take its place in the sort of fiction in which the sleuth or spy is a type of antihero, in the style of *The Third Man* or *The Spy Who Came In from the Cold.* These works are characterized by their deliberate refusal of the romantic, of the prestige traditionally attached to the classic detective or spy, such as Sherlock Holmes or James Bond.

Certain passages in *Molloy* can also be read as modern transpositions of the Ulysses legend. Molloy's stay in the police station, for instance, has affinities with Odysseus' encounter with the Cyclops, and the young woman who approaches Molloy on the beach suggests Nausicaa. A more striking example is the return of Moran-Odysseus. Although he finds no Penelope and slaughters no suitors (his servant Martha has already left and his bees have died), he cleans the slate anyway ("all there was to sell I have sold") and can receive Jacques-Telemachus back under the paternal roof. And we can certainly see in Edith a new Calypso and in Lousse the witch Circe, for Lousse puts a drug in Molloy's beer and holds him, he believes, by a spell; although she does not transform him into a pig, he does replace the dead dog which "she had loved like an only child." A closer look at the Lousse-Circe parallel will enable us to interpret the hidden meaning of this strange novel.

Leopold von Sacher-Masoch's hero Severin speaks in these words of the legendary sorceress:

I am once again seated under the arbor and reading in the *Odyssey* the story of the charming sorceress who transformed her worshippers into savage beasts. A most delightful image of love among the Ancients.[4]

The metaphysic of suffering in Sacher-Masoch can serve as Ariadne's thread in the exploration of the Beckettian labyrinth, as I hope to demonstrate. According to Gilles Deleuze's masterly exposition, Sacher-Masoch's system is based on the concept of a "wrong done to the father." It is to atone for this wrong, and at the same time avenge himself on the father for the guilt feelings the latter inspires, that Sacher-Masoch's hero goes through the following process:

The masochist would seek to identify himself with the mother in order to offer himself to the father as a sexual object, but, encountering now the danger of castration which he had tried to avoid, he would choose "to be beaten", both as a means of warding off castration and as a regressive substitute for "being loved"; the mother would then take on the role of the beating agent through the repression of the homosexual choice. Or, alternatively, the masochist would cast the wrong on to the mother . . . and would turn this to advantage, either in order to identify himself with this bad mother under cover of the projection and attain thereby to the possession of the penis (perversion-masochism), or on the contrary in order to thwart this identification, while preserving the projection, and offer himself as the victim (moral masochism).[5]

These themes can clearly be discerned in *Molloy*. The father in Beckett's writings figures most often as one set up in judgment, or as a tyrant, or else as a maleficent deity: he may be called Godot, or Mr Knott, or Youdi, to cite only a few names. In *Embers* Henry timorously addresses directly the spirit of his dead father:

4. Gilles Deleuze, *Présentation de Sacher-Masoch, avec le texte intégral de la Vénus à la fourrure* (Paris: Editions de Minuit, 1967), pp. 133–34. For the sake of convenience I translate the French not only of Gilles Deleuze's introduction but also of Aude Willm's careful rendering of the original German novel. It hardly needs saying that throughout this essay I use the terms "masochist" and "sadist" in their scientific senses and am in no way suggesting the existence of any "perversion" in the characters or anyone else.
5. Ibid., p. 92.

You would never live this side of the bay, you wanted the sun on the water for that evening bathe you took once too often. But when I got your money I moved across, as perhaps you may know. We never found your body, you know, that held up probate an unconscionable time, they said there was nothing to prove you hadn't run away from us all and alive and well under a false name in the Argentine for example, that grieved mother greatly. I'm like you in that, can't stay away from it, but I never go in, no, I think the last time I went in was with you. [96–97]

Like all Beckett's texts, this densely-wrought passage calls for detailed exegesis. Here, as in Camus' *L'Etranger*, the sea represents the mother whose person is denied firmly to the son. After the death of the father (whose body was never found, a symbol of the repression by the son of the paternal image), the son finds the courage to defy his interdicts by crossing the bay and thereby indulging his own incest-fantasy. But the son's temerity is a relative thing, for he still depends on the father: before he disappeared, the father "glared" at his offspring, calling him a "washout," (102) and thus he denied all valid connection between his wife and their son.[6]

The idea of a wrong committed against the father is one of the leading themes in *Molloy*. The narrator of the first part confesses at once that he is "scolded" by "this man who comes every week" if he has written nothing. He asserts, two pages further on, "it's my fault," only to ask at once: "Fault? . . . But what fault?" A little later, Molloy declares that C "was innocent, greatly innocent" and adds, after some reflection: "What business has innocence here? What relation to the innumerable spirits of darkness? It's not clear." It is not clear, in truth; it cannot be clear, for the memory of the crime for which one feels obscurely guilty has been repressed. The crime was that of wishing to usurp in the mother's affections the position of the father. And yet the longing to take the father's place is quite overt. Molloy's confession begins thus:

6. The French translation, *avorton,* makes this quite clear in *La Dernière Bande suivi de Cendres* (Paris: Editions de Minuit, 1960), p. 46.

I am in my mother's room. It's I who live there now. I don't know how I got there. . . . I sleep in her bed. I piss and shit in her pot. I have taken her place. I must resemble her more and more. All I need now is a son. [7–8]

The father is so firmly excluded that the son imagines, in accordance with a typically masochistic progression, that he is the fruit, not of sexual relations between the hated father and the adored mother (relations which take on the aspect of rape, in the child's eyes), but of parthenogenesis.[7]

None of this of course relieves the son of "anxiety," and the words "fellow-convict" and "justice" occur frequently under his pen. But he is incorrigible and wishes to cede nothing of his recently-assumed prerogatives:

Shall I describe the room [his mother's]? No. I shall have occasion to do so later perhaps. When I seek refuge there, beat to the world, all shame drunk, my prick in my rectum, who knows. [24]

Molloy, the writer, has already taken up residence in his mother's room, as he explains at the beginning of his confession, but he is concerned that events be recounted in chronological order and so in this early passage uses a future tense, "when I seek. . . ." More significant is the vulgar detail, "my prick in my rectum," which calls for two comments. First, the expression reflects the circular nature of Molloy's confession, which I drew attention to earlier. Second, the perspicacious reader will not fail to notice that the narrator denies the father by symbolically robbing him of his virile member: since he cannot endow the mother with a penis, he obliges the father not only to appear as a woman but also to render his sexual organ inoperative. The paternal penis, placed in the manner Molloy describes, is thus reduced to autoeroticism and autofecundation and thereby rendered incapable of harming the sacred, quasi-virginal image of the mother. In this connection another passage is revealing: Molloy is grateful to his mother for having made a serious attempt to

7. Deleuze, p. 82.

abort him (a truly masochistic theme of punishment inflicted by the woman), and he adds: "I also give her credit for not having done it again, thanks to me, or for having stopped in time, when she did" (23). He thus pays homage to "that poor old uniparous whore" for having fled his father's caresses and thereby guaranteed that he be "the last of [his] foul brood" (23).

The narrator is so strongly attracted by the mother-figure that he sometimes confuses the three women of classic masochism to which Gilles Deleuze has drawn attention, the harlot-mother (Edith in Molloy's story), the sadist-mother (Lousse), and the ideal mother who stands between the two extremes (Mag, the "true," uterine mother).[8] In a key passage Molloy clarifies an idea which disturbs him, not without reason:

> And I am quite willing to go on thinking of her [Lousse] as an old woman, widowed and withered, and of Ruth [Edith] as another, for she too used to speak of her defunct husband and of his inability to satisfy her legitimate cravings. And there are days, like this evening, when my memory confuses them and I am tempted to think of them as one and the same old hag, flattened and crazed by life. And God forgive me, to tell you the horrible truth, my mother's image sometimes mingles with theirs, which is literally unendurable, like being crucified, I don't know why and I don't want to. [79]

Why "crucified" exactly? Because, as Gilles Deleuze has explained, "the two great masculine characters in Sacher-Masoch's work are Cain and Christ"; similarly in Beckett's writings, as I have shown elsewhere.[9] For both authors Cain and Jesus typify men who deserve praise for killing the representation of the father, Cain in assassinating his brother, Christ in destroying the incarnation of the father by dying on the cross in an ultimate act of masochistic self-immolation. For their courageous acts both heroes suffered. This suffering explains not only their appeal to Sacher-Masoch, but also the

8. Ibid., pp. 42–50.
9. Ibid., pp. 83–85; *The Novels of Samuel Beckett* (for references, see the Index Nominum, p. 253).

words of Molloy: "I have gone in fear all my life, in fear of blows" (punishment dreaded but also sought after), and the words of Estragon in *Waiting for Godot:* "All my life I've compared myself to [Christ]" (Act 1, *ad fin.*).

"The trebling of the mothers has literally expelled the father from the masochist universe. . . . The masochist contract excludes the father, and transfers to the mother the responsibility for enforcing and applying the paternal law." [10] This is why Molloy speaks not only of "settling this matter between my mother and me" (87) but also of "establishing our relations on a less precarious footing" (118). The first phrase seems to refer to Molloy's concern to elicit information about his father, whose name he confesses to be ignorant of (21). The second indicates a contract analogous to those which Gilles Deleuze expounds. [11] The quasi-judicial nature of this contract is indicated by Molloy himself:

I would have had the feeling, if I had stayed in the forest, of going against an imperative, at least I had that impression. But perhaps I was mistaken, perhaps I would have been better advised to stay in the forest, perhaps I could have stayed there, without remorse, without the painful impression of committing a fault, almost a sin. For I have greatly sinned, at all times, greatly sinned against my prompters. And if I cannot decently be proud of this I see no reason either to be sorry. But imperatives are a little different, and I have always been inclined to submit to them, I don't know why. For they never led me anywhere, but tore me from places where, if all was not well, all was no worse than anywhere else, and then went silent, leaving me stranded. So I knew my imperatives well, and yet I submitted to them. It had become a habit. It is true they nearly all bore on the same question, that of my relations with my mother, and on the importance of bringing as soon as possible some light to bear on these and even on the kind of light that should be brought to bear and the most effective means of doing so. [116–17]

Like Sacher-Masoch's hero, Molloy elects to serve the dominating mother in a world from which he makes every

10. Deleuze, pp. 56, 81.
11. Ibid., pp. 66–70.

effort to exclude the father (on whose behalf "this man" fetches the manuscript pages every Sunday) . These efforts are vain, however, because the father triumphs in the end. It is no doubt a Pyrrhic victory, but it presents analogies with the flagellation inflicted on Severin by the Greek: a conclusion which "characteristically marks the aggressive and hallucinatory return of the father to a world which had symbolically annulled him." [12] This tyrant-father nonetheless allows the son to resettle in the mother's room after the suppression (of which Molloy knows nothing, he tells us) of the mother, and thus to satisfy, under the paternal aegis, "a deep and doubtless unacknowledged need, the need to have a Ma, that is a mother" (21) . All has returned to normal: the paternal authority, though briefly challenged, remains unaffected.

The riddle of the second part of the novel, made up of Moran's report, is solved by the perception that Moran is a younger Molloy (his physical condition at the end of the story is exactly that of Molloy at the beginning) and that the Moran, who finally decides to exile himself from the world of men, resembles the bum Molloy who has difficulties with the police. It then becomes probable that the "chambermaid," by whom Molloy thinks he may have had a son (8, 79) , is the servant Martha. She is Moran's mother, but he is unaware of the fact; when he is sent to look for Molloy, he sets out, of course, like Telemachus, *in search of his father.*

The two parts thus complement each other in a particularly profound way. Molloy, who is the masochist-type, sets out to find his mother; Moran, who is the sadist-type, goes to look for his father. Molloy strives to eradicate the paternal image, Moran the mother's (he is ungentle to his mother Martha, and he had no regrets when his wife Ninette died giving birth to his son, typically named after himself) . Molloy gloats on his heterosexual encounters, Moran on his onanism, for "the sadist

---

12. Ibid., pp. 57, 244; *Molloy,* end of part 1.

does not recoil from his ultimate aim, the effective cessation of all procreation; . . . sadism offers the active negation of the mother and the inflation of the father, the father above every law."[13]

This makes clear the reasons for the father-cult which is a basic feature of the second part of the novel: this panel of the diptych is the sadistic counterpart of the masochism of the other, and the work as a whole is a profound study of the sado-masochistic syndrome which is so firmly rooted in our psyche.

The interpretation that Moran is unknowingly the son of Molloy and Martha (the *M*'s significantly link them as members of the same family) is supported by a curious detail which Moran ingenuously reports:

I carried this sudden cordiality so far as to shake her by the hand, which she hastily wiped, as soon as she grasped my intention, on her apron. When I had finished shaking it, that flabby red hand, I did not let it go. But I took one finger between the tips of mine, drew it towards me and gazed at it. And had I had any tears to shed I should have shed them then, in torrents, for hours. She must have wondered if I was not on the point of making an attempt on her virtue. I gave her back her hand, took the sandwiches and left her. Martha had been a long time in my service. [165]

Martha's alarm comes from the fact that she thinks her son is about to overstep the Oedipal interdict. We know that the Oedipus myth is one with which Beckett is very familiar: Bruce Morrissette tells us that Beckett was the first to recognize the legend of the incestuous parricide in the detective plot of Robbe-Grillet's *Les Gommes*,[14] and in *Watt* we read of "Watt's Davus complex (morbid dread of sphinxes)" (251).

The theory that Molloy and Moran are the same person (an interpretation put forward by Bernard Pingaud and other critics) is invalidated by the categorical way in which Moran

13. Deleuze, p. 53.
14. *Les Romans de Robbe-Grillet* (Paris: Editions de Minuit, 1963), p. 53 n.

establishes a clear distinction between his mother (Martha, in all probability), his son's mother (Ninette), and Molloy's mother (the woman whose room Molloy occupies, that is, Moran's grandmother) (230).[15] No one would deny that the two men resemble each other, or even that Moran in a sense becomes Molloy, but we are not justified in assuming that no distinction is made between them.

Nonetheless, the resemblances between father and son in *Molloy* are even closer than has been generally noticed. In the context of what I said earlier about Moran's sadism, it should be noted that as his story unfolds Moran gradually changes, and from a good citizen and practicing Catholic turns into a skeptic in religion and a social renegade indifferent to bourgeois ideals. But the most significant change concerns his sadism, which attains its paroxysm in the murder of his persona in the woods. After this act of a violence surpassing even Molloy's brutality to the charcoal-burner, Moran turns slowly into a masochist insofar as he sees himself "being reborn of the woman alone, having a second birth" and becoming "the Man . . . without sexual love, property, country, antagonisms or work."[16] It is the voice common to both Molloy and Moran which gives birth to the new Moran, just as it had whispered "don't fret Molloy, we're coming" at the forest's edge. Moran expresses his rebirth in these terms:

I have been a man long enough, I shall not put up with it any more, I shall not try any more. I shall never light this lamp again. I am going to blow it out and go into the garden. . . . My birds had not been killed. . . . I tried to understand their language better. Without having recourse to mine. . . . I have spoken of a voice telling me things. I was getting to know it better now, to understand what it wanted. It did not use the words that Moran had been taught when he was little and that he in his turn had taught to his little one. So that at first I did not know what it

15. For the role of Ninette, Moran's late wife, see also *Molloy,* p. 238.
16. Deleuze, p. 87. In *Molloy,* Moran is ordered to take his son with him on this his last mission in view of the importance of the psychological transformation he will undergo as a result of the mission.

wanted. But in the end I understood this language. I understood it, I understand it, all wrong perhaps. That is not what matters. It told me to write the report. [240–41] [17]

What are we to deduce from all this? That the image of the mother dominates this novel as fruitfully as it does Camus' *L'Etranger*. Both Moran and Molloy are happy to take up a uterine position, and Molloy's hat is of course a figure of the caul.[18] Erich Fromm has said that one of the deepest longings in everybody is to keep the tie to mother. It is this aspiration which gives *Molloy* its profoundly disturbing quality and makes of this great novel its author's masterpiece: a masterpiece of satisfying unity in that a sadist-type, sent in search of a masochist-type, is imperceptibly transformed into the type sought. The circularity of the work thus lies deeper than in form alone. It is the circularity of psychological tensions resolved; as such it brings comfort. *Molloy* is therefore a novel not of mental sickness, but of an arduously won, and therefore doubly precious, mental health.

17. Significantly, Martha, Moran's probable mother, has disappeared from the scene. As for the "voice," it no doubt represents the feminine aspect of the godhead (*la voix*, in French), the male facet of which is represented by Youdi (cf. Yahweh, the sender of Gaber, i.e., Gabriel, and also the Latin *iudex*, judge). At the end of both parts of the novel these two forces remain in uneasy equilibrium: Molloy and Moran respond to the voice, but they also obey the orders of the male overlord.
18. See references to "Hats" and "Womb" (in the Index Rerum) in my *The Novels of Samuel Beckett*, pp. 255–56.

A Poet's Initiation

Lawrence E. Harvey

Poetry is a precipitate, says Beckett, a dead residue, an outrageous simplification and isolation, stabilized fragments torn from an obscure and fluid complexity beyond understanding. And criticism, bending over the residue, as archeology over a hominid splinter, dreams of the antecedent mystery. Knowing the gulf that divides dream from mystery, a critic may fashion his fantasy, not as one builds a bridge, but on some theory of correspondences. It was perhaps with a great deal of humility and a deep intuition of the distance that separates us even from present reality, in ourselves and beyond us in others, that the two ingredients in the word "verisimilitude" were brought together. To abandon all hope of relationship, however, is difficult.

At first any link, even fragile, even paradoxical, between the origins of Samuel Beckett and his first volume of poetry, *Echo's Bones and Other Precipitates,*[1] which he published at the age of twenty-nine, seems difficult to establish. At a very young age his hard-working father had founded a company of quantity surveyors and bought a home and property in the elegant suburb of Foxrock, south of Dublin. Interested and active in sports, sociable, almost always in good spirits, he would take his son on cross-country hikes in the Wicklow mountains of a Sunday, or on occasion to the golf course or the beach for swimming. They had long talks and laughed together over the jokes that Willie Beckett loved to tell. He had left school at the age of fourteen or fifteen, but intelligent and sensitive if not

Lawrence E. Harvey is Professor of Romance Languages and Literatures at Dartmouth College.
1. Paris: Europa Press, 1935.

well educated, he encouraged his son in his intellectual pursuits, and he was very proud of his successes at school and later at Trinity College. Until the day of his death, as a loving father might, he carried with him the letters that his son sent him.

More austere by nature, more religious than her husband, Molly Beckett was hardly less tender and affectionate. She had worked before her marriage as a nurse at the hospital in Dublin. Calm and sure, she was a pillar of strength during the usual minor family crises—accidents, sickness, childhood sorrows. Entirely devoted to her husband, her children, her house, and her garden, she was respected and loved in the circle of the family friends.

This happy and propitious climate extended beyond hearth and home, for Sam followed his older brother Frank to the best private schools, where his athletic triumphs were no less significant than his scholarly victories, because they brought him friendships that might otherwise have come less easily. In brief, just about everything militated in favor of happiness during the early years, and certainly the young Beckett was hardly unhappy. Nonetheless, life had not forgotten his portion of suffering, and nature had equipped him with a sensibility that magnified it excessively, a courage that refused to turn away, and an intelligence that demanded, fruitlessly, a satisfactory explanation.

"You might say I had a happy childhood . . . although I never had much talent for happiness. My parents did everything possible to make a child happy. But often I felt very much alone." Little by little, through his reading and his studies, he penetrated into a world where his parents were less and less able to follow. Their middle-class life in Ireland, somewhat too organized in its values perhaps (and yet admired by him then and still), came to seem conventional and progressively less real. The early and very important influence of Descartes was scarcely calculated to reconcile the little world of his mind and the big world outside.[2] Prolonged stays in Italy, France, Germany, and England, preceding the years of wandering to come, no doubt contributed to undermining the Dublin macrocosm and substituting for it the microcosm that went always with him. And yet, another element that was part of the complex of events and reasons leading to the January 1932 rupture was probably decisive.[3]

Since very early childhood, the future author had evidenced an extreme sensitivity to all forms of suffering. On one occasion, very moved by the pitiable state of a canary wounded by a cat, he prayed God on his knees to make it recover. Later, the death of a lobster thrown into a pot of boiling water under his horrified gaze was enough to prevent him from eating this particular crustacean for many a year.[4] But what was much more serious, this cruel phenomenon soon appeared in the big world of men. His mother underwent a difficult operation. A very dear cousin died of tuberculosis, which carried off her father as well. Beckett, a good friend, was with him during the last months in a Wicklow sanitorium. It is hard not to imagine the poet of *Echo's Bones,* there as later under similar circumstances, at grips with an implacable enemy, sick himself with the suffering of another, refusing to let go, a bitter and helpless witness. The difficulty, outlined long before, found sardonic expression in "Ooftish," a poem published in the spring of 1938 in *Transition.* After an accumulation of miseries, maladies, and misfortunes (which are not without paradoxical kinship to the "pathogenic litanies" of the medieval ascetic, Jacopone da Todi), the poet concludes that

2. See *Whoroscope,* a long poem published in 1930. This, as well as the other poems discussed in this essay, can be found in *Poems in English* (New York: Grove Press, 1961).
3. An Assistant in Romance Languages and Literatures at Trinity College, Dublin, Beckett left Ireland and renounced an academic career once and for all.
4. Beckett incorporates the event in a short story, "Dante and the Lobster" (1932). This story is in *More Pricks Than Kicks* (London: Chatto & Windus, 1934).

all this can be summed up in the "blood of the lamb." And we understand a little better perhaps what Estragon means in *Waiting for Godot* when he declares, "All my life I've compared myself to [Christ]." We are struggling, clearly, with the old, old knot that is so difficult to untie, the ancient question everlastingly asked about innocence (at least relative innocence) that suffers. An event of capital importance aggravated this preoccupation and prepared the terrain that was to produce *Echo's Bones*. William Beckett, father of the poet, was struck down by a heart attack and died in June 1933. Overwhelmed, the young man wrote a friend, "What am I to do now but follow his tracks over the fields and hedges." He had come back to Ireland a little less than a year after the   • rupture, that is to say in the autumn of 1932, penniless and, as he said, "tail between my legs." He left again now and settled down in London, where he wandered about the city for two years. Depressed, in what he was to call later "a confused state," searching, tempted to part company with a cruel and incomprehensible world, he read, walked, tried to write. It is to this somber period of his life that we owe the novel *Murphy* and the collection of poems entitled *Echo's Bones*.

The first lines of the second poem in the collection ("Enueg I") are a synthesis of all the poet's experience of hospitals, all the times he kept vigil at the bedside of the sick and dying. "Exeo in a spasm/ tired of my darling's red sputum/ from the Portobello Private Nursing Home." These lines tell us as well of his imperious need to flee, to liberate himself from a suffering he can no longer sustain. It is as though the spasms of the dying person became contagious, began to infect the poet himself. At the same time, the word *exeo*, set off in Latin by the poet, suggests (much better than the English word) not only the departure from the hospital but from life also. Obviously, the two exits often coincide, and when the narrator leaves, he finds signs of death everywhere about him.

The lines quoted are not only a synthesis; they are also a very precise allusion to the death of close relatives from tuberculosis. The poet's flight takes the form of a long walk. From the hospital, a very real one in Dublin, his course describes a great circle that runs along the Grand Canal, passes through two villages, the Fox and Geese and Chapelizod, and returns beneath the heights of Kilmainham along the quais of the Liffey—a symbolic circle, no doubt, for he resists the calls of death hidden everywhere along his way ("the fingers of the ladders hooked over the parapet,/ soliciting") —and returns to the city of man, without, however, reconciling himself to man's condition.

The poem's point of departure is also in the interior life of the poet, in the literary recollections that are as real for him as the beings and events of the world outside. The word *exeo* itself reminds us that the very title of the book comes from mythology, via the *Metamorphoses* of Ovid (bk. 3) , where we read, among others, this significant passage: "The cares that keep her from sleep exhaust her miserable body; emaciated, her skin dries out; all the sap from her members evaporates. Only her voice and bones remain; her voice is intact; her bones, they say, have taken the form of a rock." The key word for our present purpose, "evaporate," signals in an immediate and final way the disappearance of the nymph. In the original Latin text the verb is *abeo,* synonym of *exeo,* and bearing like it the two meanings, *to leave* and *to die.*

The fate of Echo is especially interesting in the context of the poem because of her relationship with Narcissus. If an overly simple identification of the poet with Narcissus is undesirable (he reveals himself also perhaps in the situation of the unfortunate Echo) , it is important nevertheless to insist on the theme of painful separation. Nor is narcissism without analogy to the attitude of the poet who ignores the calls of the outside world in order to heed inner voices, and doing so destroys himself in a sense, leaving behind only the flower that is his poetry. The voice of the nymph persists, but Echo's crippled immortality suggests an inadequate, fragmented poetry (cf. the style of *How It Is*) . In like manner the indestructible rock of his poetry seems to him appallingly cold and hard by comparison with the warmth and beauty that was life.

This same poem ends with another allusion (to "Barbare," one of the *Illuminations* of Rimbaud) where the conflict between the big world and the little, here an opposition between brutal reality and the no doubt illusory beauty of art, is presented in a more explicit way: "Ah the banner/ the banner of meat bleeding/ on the silk of the seas and the arctic flowers/ that do not exist." [5] If, as I believe, such a conflict was central in the life and art of the young poet and has remained so for him, it will be important to analyze the problem in some detail as it appears in the collection *Echo's Bones*. This is the aim in the following pages.

The outside world with which the narrator makes contact from time to time often takes on the aspect of a surface that dissolves under his penetrating gaze. Riding a bicycle, dressed in a dirty slicker, he "court[s] . . . the sneers" of the stylish young couples he passes. But for him society's trappings hardly conceal the less avowable reality beneath, and he sees "these fauns these smart nymphs"—another possible allusion to the destiny of Echo ("Sanies I"). In a similar way, the Portobello Private Nursing Home, a euphemism that the alliteration (introduced by the poet, who adds the word "private") seems to mock, hides "its secret things." Elsewhere young spectators watching an Irish hockey match, decked out in their Sunday best and ironically termed heroes, come down from Kilmainham to drink beer; but their clothes fail to conceal their sweating bodies from the poet's eyes, and the beer—"a pint of nepenthe, or moly or half and half" ("Enueg I") —is reduced to its true function, an aid to forgetfulness of sorrows hardly masked by an artificial gaity. Once in a while the reverse movement occurs, and the narrator, on foot this time,

5. "Le pavillon en viande saignante sur la soie des mers et des fleurs arctiques, (elles n'existent pas)."

provides us with a different image of two worlds separated. In
"Sanies II" the outer is symbolized by rags and the inner by a
happy body: "coming from the bath . . . / happy body/ loose
in my stinking old suit . . . / spotless then within the brown
rags. . . ." The lines suggest the possibility of a happiness
independent of social norms. Usually, however, only the dead
escape the pressures of convention, "breaking without fear or
favour wind/ the gantelope of sense and nonsense run"
("Echo's Bones").

Superficial, conventional, the world is also painful, "all
things . . . pressed down and bleeding" ("Serena I"). In an
allusion to the Bible, the poet turns values upside down and
puts a negative sign on existence: "the prone who must/ soon
take up their life and walk" ("The Vulture"). We find in
several poems images of contortions and convulsions, of
tremblings and shakings, of dissolution and crumbling, of
stagnation, rotting, and wasting away. The tower chosen in
London is the Bloody Tower. An adder at the zoo broaches its
white rat: innocence that dies a horrible death. An ambulance
passes filled with sighs and palpitations. In another biblical
allusion, the poet depicts for us a fly that "could not serve
typhoid and Mammon" ("Serena I"). Finally, in a line that is
curiously medieval, he sets in bold relief the illusory nature of
existence, for the worms make no mistake about it; the dead
revelers who have finally found asylum are "taken by the
maggots for what they are" ("Echo's Bones"). Perhaps this
somber vision is best summed up and explained by the very
discreet allusion, already touched on, to the author of the
Inferno; for the "secret things" are indeed "le segrete cose" of
Dante, and behind the door of the Portobello Private Nursing
Home we can expect to find what we come upon just beyond
the terrible Gate of Hell: [6]

> Quivi sospiri, pianti e alti guai
> Risonavan per l'aere sanza stelle,

6. "[Virgil] mi mise dentro a le segrete cose" (3. 21).

Per ch'io al cominciar ne lagrimai.
Diverse lingue, orribili favelle,
Parole di dolore, accenti d'ira,
Voci alte e fioche, e suon di man con elle,
Facevano un tumulto, il qual s'aggira
Sempre in quell' aura sanza tempo tinta,
Come la rena quando turbo spira. (3.22–30)

Beckett has not forgotten the reply made long years ago to the family maid who had been terrified by a fire-and-brimstone sermon she had just heard: "Hell is now." Although it would no doubt be a mistake to reduce the poet's morbid anguish to a single and unique event, it becomes perhaps a little more understandable when we read the very moving poem "Malacoda," one of the most touching tributes ever rendered by a son to a dead father and a mourning mother, and also when we realize that almost half the poems in the collection were written in the eighteen months following Willie Beckett's death.

We may object that others have resigned themselves with less sorrow and anguish to greater suffering. Perhaps the poet's problem is often that he must accommodate two warring selves, a chronic idealist and an insistent realist. We have already noted a nostalgia for an ideal world—accompanied by a clairvoyant refusal—apropos of the quotation from Rimbaud's *Illuminations*. It is not difficult to multiply poetic examples of a conflict that is never resolved definitively into total despair, although hope is frail and often battered. In "Enueg II" a cloud comes "too late to brighten the sky." In "Alba" love, beauty, forgiveness do not suffice, nor compensate for absence, darkness, death: "so that there is no sun and no unveiling/ and no host/ only I and then the sheet/ and bulk dead." In "Sanies II," in spite of the comic tone and verbal antics, the happy land soon becomes a nightmare place where cruelty creeps in, the dream evaporates, and the poem ends on a *kyrie* that brings us back to painful reality. Finally, numerous expressions like "scarlet beauty in our world dead fish adrift" in "Serena I" translate the disarray of a spirit caught in a tug of war between its loves and its sufferings and tormented by the idea of the impassable distance between the Eden it needs and the hard exile into which it has been plunged.

The experience of exile—reinforced for Beckett by his early life as Protestant in a Catholic country, as intellectual in a bourgeois family, as artist in academia, and at this particular time by his very real exile as a vagrant Irishman in London—is apparent everywhere in his poetry, but in a particularly striking and concentrated way in the images of the poem entitled "Enueg I." Here we see "a dying barge . . . in the foaming cloister of the lock"; "on the far bank a gang of down and outs"; a child excluded from a game at which the narrator himself is no more than a spectator; the narrator described again, "derelict, as from a bush of gorse on fire in the mountain after dark,/ or, in Sumatra, the jungle hymen,/ the still flagrant rafflesia." Further on in the poem: "a lamentable family of grey verminous hens,/ . . . half asleep, against the closed door of a shed,/ with no means of roosting" and finally, "a small malevolent goat, exiled on the road,/ remotely pucking the gate of his field." Such an accumulation of figures makes interpretation easy enough. However, if the images reveal the solitude of the poet, they are not without ambiguity. The child, reassured, *chooses* after all not to try again to enter the playing field from which he had been once rejected, and the goat seems only half ready to give up his liberty. Similarly, the darkness of the mountain or the jungle appears barely preferable to the fire that destroys as it illuminates or to the putrid beauty of the parasitical flower. Only the river that beckons offers momentarily a possible escape to one who knows neither how to adapt to social existence nor how to suffer total isolation. He does not respond to the call, however, and "Enueg I" remains without true conclusion.

There are, in effect, other solutions, and Beckett's poems function as imaginative modes for exploring and testing conceivable alternatives. Caught in the anguish of such a dilemma, what are the options for a being at once demanding and lucid? First of all revolt, now through violence, now through obscenity. At sunset in the mountains, he interprets after his fashion the movements of his sleeping, dreaming dog: "snarl and howl in the wood wake all the birds/ hound the harlots out of the ferns/ this damfool twilight threshing in the brake/ bleating to be bloodied/ this crapulent hush/ tear its heart out" ("Serena II") . The need for violence, curiously accompanied at times by an equally irresistible compassion, becomes masochistic in one poem—without however ceasing to be completely lucid. The burlesque scene of flagellation, done in a mixture of English, Latin, Italian, and French, is a demonstration of verbal virtuosity quite as much as a psychological catharsis. Sometimes revolt is under the sign of irony or bitter sarcasm, and sometimes it takes the form of classical understatement translating a calm but hopeless opposition, a simple refusal that knows its own futility before that which is unacceptable and at the same time inevitable. Such is the "nay" that ends "Malacoda."

In several poems a religious solution seems to offer the possibility of a satisfactory reconciliation. A trip to western Ireland occasions thoughts of the Blessed Isles. Croagh Patrick, mountain of the Irish saint and goal of pilgrims, presents itself only to be engulfed at nightfall along with all the condemned land ("Serena II") . The poems are sprinkled with explicit allusions to Christ, but He appears not as Savior but as Man the victim of fathomless injustice. In the last lines of "Serena III," which refer both to a town south of Dublin and to the Rock of Ages in the Protestant hymn (and beyond to the Old Testament) , he definitively rejects the religious solution: "Hide yourself not in the Rock keep on the move/ keep on the move."

His quest, renewed always one more time, does not at all exclude attempts to adapt himself to life in the society of men, to find his "place in the sun." Even the humble fly succeeds, and the adder is warm and well fed in her well-lighted glass home; but as the allusion to Pascal suggests, it seems that human space has been wholly usurped. Lacking the talent of a Defoe or an Aretino, he is unfortunately incapable either of prostrating himself abjectly before The City, or of conquering it by force ("Serena I").

And so only flight is left. To escape what one can neither win nor vanquish seems the last hope. But escape where? The vultures at the zoo in London gaze fixedly toward distant Ireland, but "the harpy is past caring" ("Serena I"). She has no doubt accepted her cage—prison or refuge, depending on need. As for himself, he muses, "in Ken Wood who shall find me/ my breath held in the midst of thickets/ none but the most quarried lovers." The line returns again and again in "Serena I," a refrain that is almost obsessive. Such a choice (one of many examples scattered through the poems of enclosed, protected places) can scarcely fail to suggest both womb and grave. A Freudian's field day! Still, meaning is hardly hidden, and in "Sanies I" the poet makes things quite plain: "ah to be back in the caul now. . . ." (It is perhaps appropriate to mention here the old superstition that a child born with its head enveloped by the caul will be lucky. The caul was supposed to protect against drowning, and there may well be a relation between this notion and the attachment to hats so characteristic of many Beckett protagonists.) The tomb is just as attractive: "asylum under my tread all this day" ("Echo's Bones"). The juxtaposition of beginning and end, womb and grave, occurs in *Waiting for Godot* in the striking image of the women who give birth astride a tomb. Here, the young man walks on and on toward he knows not what. There, the old man has stopped walking and waits—for he knows not what. In the last poem in the collection the themes of flight and suicide, that definitive flight, come close to joining, as in "Serena I," but in the last analysis the tension remains unresolved. Although he does not reply to the call of death, he cannot give up the day-long wanderings across fields and through towns that bring the pseudo-death that is physical exhaustion and spent nerves. The tortured spirit is finally calmed—"mind annulled/ wrecked in wind" ("Enueg I") .

He has other aids to living—and above all an inexhaustible compassion. Human beings but also animals and even the common housefly merit his fraternal concern ("Serena I") . They too are marked for suffering, exile, and death. Then also his instinct for the comic can lay bare the burlesque face of the macabre and put a merciful distance between the self that suffers and the self that watches. Finally, a tenacity that refuses surrender serves him well during downcast times—perhaps, too, a grain of pride that rejects facile illusions and draws spare comfort from a hard but accurate realism.

The true solution, however, is his poet's art. As the poems themselves make clear, the closed-in place is not solely the womb, nor the grave that resembles it. It is something more positive than these two forms of movement toward nothingness. The place of refuge is above all the little world hidden inside the skull. Even while it recalls death, always present beneath the appearances of life, the image of the skull suggests the microcosm so admirably evoked in the novel *Murphy,* written during the same period. "Who knows," asks the narrator "what the ostrich sees in the sand?" (176) . Working in an asylum for mental patients, Murphy came to loathe "the complacent scientific conceptualism that made contact with outer reality the index of mental well-being. . . . [All his experience] obliged him to call sanctuary what the psychiatrists called exile and to think of the patients not as banished from a system of benefits but as escaped from a colossal fiasco" (176–78) . As for Murphy himself, he considered what he called his mind "not as an instrument [designed to record facts from the outer world] but as a place, from whose unique delights precisely those current facts withheld him" (178) . As far as he was concerned, therefore, there was an absolutely fundamental conflict between the two worlds. "His vote was cast. 'I am not of the big world, I am of the little world' " (178).

It would be difficult to overstress the importance of this passage. However, the link between inner asylum (the key word in "Echo's Bones") and artistic creation comes not in the novel but in the poetry. "The Vulture," of special importance because of its initial position in the group of thirteen poems, was inspired by lines from Goethe that contain a comparison between a soaring bird scanning the earth for prey, its wings motionless, and the lyric that hovers on the edge of becoming. In Beckett's poem, the vulture drags "his hunger through the sky/ of my skull shell of sky and earth." (Here already we have the tendency to interiorize that creates the microcosm.) Then the bird, dropping toward an intended victim, finds itself "mocked by a tissue that may not serve/ till hunger earth and sky be offal." An esthetic point of view that helps to explain the entire collection can be discovered lying half hidden in the lines of this opening poem. In effect, the microcosm of the imagination can be not only a place to live but also the little world of a literary work. Any attempt to isolate it totally from the big world would no doubt be vain, but there is certainly a tendency in this direction. Implemented, it will produce an individualistic art concerned above all with the exploration of the self, an introspective art difficult of access, hardly popular in any sense, but singularly "modern." It will reflect the need of those living at a time when social institutions disintegrate and reform unceasingly to take stock, to find (at least to seek) a more stable inner reality. So much the worse if this reality turns out to be as shifting and elusive, similarly destined to disintegration, equally unreal.

The macrocosm, after all, must feed the little world of the mind—but only after a metamorphosis has taken place. A death must intervene before the poem can be born. *Echo's Bones* is indeed under the sign of Ovid, and the poet's theme as well as practice is poetic metamorphosis. A Freudian interpretation would miss the mark if it failed to take account of the essential metaphoric movement that extends the imagery of enclosures and makes both womb and tomb figures of the microcosm of transforming imagination. In "Malacoda" the narrator is a stage manager who oversees the funeral preparations. "Mind the imago it is he," he says of the corpse. The word *imago,* as a term taken from entomology, evokes the world of Ovidian metamorphoses. At the same time, in its psychoanalytical meaning, it suggests the idealization of the father, as "incorruptible" now as the demon "in the vestibule." But mythology and psychoanalysis merely provide materials. It is art that makes possible the last and best transformation of reality. Only the poet can fix forever the ideal vision that in its way corrects the cruelty of the human condition. We find a similar metamorphosis of the funeral wreath that adorns the coffin. Composed, in the poem, not of natural flowers that time fades, this last homage of an aggrieved son is a still life by the artist Van Huysum, famous as a painter of flowers. The vision is negative in a sense, for it rejects nature in favor of the perfection of art. Not an easy perfection however. The *limae labor* of the conscious poet can be as hard and as cruel as the "peristalsis" of the adder that swallows its rat ("Serena I"). All the same, for him too it makes survival possible.

As exorcism, such art diminishes the pain of living and gives its due, however small, to a vanished Eden. Realistic, on the other hand, it dissolves the surfaces of conventional day-to-day existence and makes contact with a harder but truer condition. Idealism and realism coexisting side by side—in poetry as in life. In the recent play, *Happy Days,* a moving refrain that breaks the monologue when endurance declines and all else fails implies a courage still set against the deepening silence: "Sing your song, Winnie." As then, so now when wandering has become waiting, the seeker's strength and the sufferer's refuge seem to remain the song that is art.

The Laughter of Sad Sam Beckett

Ruby Cohn

In *Watt,* Beckett's last novel to be written directly in English
and only now being translated into French, a character named
Arsene explains:

> The bitter laugh laughs at that which is not good, it is the ethical
> laugh. The hollow laugh laughs at that which is not true, it is the
> intellectual laugh. . . . But the mirthless laugh is the dianoetic
> laugh, down the snout—Haw!—so. It is the laugh of laughs, the
> *risus purus,* the laugh laughing at the laugh, the beholding, saluting
> of the highest joke, in a word the laugh that laughs . . . at that
> which is unhappy. [48]

Arsene's laughs undercut three human ideals—the good, the
true, and the happy. In sharp contrast to the laughter aroused
by classical comedy—*Castigat ridendo mores*—Arsene's
laughter is aroused by desiderata rather than mores. Since the
ethical laugh mocks goodness, and the dianoetic laugh mocks
suffering, these two laughs are almost polar opposites. An
executioner would evoke the ethical laugh, and his victim
would evoke the dianoetic laugh. But Beckett's characters are
often executioner *and* victim, Cain *and* Abel, swinging from
sadism to suffering without reason but with a good deal of
rhythm. This is made explicit in *How It Is,* where Everyman
and all men are statistically counted as both victim and
executioner; the more one suffers, the more wildly one laughs:
"All suffering of all time is mine but it doesn't phase me and
it's the wild laugh in every cell." Beckett's dramas do not
abound in laughter, but most of the extant laughter is attracted
by these magnetic poles, cruelty and suffering, which inspire,
respectively, the ethical and the dianoetic laugh.

Ruby Cohn is a fellow of the California Institute of the Arts.

In *Waiting for Godot,* Beckett's best-known work, there are eight laughs in toto, and Arsene's analysis is relevant to them all. Four of the laughs belong to Pozzo, two to Didi, and two to Gogo; Lucky never laughs, which emphasizes the irony of his name. Of the eight laughs, seven occur in act 1 of *Godot,* and only one in act 2. Proportionately, this contrasts with Beckett's manipulation of the celebrated phrase, "We're waiting for Godot," which occurs only three times in act 1 and ten in act 2. Just as repetition of the waiting phrase insists upon the long, long duration of that wait, so the gradual disappearance of laughter contributes to the dull desolation of that wait. Moreover, this reduction of laughter in the play as a whole is reflected in the reduction of the laughter of the principal laugher, Pozzo.

Pozzo's first laugh, on examining Didi and Gogo, is an "enormous laugh." The next two times, the scenic directions state merely: "He laughs." and the last time, "he laughs briefly." All four laughs of Pozzo occur in act 1 of *Godot,* for by act 2, along with the loss of pipe, atomizer, watch, and sight, Pozzo has lost the power to laugh. And perhaps even the memory of laughter, since he no longer speaks of it.

In contrast to this marked deterioration, the limited laughter of Didi and Gogo is constant—a constancy that may perhaps be linked with the constancy of their wait for Godot. Didi's two laughs are hearty, and those of Gogo are noisy. Because he suffers from prostate trouble, Didi's two laughs are painful to him, and he laughs no more after the first few minutes of the play. Gogo, on the other hand, delays his one-laugh-per-act until the entrance of Pozzo and Lucky. Like many of the laughs which the two friends evoke from the theater audience— described in French only as "aspects riants"—their own stage laughter is problematic in origin, but is susceptible to Arsene's analysis.

Quite early in the play, before Godot is mentioned, but when time already has to be passed, Didi has the bright idea that the two friends should repent, but he is at a loss when Gogo asks *what* they should repent. Then Gogo suggests that they might repent being born, and Didi breaks into his hearty laugh, which pubic pain compels him to stifle, complaining, "One daren't even laugh any more." Didi's first laugh is thus bounded by suffering—the fact of being born and the fact of prostate trouble. Though Didi tries to substitute a painless smile for the painful laugh, he decides, "It's not the same thing."

Beckett's scenic directions attach Didi's second laugh to his first, since it is "stifled *as before,* less the smile" (my italics) . This second laugh, which follows the first after a few minutes of playing time, punctuates the friends' stichomythic exchange about Godot, through which seeps anxiety about their own situation. "Where do we come in?" Gogo wants to know. When Didi replies cryptically, "On our hands and knees." Gogo asks innocently, "We've no rights any more?" Whereupon Didi explodes into his last laugh of the play. By Arsene's analysis, that laugh borders on both intellectual and dianoetic, for the truth of their rights seems preposterous, and their unhappiness is evident, deprived of rights as they are. Even the right to laugh seems to have disappeared for Didi, who declares, "You'd make me laugh if it wasn't prohibited."

Though Gogo's laughter does not seem to be prohibited, it too is ambiguous. In act 2 of *Waiting for Godot* Gogo laughs noisily when Pozzo inquires whether the two bums are friends. There is some doubt about whether Gogo is laughing because he thinks that they *are* friends, or are *not* friends, but he apparently knows the truth that arouses his intellectual laugh. And even as Gogo indulges in his intellectual laugh, the theater audience is indulging in a different intellectual laugh, for, as Didi points out, Pozzo couldn't be less interested in whether or not the two bums are friends. What he wants to know is whether they are friends of *his:* Gogo laughs at the truth which he misunderstands in Pozzo's question, and we laugh at his misunderstanding.

Gogo's first laugh—evidently a series of laughs, embraced by the scenic directions "laughs noisily" and "convulsed with merriment"—is also inspired by Pozzo, since he "laughs noisily" when Pozzo cannot find his pipe. Gogo's laugh at Pozzo's loss is an example of Arsene's *risus purus,* and that purity is emphasized when Pozzo is "on the point of tears" while Gogo is "convulsed with merriment" at the offstage urination of Didi, which also involves suffering. Gogo's laugh begins at the unhappiness of Pozzo, and continues at the unhappiness of Didi; in the equation for a straight line $y = mx + b$, Beckett's m stands for mirthless.

Although both friends laugh, and Lucky weeps, Pozzo alone indulges in both tears and laughter, and he includes both reactions in a philosophical pronouncement: "The tears of the world are a constant quantity. For each one who begins to weep somewhere else another stops. The same is true of the laugh. (*He laughs.*)" Within his tightly closed system, then, he has just deprived someone of laughter by laughing himself, and since, in the remainder of that speech, Pozzo suggests that laughter at large is associated with happiness, he has perhaps deprived someone of happiness too.

In *Endgame,* however, Nell declares, "Nothing is funnier than *un*happiness." (my italics) and, fitting action to paradox, she shortly afterward tries to cry. In *Endgame,* both Nagg and Nell, the older generation, seem able to manage Pozzo's switch from tears to laughter. Nevertheless, the play provides less variety than *Godot*—a reduced world and a *reductio ad absurdum.* The tree and road have shrunk to a "bare interior." The moon and firmament of *Godot* blend to the gray light of *Endgame.* And although we still have two couples in *Endgame,* one is confined to garbage cans, and Clov alone is minimally mobile while Hamm lives in his wheelchair. But more fully than in *Godot,* there is exploration of the relationships between the four characters on stage, and none without cruelty, none without comedy. These facets are reflected through the stage laughter; for in this play where Nell announces that nothing is funnier than unhappiness, *all* the characters laugh, three of them singly, and three in duets. Thus, the laughter of *Endgame* differs from that of *Godot* where no two characters laugh simultaneously.

Of the sixteen laughs of *Endgame*—twice the number in *Godot,* though the play is otherwise sparer—seven belong to Clov alone, and five are finished before a word of dialogue is heard from the stage. Such petty calculations would suit Clov admirably, bent as he is on order. Just as Clov's "Finished" is the *opening* word of the play, so his "Brief laugh" is the first human sound of the play that Beckett himself described as "more *in*human than *Godot*" (my italics) . Clov's five brief laughs are part of the ritualistic opening of the play, substituting for the invocation. The opening action, which can take many minutes on stage, may be summarized as much ado about nothing. As the focus of *Godot* was on all that waiting, so the focus of *Endgame* is on all that ado.

Early in the play, even before Clov's first laugh, we have a literal representation of the *reductio ad absurdum.* Clov looks up at the window and realizes that he needs a ladder to see through it; he has evidently been reduced to the present self we see. Hamm asks him later, "Have you shrunk?" In Beckett's entropic play there is ubiquitous shrinkage. When Clov does look out of the window on the left, which we later learn is the sea, perhaps he laughs because the sea has shrunk; more probably perhaps, his second laugh may indicate that the earth has shrunk. Or, to recall Arsene's categories, perhaps he laughs because earth and sea are neither good nor true. We never know. He laughs, too, after looking into each garbage-can, perhaps at the unhappiness of Nagg and Nell, though the audience does not yet know that the garbage-cans contain these human derelicts. As far as we can see, Clov's opening laughs are at four successive things—window, window, garbage-can, garbage-can—before his brief laugh at Hamm breaks the symmetry. By gesture and laughter, Clov virtually gives life to things so that we will hear words from Nagg, Nell, and especially Hamm. And for this family, words are synonymous with life.

When they both emerge from their garbage-cans, Nagg and Nell strain to kiss each other in a grotesque parody of love. When they fail to meet, Nell asks, "Why this farce, day after day?"—a line that Clov will later echo though he is not on stage to hear Nell's question. Elegiac about the past, Nagg and Nell share a decrescendo of three laughs in recollecting their honeymoon—a decrescendo that seems to be a *risus purus* at their own unhappiness, for on their honeymoon occurred the accident in which they lost their legs.

These three shared laughs exhaust Nell's laughter, but Nagg is ready to laugh at the suffering of others as well. When Hamm announces that he has a heart in his head, Nagg "chuckles cautiously," and Nell admonishes him not to laugh even though "Nothing is funnier than unhappiness." But Nagg nevertheless does most of the laughing in the play—eight laughs compared to Clov's seven. Nagg shares the three-laugh decrescendo with Nell, at the joke of losing their legs. Nagg shares a hearty laugh with Hamm at the word "honor." Nagg laughs twice at his own joke about the worthlessness of God's created world, and he laughs once when Hamm claims to have a heart in his head, stifling a last laugh when Hamm repeats this obliquely, "Something dripping in my head, ever since the fontanelles." In these eight laughs, Nagg encompasses Arsene's hierarchy: God's world is not good, and Nagg's laugh is ethical; Hamm's honor is not true, and Nagg's laugh is intellectual; Hamm's suffering from a heart in his head, and Nagg's suffering from his leglessness evoke Nagg's dianoetic laugh at unhappiness. Nagg's laughter affirms the meaning of his name —to nag.

Though Hamm is at the center of the play, and though he talks long and loud about his unhappiness, he does not seem to find it funny. Though Hamm talks about laughing with Clov, though he joins Nagg in a laugh about his honor, Hamm

laughs *alone* only once, during his chronicle. Confronted with
the crawling father begging food for his child, the narrator
broods, "And then I imagined already that I wasn't much
longer for this world." Hamm uses a narrative tone for his
chronicle, but much of it seems to be relevant to himself, and
the laughter may be a response to the untruth of his remark,
since his own life has dragged on. There are also implications
of the ethical laugh, since life is clearly not good, and the laugh
may be reaching toward the *risus purus* since life, all life in
Endgame, is unhappy.

In contrast to Hamm's lone laugh that seems to summarize
Arsene's hierarchy, Clov's two lone laughs during the course of
the play are as puzzling as his laughter in the opening ritual.
About one-third of the way through *Endgame* Clov echoes Nell's
line, "Why this farce, day after day?" and ruminating, Hamm
asks Clov, "We're not beginning to . . . to . . . mean
something?" Clov snaps back, "Mean something! You and I,
mean something! *(Brief laugh.)* Ah that's a good one!" Clov's
brief laugh seems to be intellectual and to doubt the truth of
their meaning anything. But what would they mean if they did
mean something? Hamm continues to contemplate this
possibility until he is shocked into alarm at another possibility
—that of a flea in Clov's trousers.

Clov's last laugh, separated from the next to last by some half
hour of stage time, is the last laugh in *Endgame.* As in *Godot,*
stage laughter thins down to zero. Clov's last laugh is his
heartiest: "Clov *bursts out* laughing" (my italics). But there is
no presumption in *Endgame* that he who laughs last laughs
best. The burst of laughter is inspired by the following passage
from Hamm's chronicle: "Crawling on his belly, whining for
bread for his brat. He's offered a job as a gardener. Before—"
Hamm, as author, is most anxious to pinpoint the source of
Clov's laughter. "What is there so funny about that?" he
demands of Clov, who replies, "A job as gardener! Is that what
tickles you?" Hamm insists, and Clov is not sure, "It must be
that." Persisting, Hamm inquires, "It wouldn't be the bread?"

And, more uncertain, Clov replies in a near-pun, "Or the brat." Whereupon Hamm, in a sweeping statement, seems to sum up his chronicle and the whole of *Endgame:* "The whole thing is comical, I grant you that." A dianoetic comedy at pervasive unhappiness.

For the last time, Hamm suggests that he and Clov "have a good guffaw the two of [them] together." But Clov has had his guffaw for the day, and there is no further laughter in the last half hour or so of the play. Just before Hamm's final soliloquy, Clov recites what may be *his* chronicle or merely his future: "I open the door of my cell and go. I am so bowed I only see my feet, if I open my eyes, and between my legs a little trail of black dust. I say to myself that the earth is extinguished, though I never saw it lit. (*Pause.*) It's easy going. (*Pause.*) When I fall I'll weep for happiness." In *Endgame* the totality of the action and reaction supports Arsene's spectrum of laughter; one weeps for happiness, and nothing is funnier than *un*happiness. The entropic symmetries of design in Beckett's two French plays are bolstered by the symmetries of the stage laughter.

In Beckett's other plays, written originally in English, symmetries disintegrate. The two radio dramas and the monodrama, which precede or follow *Endgame* by a year, elevate laughter almost to a climax, and all three plays resemble *Endgame* rather than *Godot* in that solitude is paradoxically emphasized through laughter in duets. Before the duet of *All That Fall,* Mrs. Maddy Rooney bursts into two wild laughs and a giggle. On the surface of sound in this radio play, *All That Fall* seems to be a return to a more realistic mode, and Maddy Rooney's two wild laughs and giggle seem to spring from a traditional domain of sexual suggestion. Maddy Rooney is in her seventies; her name is a diminutive for "mad ruin." But though her massive flesh may be weak, her sexual spirit is very willing. Her first wild laugh follows her invitation to the elderly Mr. Tyler: "Oh cursed corset! If I could let it out, without indecent exposure. Mr. Tyler! Mr. Tyler! Come back and unlace me behind the hedge!" Her second wild laugh, which occurs soon after the first, precedes her greeting: "Well, if it isn't my old admirer, the Clerk of the Course, in his limousine." There follows a scene of obscene innuendo, which is summarized by the name of Maddy Rooney's old admirer, Mr. Slocum. And it is during this suggestive scene that Maddy giggles, "Oh glory!. . Up! Up!. . Ah!. . I'm in!" As Mr. Slocum pants.

But even in such semi-traditional comedy, the laughs and giggle are preceded or followed by sobs and tears. So that Beckett provides a counterpointed preparation for the climactic laugh of the play, when Maddy is leading her blind husband, Dan, home from the train station. As they walk, they hear a record of Schubert's *Death and the Maiden*, which emphasizes the series of dead maidens mentioned in *All That Fall*, and Maddy starts to cry, mingling her tears with the wind and the rain. Dan asks her about Sunday's preacher and text, to which she replies with the words of a psalm: "The Lord upholdeth all that fall and raiseth up all those that be bowed down" (145:14). After a moment's silence, the old couple join in wild laughter. And that wild duet derives directly from Arsene, casting doubt on the goodness of God, on the truth of His mercy, and on ultimate happiness in His care.

In Beckett's next radio play *Embers* there is another laughing duet between man and wife, but it is neither so climactic nor so pointed as the one in *All That Fall*. The very act of laughing has been previously denigrated in the conversation between Henry and Ada. It is Ada who is the first to laugh, at her own dubious joke about the horses she fancied, who stood still and marked time with their four legs. But she laughs alone at what may be a dianoetic joke, and she wants Henry to join her: "Laugh, Henry, it's not every day I crack a joke. (*Pause.*) Laugh, Henry, do that for me. . . . You laughed so charmingly once, I think that's what first attracted me to you. That and your smile. (*Pause.*) Come on, it will be like old times. (*Pause. He tries to laugh, fails.*) " Henry suggests:

"Perhaps I should begin with the smile. (*Pause for smile.*) Did that attract you? (*Pause.*) Now I'll try again. (*Long horrible laugh.*) Any of the old charm there?"

Despite its horror, however, that first laugh seems to teach Henry how it's done, and he is able to muster four laughs at the sea that makes him suffer: "And I live on the brink of it! Why? Professional obligations? (*Brief laugh.*) Reasons of health? (*Brief laugh.*) Family ties? (*Brief laugh.*) A woman? (*Laugh in which she joins.*) " All four are intellectual laughs at that which is not true, but their joint laughter at "A woman?" may imply a shift to laughter at the mutual unhappiness they cause each other—particularly since the woman Ada may be dead, and the line which follows their laughing duet, and which is not followed by laughter, is: "Some old grave I cannot tear myself away from?" What we hear in the play are the dying embers of Henry's life before he commits it to "some old grave." Henry's last laugh in the radio play is a long laugh at the mention of tears.

Krapp's Last Tape, a monodrama for the stage, was written in the same year as *Embers,* and the rhythm of its laughter is comparable. Henry indulges in three intellectual laughs before Ada joins him. Krapp, on the other hand, begins his stage laughter in a duet with his recorded voice, before he laughs alone. In this memory play, Krapp listens to the tape-recording of his memories: "Hard to believe I was ever that young whelp. The voice! Jesus! And the aspirations! (*Brief laugh in which Krapp joins.*) And the resolutions! (*Brief laugh in which Krapp joins.*) To drink less, in particular. (*Brief laugh of Krapp alone.*) " The laughter is inspired by the futility of aspiration and resolution, which have resulted in the unhappiness of the creature on stage. Krapp proceeds to summarize his life with terse irony, concluding, "Shadows of the opus . . . magnum. Closing with a— (*brief laugh*) —yelp to Providence. (*Prolonged laugh in which Krapp joins.*) " The prolonged duet recalls the wild joint laugh of *All That Fall,* with its implications that Providence, or the Lord, is neither good, nor true, nor comforting.

In *Happy Days* such laughter, and its comment on transcendence, becomes matter for meditation in Winnie's first day on stage. Again, Beckett prepares us for a climactic duet which contains Winnie's only stage laugh, though she smiles some thirty-five times. In several of her quotations, Winnie has coupled sadness and gladness, and her first mention of laughter is similarly ambivalent.

Winnie's problem, like that of the characters of *Godot* and *Endgame,* is to pass the time, in her case "between the bell for waking and the bell for sleep." Her last inspiration in a series of ideas for action, limited by the fact that she is buried up to her waist, is: "Or a brief . . . gale of laughter, should I happen to see the old joke again. *(Pause. Smile appears, broadens and seems about to culminate in laugh when suddenly replaced by expression of anxiety.)* " The thought of the mysterious "old joke" is not adequate to evoke her laughter. And when Winnie does manage to laugh on stage, it is not quite the gale she envisioned, but is nevertheless prolonged.

The big event in Winnie's first happy stage day is the sighting of the emmet which "has like a little white ball in its arms." To this description her husband Willie comments monosyllabically, "Eggs." He then repeats that comment, "Eggs." and expands it with a relatively rare word, "Formication." A word he repeats. The word means a sensation of ants creeping over the skin, but it is unlikely that most theater audiences will share Willie's erudition, and they will probably confuse it with the more familiar word, "fornication." Perhaps Winnie herself confuses the two, but formication or fornication, Winnie replies with a monosyllable, "God." After a pause, we hear the most extended duet of laughter in all Beckett's drama, which is followed in turn by Winnie's association of her laughter with her own particular piety:

(*Willie laughs quietly. After a moment she joins in. They laugh
quietly together. Willie stops. She laughs on a moment alone.
Willie joins in. They laugh together. She stops. Willie laughs on a
moment alone. He stops. Pause. Normal voice.*) Ah well what a joy
in any case to hear you laugh again, Willie, I was convinced I never
would, you never would. (*Pause.*) I suppose some people might
think us a trifle irreverent, but I doubt it. (*Pause.*) How can one
better magnify the Almighty than by sniggering with him at his
little jokes, particularly the poorer ones? (*Pause.*) I think you
would back me up there, Willie. (*Pause.*) Or were we perhaps
diverted by two quite different things? (*Pause.*) Oh well, what does
it matter, that is what I always say, so long as one . . . you know
. . . what is that wonderful line . . . laughing wild . . . something
something laughing wild amid severest woe. [30–31]

That "wonderful line" is quoted from a poem whose dark
vision Beckett shares—Thomas Gray's "Ode on a Distant
Prospect of Eton College." A Greek epigram from Menander
which precedes the poem is translated, "I am a man; sufficient
reason for being miserable." And the poem reflects upon the
disasters that will inevitably destroy the carefree youths of Eton
College. Typical of the whole poem is the stanza that trembles
in Winnie's memory:

> Ambition this shall tempt to rise,
> Then whirl the wretch from high,
> To bitter Scorn a sacrifice,
> And grinning Infamy.
> The stings of Falsehood those shall try,
> And hard Unkindness' altered eye,
> That mocks the tear it forced to flow;
> And keen Remorse with blood defiled,
> And moody Madness laughing wild
> Amid severest woe.

It is *madness* that laughs wildly amid severest woe in the poem
by a man whose outlook matches his name—Gray—described
by Clov as "light black from pole to pole." Similarly, it is a kind
of madness that evokes the single laugh in Beckett's most recent
short dramatic piece—that of W2 in *Play*. Hoping against hope
that she is "perhaps a little unhinged already," then doubting

that hope, the Other Woman of a purgatorial triangle breaks into a "peal of wild laughter," which is cut short, heard again, cut short again, without conclusion.

The conclusion of Gray's poem is well known: "No more; where ignorance is bliss,/'Tis folly to be wise." In Beckett's drama, however, there is neither bliss nor a single truly happy day. If it is folly to be wise, it is the only folly from which Beckett's characters are preserved, since there is so little wisdom to be had in his world. But what little there is may flicker forth from that triad of laughs which Arsene called "excoriations of the understanding."

Beckett's Metaphysics of Choiceless Awareness

Rosette Lamont

It is a gray world at the edge of silence. Humans and objects, bathed in the shadowy light of the twilight of the gods, stand strangely apart. Alienated from the unifying act of discourse, these would-be writers and ham actors endure their exile from the temporal sequence implicit in syntax and logic. Devoid even of the rudimentary definition of sex, Beckett's neuter organisms move nevertheless in pairs: aged married couples, old friends who appear at times to be ectoplasmically connected, master and slave tied to one another by tyranny exercised and borne. These crepuscular creatures move in a no-man's-land of vague memories and unformulated hopes, a world either barely created, or emerging from some cataclysmic occurrence. They celebrate the ritual drama of old age, a prologue to the final humiliation of death.

Although these mirror images suggest the irrevocable duality of spirit and flesh, their almost total loss of identity and individuality frees them of contingency. Even their names sound like the distorted double echo of a single name uttered in the void. Reverberated, Godot might become either Gogo or Didi, a child-like nickname for God or Dieu. But it is also the existence of these beings in a world running its course to entropy which, however insignificant and evanescent, imparts meaning to the universe. In his effort toward ever growing abstraction and purification, Beckett captures with loving irony that precise moment in time when life has almost deserted the body, but consciousness lingers on, the spirit's afterglow. Such is his endeavor in *Malone Dies,* and, more

Rosette Lamont is Professor of French and Comparative Literature at City University of New York.

recently, in a short piece published in 1965, "Imagination Dead Imagine."

In the more recent piece, two white bodies are depicted lying on the bare floor of a rotunda, each within a semicircle. The space which encloses them is white, and while light prevails, a burning heat fills the void. It is a joyless Paradiso. Soon the light begins to fail, and heat is proportionately reduced till the atmosphere becomes that of the Inferno of Baudelaire's "De Profundis Clamavi": pitch black and ice cold. Halfway through the piece, the reader is informed that the bodies are those of a woman and her "partner." They lie "back to back head to arse." The presence of life within these bodies, lying so still, can be ascertained by lifting a mirror to their lips: it mists. A film of icy sweat covers the motionless flesh and, upon close scrutiny, one can detect the brief opening of an eye though "never the two gazes together except once, when the beginning of one overlapped the end of the other, for about ten seconds."

Unlike the more agitated co-prisoners of this planet— Molloy's expression for human and animal life—the future dead of "Imagination Dead Imagine" assume, in their wisdom, their final position. Through their total immobility they manage to transcend the fever and the fret of daily living. For Beckett, as for his favorite painter, Bram van Velde, "art is not necessarily expression." [1] Beckett tries to achieve that "melancholy of abstract objectivity" [2] which, according to Jung, is the particular quality of Joyce's *Ulysses*. In his essay, "Being without Time: On Beckett's Play *Waiting for Godot*," Günther Anders reminds us that Beckett's antiheroes are *"abs-tracti,* which means pulled away, set apart." [3] Certainly this is true of the creatures of "Imagination Dead Imagine,"

1. Samuel Beckett, "Three Dialogues," *Samuel Beckett: A Collection of Critical Essays,* ed. Martin Esslin (Englewood Cliffs, N.J.: Prentice-Hall, 1965), p. 20.
2. Quoted by Eva Metman, "Reflections on Samuel Beckett's Plays," ibid., p. 130.
3. In *Samuel Beckett: A Collection of Critical Essays,* ed. Martin Esslin, p. 141.

beings isolated in a vacuum, illustrations for the philosophy of Gorgias of Lentini who, according to A. J. Leventhal, propounded:

1. Nothing is.
2. If anything is, it cannot be known.
3. If anything is, and cannot be known, it cannot be expressed in speech.[4]

Caught in an attitude of hieratic dignity, the living dead of Beckett's somber fable appear as grotesque *gisants,* at once statues of themselves and mummies, awaiting transfer from morgue to mausoleum. The next phase would be the surrender of consciousness, but this is where Beckett stops for "No, life ends and no, there is nothing elsewhere." Clearly, the man and woman of "Imagination Dead Imagine" would take Hamlet's advice and absent themselves from felicity a while longer. Awareness then is what matters for Beckett, though he may exorcise in a series of ever tightening statements, or questions, the existentialist illusion of the necessity of ethical choice. He seems to prefer the Buddhist ideal of choiceless awareness, more suited to a dramatist whose concern is with the irrevocability of human suffering.

It has been one of the clichés of contemporary criticism to emphasize the elements of inaction in Beckett's fiction and drama. Actually, we can observe how, from one work to the next, Beckett has approached "an art unresentful of its insuperable indigence and too proud for the farce of giving and receiving." [5]

Beckett's novels and plays are circular in structure, evolving from point zero in limbo, and returning to that point, or its vicinity. But though one cannot speak of action in connection with Beckett's world, it becomes clear as one enters his particular universe that acts of the mind are taking place. In *Waiting for Godot,* Vladimir and Estragon may not stray far

4. "The Beckett Hero," ibid., p. 46.
5. Beckett, "Three Dialogues," p. 18.

from their place of waiting, yet they come to realize that patient expectation of *something* or *someone* has meaning in itself, that it represents in fact the enduring hope of mankind. Vladimir states: "At this place, at this moment, all mankind is us, whether we like it or not."

As to the sense of failure which is an inherent part of the morass of non-action if not inaction—the refusal to act rather than the inability to take action—it must be the climate of the work of one who believes that "to be an artist is to fail, as no other dare fail." [6] This is a defiant failure. In speaking of Bram van Velde, Beckett states that to "shrink from [failure is] desertion." [7] Not unlike Mallarmé whom he resembles in his quest for the absolute, the dramatist wishes that he could become a "sublime raté." The French Symbolist poet defined this condition as the situation of the artist whose goals are so high that he can never hope to reach them. Thus, what appears at first glance to be a manifestation of resignation, is perhaps only the surface immobility of one readying himself for the leap which is to take him to that place which Poe, and after him Baudelaire, call "anywhere out of this world."

One of Beckett's favorite characters is Dante's Belacqua, one of the more grotesque and pitiful figures of the *Divine Comedy*. At the same time, the inescapable element of humor inherent in the attitude of one too lethargic to start the sharp climb up Mount Purgatory could not elude the attention of a writer nicknamed Oblomov by his friends. Goncharov's antihero does indeed seem to be a nineteenth-century reincarnation of Belacqua. Visited by friends whom he receives reclining on his bed—his favorite position—Oblomov listens to their plans for the day, or to the tales of their round of activities with nothing but pity in his heart. These occupations strike him as exhausting and vain. In *Samuel Beckett: The Language of Self,* Frederick J. Hoffman declares: "This tendency to resume

6. Ibid., p. 21.
7. Ibid.

the horizontal as the best position from which to contemplate
the world is of course Oblomov's besetting sin." [8] One could
object to this statement and say that perhaps the major
difference between Belacqua and Oblomov lies in the fact that
the sin of sloth of the first, the creation of a medieval poet,
becomes a virtue in the second. Belacqua is condemned to
linger at the core of nothingness, in a region at the antipodes of
Jerusalem, before being admitted to the locus where he can
begin working toward his salvation. Seated in a fetal position
in the shade of a rock, he refuses to be born anew to that other
life which he can reach only through suffering and redemption.
Oblomov, on the contrary, enveloped in his Eastern dressing
gown which lends him the appearance of a benign Buddha,
clearly dominates the friends who have come to call on him.
Belacqua sees his friends pass him by as he sits on the side of
the road, whereas Oblomov makes his friends welcome in the
slightly dusty oasis of his small apartment. The passive attitude
of Oblomov's effeminate body, his calm, radiant features
suggest the guru. Uninvolved in the materialistic world,
Oblomov transcends the vulgar cares of those who spend their
time selling or buying. His quietist philosophy permits
spiritual access to the "whole ark of hope and consolation." [9]
Passive only in relation to the general pursuits of Western
society, this Eastern *barine* nevertheless admits to an active
love of man. It is this sentiment which renders him worthy of
belonging to the saints of Nirvana.[10]

The early fiction of this "Irish Oblomov"—the title of an
article on Beckett by V. S. Pritchett—features a Belacqua

8. (New York: E. P. Dutton, 1964), p. 15.
9. Ivan Goncharov, *Oblomov*, trans. David Magarshack (Harmondsworth,
England: Penguin, 1954), p. 100.
10. The idea of the saintly aspects of Oblomov's character was
formulated for the first time by Dr. Yvette Louria who presented a paper
written by her and Dr. Morton Seiden, "Oblomov and the Christian
Vision," at the annual meeting of the MLA, in New York City, during
December 1964.

Shuah, "the picaresque hero" of a series of stories collected
under the title *More Pricks Than Kicks*.[11] This comic Dubliner
is a passive Don Juan who allows himself to be pursued by a
variety of ladies, not all lady-like, and goes so far as to plan
marriage and to commit it on more than one occasion despite
his own revulsion at the idea of a consummation so devoutly
wished by the more active females. Having escaped on three
occasions from this prefiguration of death, Belacqua will perish
grotesquely in the course of an operation on his head and foot.
Sick in body and mind, this "hollow man" who knows only too
well that the Shadow falls between "the motion/And the act
. . . the desire/And the spasm," [12] crosses with the ease of one
used to existing in limbo the thin boundary line between being
and non-being. The green waters of the Liffey, if not of the
Lethe, which flow through the veins of this "spleenetic"
creature, as indifferent to his surroundings as the apathetic
prince of Baudelaire's "Spleen LXXVII," will no longer feed
his unhasty heart. As to the hasty doctor who has rushed over
for the operation from the wedding at which he was—oh,
irony!—best man, he will fail to notice that the patient
etherised upon the table has given up the ghost. The title of the
story in which the demise of Belacqua is told is "Yellow," the
color of bile. Whether the title suggests cowardice, the dark bile
of Baudelaire's Spleen poems, or simply the fog and mist of
Northern Ireland, the end of Beckett's Belacqua is
characteristically undramatic. As to the family name of this
Belacqua, it reveals, as Ruby Cohn points out, his preference
for solitude—"A biblical Shuah was the mother of Onan, and
onanism may be related to Belacqua's solipsism." [13] If one did
not fear to uphold a physiological absurdity, one could say that
Beckett's Belacqua is the heir of Joyce's Leopold Bloom.

11. Ruby Cohn, *Samuel Beckett: The Comic Gamut* (New Brunswick,
N.J.: Rutgers University Press, 1962) , p. 18.
12. T. S. Eliot, "The Hollow Men," *The Complete Poems and Plays* (New
York: Harcourt, Brace & World, 1952) , pp. 56–59.
13. Cohn, p. 28.

"I am working with impotence and ignorance," Beckett said at one time to an interviewer.[14] The antiheroes of his novels and plays, be they Murphy, Malone, Watt, Gogo and Didi, or the nameless creatures of the more recent works, are all non-doers. Theirs is a heroism in reverse. Instead of embarking upon a continuous expansion in space and time through conquest and recognition, they contract in an infinite quest of their inner essence. They subtract themselves from the locus of human existence, history, and choose the realm of make-believe, storytelling. Yet they have in common with the hero of tradition a need for complete possession of self at the price of solitude and estrangement. In their own way they are extremists, enemies of mediocrity. In *Journey to Chaos,* Raymond Federman writes:

the fundamental idea behind Beckett's fiction may be termed an affirmation of the negative. This paradoxical artistic undertaking becomes an investigation, an exploitation of opposites. Beckett substitutes ignorance for knowledge, impotence for creativity, lethargy for efficiency, confusion for understanding, lunacy for rationality, doubt for certainty, illusion for reality.[15]

Beckett's world is divided between the doers and the non-doers. The first belong both to the race of masters and to that of slaves. Since the masters of Beckett's fiction, or of his theater, are invariably crippled in some way, blind or paralyzed or both, they depend on their *knooks,* and this dependency turns them into their servants' slaves. Once active they are acted upon, or they can act only through another. Thus the slaves are forced to become doers and to take on some of the duties and responsibilities of their impotent masters. The non-doers are passive onlookers for whom action is a game they enjoy watching or aping. In comparison with the masters, these non-doers may be ill-fed and ill-clad but they possess the

14. Raymond Federman, *Journey to Chaos: Samuel Beckett's Early Fiction* (Berkeley and Los Angeles: University of California Press, 1965), p. 6.
15. Ibid.

freedom of imagination, objectivity, and humor. If the tie
exists between two antiheroes it is one of concern and genuine
friendship. Their occupations have nothing to do with power
struggle. They play at storytelling and story-acting, at being
and non-being. This reenactment of the human situation
allows them special entry to the core of significance. Tuned to
the inevitable catastrophe of the final dissolution of the spirit,
they perceive a world in which the distinction between living
and having lived, between sanity and madness fades into a
constant oscillation, a muted universality. It is through
language that they are able to stand outside themselves, for
language is reality minus time. By playing the supreme game of
literature and theater, Beckett's non-doers can summon forth
the treasure of images contained in the receptacle of our
vocabulary. As Roland Barthes stated in his lecture, "Flaubert
et le travail du style," given in New York on 14 November
1967: "The writer knows that the world is a dictionary which
he must reproduce in that other dictionary, his work." Thus,
Beckett's non-doers exist in that non-linear space of language,
that *flumen orationis* which carries the multiplicity of
possibilities contained in the Word. By existing on the plane of
non-action, they themselves become that multiplicity. Having
become the world they have no need of world, and they could
say, like the speaker of Yves Bonnefoy's "Le dialogue d'angoisse
et de désir":

Nous n'avons plus besoin
D'images déchirantes pour aimer.
Cet arbre nous suffit, là-bas, qui, par lumière,
Se délie de soi-même et ne sait plus
Que le nom presque dit d'un dieu presque incarné. [*Pierre Ecrite*]

A tree, as abstract and indeterminate as the two clown-bums
who debate whether to hang themselves from its meager
branches, stands at the center of the stage in *Waiting for
Godot*. Bare in act 1, it will acquire sparse foliage in act 2, and
thus reveal the passage of time. Gogo and Didi do not stray far
from the shade of that tree, if a leafless tree can be said to give

shade. What kind of tree is it? Vladimir suggests it might be a willow, and that, since it is bare, it must be dead. "No more weeping," is Estragon's only comment. Could a weeping willow be that "tree of life" mentioned in Proverbs 13:12, or is this one of Beckett's ironies? Didi quotes from Proverbs, but his lapse of memory is revealing in itself: "Hope deferred maketh the something sick, who said that?" Not only has he forgotten the source of his quotation, but the word he leaves out is "heart." Also, he omits the rest of the proverb: "but when the desire cometh, it is a tree of life." Hope may be deferred, the waiting for Godot prove endless, but the seemingly dead tree of life sprouts leaves sometime between the two acts of the play.

In Ecclesiastes we read:

Two are better than one; because they have a good reward for their labour.

For if they fall, the one will lift up his fellow: but woe to him that is alone when he falleth; for he hath not another to help him up.

Again, if two lie together, then they have heat: but how can one be warm alone? [4:9–11]

Waiting for Godot is structured upon the antinomy of the two races of men. In contrast to Gogo and Didi, the fraternal pair—the nicknames suggest older brother and younger brother for the reader or spectator even superficially versed in Chinese—we have the Pozzo-Lucky couple. Gogo and Didi choose to stay together, Pozzo and Lucky are visibly tied to one another.

At the beginning of the play, Lucky, the slave, is driven by Pozzo by means of a rope tied round his neck. More dog-like than human, he responds to the cracking of a whip he himself carries between his teeth till his master has need of it. He must also bear upon his shoulders the weight of Pozzo's possessions. (Given an Italian pronunciation the master's name means a well, but the English sound suggests wealth.) Bent under the weight of his burden the servant resembles a mule, or perhaps that most humble and useful of creatures, the biblical ass. He is also a caricature of Atlas, a name by which Pozzo calls him at a moment of fear and anger. As to his name, it is as ironic as that given by Flaubert to his patient, selfless servant in "A Simple Heart," Félicité.

At some time in the distant past, we are told by Pozzo, who is not what the French call "un puits de science," his slave originated "beauty, grace, truth of the first water." Pozzo admits that, being overwhelmed with "professional worries," he had no time for finer things such as dancing, singing, and thinking. Besides, such pursuits do not befit a master. Even the great rulers of Ancient Rome left many decisions of state to their slaves, raised to the post of minister or councillor. Now, Lucky's intellectual baggage contains only sand, but once "he used to dance the farandole, the fling, the brawl, the fandango, and even the hornpipe. He capered. For joy." Looking at Lucky's dance, Gogo wonders whether this strange, jerky movement could be called "The Scapegoat's Agony." Didi, at the sight of such writhing, puns: "The Hard Stool." But the master straightens them out: "The Net. He thinks he's entangled in a net." Entertaining though it might be to watch the wretched creature struggle within the web of an invisible net, Vladimir, the intellectual one of the pair, expresses a preference for hearing Lucky think. Pozzo is willing to offer this entertainment, but warns his new acquaintances that his slave cannot do so without wearing his hat. Hatted, the puppet hisses and gurgles, like a cooking pot covered by a lid. Once Lucky's thoughts begin to boil over, they prove to be a strange mess of pottage.

Pozzo's *knook* is the Philosopher-King gone senile or mad. Thomism, Cartesianism, Hegelianism are all strangely mixed in his poor head. The form of Lucky's monologue is an unfinished question which begins with a postulation of the existence of a personal God and ends with the image of an empty, fossilized skull. The clownish raving of Lucky concretizes that crisis of intelligibility which was already the

concern of the Sophists and rhetoricians of the fifth century.
Here a loss of faith in the adequacy of language is accompanied
by an equal mistrust of axiomatic procedures used to establish
a chain of meaning. If man's place in the universe is a matter of
syntax, then the amorphous, incomplete sentence which trickles
out of Lucky, like the sawdust blood of a stuffed doll, reflects
the fact that man has been unable to make a place for himself.
Divorced from the intelligible world of essences, from God's
word, man "wastes and pines" and, eventually, "fades away."
As to God, or the little God, Godot, asleep, or absent, he is the
victim of "apathia . . . athambia . . . aphasia." He leaves man
to his sports: "dying . . . flying . . . penicilline." Scientific
"progress" will unmake man.

Ticks, convulsions, mock-epileptic fits agitate Lucky's body
as he delivers his anti-soliloquy. Clearly, Descartes' perfect
mechanism, the human body made by the hand of God, has
suffered the same deterioration as the questioning mind. The
Cartesian centaur—Hugh Kenner's term for the Beckett man
—has turned into a sad Rouault clown whose tightrope
exercise evokes the precarious equilibrium of Western thought,
itself a mad dance over that infinite void which filled Pascal
with terror. The invisible tightrope of this "pitre châtié" is the
process of consciousness which leads the mind from essentialism
to existentialism. Lucky's linear progression along this
imaginary line is a grotesque ceremony. By watching it we
participate in the ritual dismemberment of the cultivated
mind. It croaks out its *quaquaquas* (quoi?quoi?quoi?) which
must remain unanswered. The personal God with the white
beard evoked in the opening lines of the monologue will not
appear to settle the debate of the conscience with the void. Nor
will Puncher and Wattman (Whatman?), Testew and Cunard
(Test, stew, *cul,* and testicules), Fartov and Belcher, whose
names suggest the difficult digestion which follows the ingestion
of philosophical matter, Steinweg and Peterman (stone and
stick), nor any member of the "Acacacademy of
Anthropopopometry" provide an answer since they specialize

as did their colleague, Voltaire's Doctor Pangloss, in the study and teaching of "méta-physico-théologo-cosmolonigologie" (the science of fools, *les nigauds*) . These philosophes and scholars will be unable to halt the regressive motion by which the human creature will revert to its primitive condition. Thus, though Pozzo and Lucky seem to live in Time, in contrast to Gogo and Didi who are never sure of how much time has elapsed, Lucky's monologue reveals that one can never find "le temps perdu," that indeed man will uncreate himself to the point of becoming "the empty skull in Connemara."

The shortest distance between two points is not the straight line. There are no short distances in the time-space continuum. Linear progression is actually regression. A history of philosophy may trace a line or a curve connecting all points of speculation and observation leading from the essentialism of the ancient Greeks to the phenomenological philosophers of our century, but it presupposes the rationality of analysis, man's favorite delusion. Lucky's vertiginous denunciation of the race, his eloquent silences, his own condition of near-idiocy testify to the fact that man's endeavors constitute a mass which, in Sartrian terms, is *de trop* as is the creature that generated them. Thought is reduced by Beckett to a vaudeville act which can be stopped only by having Didi seize Lucky's hat.

In order to understand Beckett's language of spectacle in this scene it might be useful to recall that in French the expression *faire du chapeau* indicates a mild form of insanity, whereas *être coiffé* means to be lucky. Thus, when Pozzo's slave begins to rave, it can be assumed that the condition is due to the presence of the bowler atop his head. It is as though the mechanism of repressed thought had suddenly slipped out of control. The proliferation of words issuing from Lucky's foaming lips reminds one of the endless buckets of water carried by the sorcerer's apprentice. In this case, the sorcerer, Pozzo, is equally horrified by his creation. This once gifted creature, endowed above all with that crowning glory of man, the quality which turns the weakest of reeds into *un roseau pensant* (Pascal) , lucidity, has been transformed through centuries of subservience into a mindless parrot. Thus, the grabbing of the hat, a bit of stage business reminiscent of the antics of vaudeville clowns, is also the only possible expression in terms of scenic language of the obvious failure of language as a mode of communication. Symbolically, the man of thought loses his crown. Having demonstrated the uselessness of his achievements, Lucky can no longer be *coiffé*. Taking the hat away from Didi, Pozzo casts it on the ground, tramples on it as though it were a snake, and shouts triumphantly: "There's an end to his thinking!" Tyranny is at last firmly established, but the restoration of peace and order signifies the instauration of the idiot, an event which could please only Tristan Tzara.

When next we see the master and his slave, now dumb, Lucky is still doing the carrying, but Pozzo has lost his sight and his strength. It is a case of the dumb leading the blind. The rope which connects the two is shorter, symbolizing the growing dependence of the master on his servant. Clearly, Pozzo did not carry out his original intention of selling his *knook*. Not unlike the exposed autonomic nervous system, the rope connects body and mind, transmitting impulses rather than commands. It is also reminiscent of an unsevered umbilical cord, although it is not clear in this case which of the two wretched creatures is the child. What is obvious is that two separate beings have joined symbiotically: the result a monstrous, indivisible mass of humanity.

It has often been said that Pozzo and Lucky are one man—that they represent the duality of mind and body—as are Gogo and Didi. This may be so with the difference that the union of the former is demeaning to both and is indeed shown as profoundly lethal, whereas the connection of the latter, symbiotic though it might be, is a warm, life-sustaining relationship. If we recall the passage from chapter 4 of Ecclesiastes quoted above, we can see that Gogo and Didi are those two who know that one cannot be warm alone. But it is the reading of verses 9 and 10 which is particularly helpful. It casts a light upon the situation of Pozzo and Lucky in act 2. As they enter, they fall. Neither is able to help the other. In fact, when Didi attempts to help Pozzo to his feet, he falls next to the blind man, and, in turn, when Gogo comes to his friend's rescue, he is dragged down on the heap on the floor. Thus, Gogo and Didi try to lift up their fellow man, but if they are unable to do so it is because Pozzo is beyond human reach. He manages to extricate himself from the pile and to crawl away. Like the wounded of Baudelaire's "La cloche fêlée," Gogo and Didi lie on the ground, as though forgotten "Au bord d'un lac de sang, sous un grand tas de morts." After a while, however, they manage to rise. "Simple question of will-power," states Didi, unaware that he could not exercise his will while Pozzo was close. Contact with Pozzo seems to be weakening. One cannot help him, one can no longer help oneself. Nothing concretizes so clearly as this scene the depleting effect of tyrannical rule.

Once Gogo and Didi have succeeded in shaking off the paralyzing influence of the tyrant, they attempt to assist him. By having him place his arms around their neck, they manage to hold him up, but in this position he is nothing but a dead weight that they are forced to drag around the stage. "How much longer are we to cart him?" wonders Estragon. This question sets Gogo off to further musing. Formerly a poet as he reminded his friend early in the play, a turn of phrase, a word, an expression propel him on the sinuous path of free association. The verb to cart summons forth a vision from classical antiquity: "We are not caryatids!" Does Estragon suggest that he and Didi must bear alone the full weight of the temple? The image seems particularly ironic in this sterile place unvisited by a god. Nor is anything more removed from the proud female pillars of the Erechteion than the two clown-bums stooping under the almost lifeless body of the tyrant they had taken for Godot.

Yet, devaluation, that essential component of the humorist's statement, is not the only feature of Beckett's bitter irony in this passage. Pozzo might be a blind divinity like the Hamm of *Endgame,* a cruel god, powerless, unknowing, unjust. If Camus could say about the hero of *The Stranger* that he is "the only Christ we deserve," then by the same token Pozzo and Hamm are the only gods who walk among us. Why wait then for the Second Coming of Godot? And in fact what justice would he mete out? The revelations of the boy-messenger indicate that Godot's rewards and punishments are nothing less than gratuitous. He is good to the goatherd but beats his brother who, like Abel, minds the sheep. Is Godot then an Anti-Jehovah as Pozzo seems to be an Anti-Christ? The goat is traditionally a symbol of lust, and we learn from Matthew that if the sheep are to be on God's right hand, the goats will be set on the left. Godot's inverted justice reminds us of the absurd judgments of Jarry's Ubu. Yet, does not Beckett suggest that the choices of Jehovah are equally mysterious? Why allow Cain to be Cain and kill kind Abel? Perhaps God is only a human being, a lost, suffering creature, for when in pain, Pozzo responds to the names of both Abel and Cain. "He's all humanity," comments Gogo.

"We're not tied? (*Pause*) We're not—" ventures Gogo, shortly before the first entrance of Pozzo and Lucky. The two friends are tied neither to Godot nor to one another. They simply choose to wait in each other's company. Didi feeds Gogo the carrots and turnips which he carries in the inside pocket of his jacket. He protects his child-like friend from real or imaginary attackers. To while away the time Gogo and Didi play games. They will even play at being Pozzo and Lucky, but they will not be very convincing in these roles. Occasionally they speak of parting, neither taking this suggestion seriously. At the end of act 1, Didi says: "We can still part, if you think it would be better." "It's not worth while now," answers Gogo. Since nothing is certain, the two friends prefer the greater certainty of staying together. Nor is this decision as negative as it seems. Not to make a choice is also a decision, not to act is action. When, at the very end of the act, Gogo and Didi do not move as they say: "Let's go," it is not because they are unable to move, but because by playing at leaving they acquire greater knowledge of their need to stay close to one another. In the beginning of act 2, after a brief separation—Is it one night or one season?—they are deeply happy to see each other. Estragon cries out: "Don't touch me! Don't question me! Don't speak to me! Stay with me!" When Vladimir questions: "Did I ever leave you?" Gogo answers: "You let me go." The negative action of allowing someone to go is apparently as decisive as a willed separation. The brief exchange between the two friends could also be a love scene, a conversation between husband and wife after a separation. In Beckett's play it acquires an abstract quality which stresses the fact that acts happen in the mind and in the heart. Gogo is still wounded at the thought that his friend permitted him to leave. His words provide a key to Beckett's opposition in the play between the bonds of tyranny and those of understanding. The dialectic of tyranny versus choiceless awareness is fully played out in the second act of *Waiting for Godot*.

Ignorant, frightened, utterly dependent on his "menial," Pozzo is nevertheless the man who cannot stay in one place. Once the whip-cracking owner of men and worldly possessions, he is unable to give up the myth of action, even when his powers fail him. Through blindness he has entered the shadowy world of indeterminate space and time, a universe which is "like nothing," the ambience which Godo and Didi have come to regard as the climate of life. Like Proust, about whom Beckett has written a wonderful monograph, Didi knows that "habit is a great deadener." But Pozzo is a doer who could never consider boredom "the most tolerable because the most durable of human evils" (*Proust,* 16) . His sightlessness, as he himself states, is that of Fortune, an absurd blindness. Unlike Tiresias, he does not possess a third eye which would allow him to envision the future. A grotesque Oedipus at the crossroads, led by the only Antigone he can have, a moronic slave, Pozzo is as cut off from any future as from his past. He does not recall

having met Gogo and Didi before—perhaps because they were
of no consequence to him except as an improvised
audience—nor will he remember them the next day. The Holy
Grail he seeks is THE BOARD.

Beckett's caricature of one of the Great Organizers of the
world is devastating. God, Absolute Monarch, President,
Trustee, Chairman of the Board, Pozzo is the living symbol of
the Establishment. Nothing must deter him. When Didi asks
him: "What do you do when you fall far from help?" he
answers, unhesitatingly, using the royal we, or perhaps
including his *knook:* "We wait till we can get up. Then we go
on. On!" Is this heroic fortitude or the need for what Pascal
termed "le divertissement"? Pascal expressed the thought that
all our misfortunes come from our inability to remain quiet in
our room. Were he to stop for one moment, Pozzo would be
faced with the clear and unbearable image of his gradual
disintegration followed by an inevitable demise. We know this
for it is Pozzo who formulates in the most striking image of the
entire play, the definition of the human condition: "They give
birth astride of a grave."

Despite such knowledge, Pozzo belongs to that race of men
afflicted by the inability to learn by suffering. This egotistical,
narcissistic traveler, in love with the sound of his voice and the
ready flow of his rhetoric, is convinced that he owns not only
the land around the road, but the road as well and all the
people on it. His stool which Lucky sets up for him whenever
he wishes to rest is a portable throne. With the grand gesture of
Henry VIII or of the Sun King, Pozzo, having eaten the
chicken, casts the bones in the direction of his slave who, too
weak to eat, lets Gogo gnaw on them. The master's greatest
concern is with his dignity. Once he has risen from his stool, he
will not linger unless begged to do so. When Gogo and Didi,
not knowing what is expected of them, fail to play the game,
Pozzo circumvents the problem by having Lucky move the stool
a few inches, as though to indicate that another spot in the
desert were infinitely more desirable than the first. After this

face-saving device which explains why he made a move to go, the master can sit down again and chat a while longer. If he deigns to address himself to Gogo and Didi, it is only because "from the meanest creature one departs wiser, richer, more conscious of one's blessings." But when these two dare question him, he sees in this a sign of future insurrection: "A moment ago you were calling me Sir, in fear and trembling. Now you're asking me questions. No good will come of this!" Pozzo's absolute mastery, his divinely delegated powers must remain unchallenged.

As to his slave, he would like to get rid of him, or so he claims in act 1, but "The truth is you can't drive such creatures away. The best thing would be to kill them." (One recognizes here the tone of a plantation owner, or a nineteenth-century Russian *barine* speaking of his serfs.) Pretentious, but only half-educated, Pozzo curses Lucky, calling him: "Atlas, son of Jupiter." Though he does not seem to know that Atlas was not Jupiter's son, he must recall that the brother of Prometheus was a foe of the gods, and that they punished him for having taken part in the rebellion of the Titans. Not that the wretched creature looks like a Titan—this is another example of Beckett's irony—but Pozzo fears a possible uprising of the slaves. In act 2, reduced to a pitiable condition, the master still calls his servant, "Pig!" and encourages Gogo to "give him a taste of his boot, in the face and the privates as far as possible." Though he cries for pity he has none for anyone else.

Paradoxically this grotesque man of action, a doer who has made the mistake of outliving the moment of his greatest power, formulates the tragedy of man's brief passage on this earth: "One day I went blind, one day we'll go deaf, one day we were born, one day we shall die, the same day, the same second." Like Ionesco's King Bérenger in *Exit the King,* Pozzo, himself a sovereign, realizes that all that must end is already finished. *Nascentes morimur,* says the poet. Pozzo communicates this apprehension to the two friends. After Pozzo's departure, Vladimir repeats, as though understanding

it for the first time: "Astride of a grave and a difficult birth,"
and he adds: "Down in the hole, lingeringly, the grave-digger
puts on the forceps."
　Does Didi's view of life and death emerge from his
confrontation with the defeated man of action? Certainly after
this meeting Gogo and Didi know that if they stay "with folded
arms" weighing "the pros and cons," this does not make them
"less a credit to [their] species." By rejecting time, logic, reason,
Gogo and Didi do not lead diminished lives. They are fully
aware that "the only possible spiritual development is in a
sense of depth" (*Proust,* 46–47). Within Beckett's quartet they
represent a superior form of existence. In their discovery of the
macrocosm of the world and the microcosm of their own
bodies, they retain receptive, uncluttered minds. They have no
ambition, no special purpose, no place to go, only a place to
wait. Instead of feeling discouraged, they claim that they are
blessed in their waiting that provides them with an answer to
the question of what they are doing here. Heroes are defeated
by time and the process of history, but antiheroes go on living,
thinking, biding their time. Although they sometimes speak of
suicide, there is always a good excuse to postpone this project:
the branches of the tree are too fragile, the rope they could use
too frayed. It is better to endure, to be. "Let's not do anything.
It's safer," Gogo suggests at the beginning of the play. Patience,
passive resistance, the silent rebellion of the spirit seem greater
virtues to the generation that has known concentration camps,
slave-labor camps, nightmares fostered by the doers of our
world. If Gogo and Didi seem to be satisfied with lingering in
limbo, in a no-man's-land, it is because as modest men they
want only to be true to themselves. Their predicaments are the
common, human ones: aching feet, sour breath, the pangs of
hunger and of fear. To feel pain is to be alive and while they
live they retain the hope of seeing Godot. If this is an illusion it
is a better one than that of power. Their willow may not be
"the tree of life," but, perhaps after all, both thieves will be
saved.

Samuel Beckett: A Checklist of Criticism

This Checklist is designed to supplement those already in print, by Ruby Cohn (*Perspective*, Autumn 1959) , by Eugene Webb (*West Coast Review,* Spring 1966) , and by J. R. Bryer (*Configuration critique de Samuel Beckett,* ed. Melvin J. Friedman, 1964) , and to anticipate the definitive Beckett bibliography, by John Fletcher and Raymond Federman, now in press with the University of California Press. In an effort to do more than simply bring the earlier listings up to date, however, I have divided the Checklist into two parts, in accordance with the practice used by the editors of *Modern Fiction Studies* in their semi-annual checklists of the authors to whom they devote special issues. Part I consists of general studies of Samuel Beckett as author and man. This section also includes studies which consider several Beckett works at one time. Part II consists essentially of studies of individual Beckett works. Immediately following each of the titles (which are listed in alphabetical order) are references to items identified more fully in part I, and following these are special studies of the work in question.

Unlike the editors of *Modern Fiction Studies,* I have not excluded either foreign references or book reviews and play reviews. With respect to foreign items, I have tried to be as exhaustive as possible because, obviously, much of the important Beckett scholarship has not been in English; but the lack of reliable and complete indexes and the unavailability of much foreign material in this country have seriously hampered this effort. I have been highly selective with book and play

Jackson R. Bryer is Associate Professor of English at the University of Maryland.

reviews in English and have listed only those which I feel make a genuine contribution to Beckett criticism. Such notices are annotated either "Rev. art.," or, in cases where they are listed as reprinted in a book (e.g., Brustein's or Tynan's volumes of their drama criticism) , "Repr. rev."

Since *Samuel Beckett Now* is designed primarily for English language readers, I have, in all cases where a book or article has appeared in both English and another language, listed the English version first, regardless of whether that version was the first published. Other versions of the item are cited in an annotation to the entry for the English version. I have made no consistent effort, however, to list all appearances of any individual piece.

Five collections of material on Beckett have been published, to date—those edited by Ruby Cohn, Martin Esslin, Melvin J. Friedman, and Terje Maerli, and *Beckett at 60: A Festschrift.* Each collection is listed as a separate entry, with full bibliographical data, but if any of the material in these volumes is reprinted from another source, this source is also listed separately, with a cross-reference to the collection. An exception, however, is Mrs. Cohn's *Casebook:* brief excerpts from reviews of *Godot* and some first-night notices reprinted therein are not listed separately.

No effort has been made to trace the incorporation of essays on Beckett into full books on him. Many of the essays by Fletcher, Kenner, Federman, and Mrs. Cohn subsequently reappeared, often somewhat revised, in their books on Beckett, but I have not indicated this fact. Similarly, I have not listed the brief biographical and quasi-critical notes on Beckett which invariably precede work by him in anthologies—most usually of modern drama.

Stylistically, the Checklist generally follows the form of the *Modern Fiction Studies* listings. Books entirely or primarily about Beckett are marked by asterisks. Where an essay or book chapter deals with Beckett among other writers, I have listed first the page numbers of the entire article or chapter and then, in brackets, the pages which are about Beckett.

For significant assistance in the preparation of this Checklist, I wish to thank the General Research Board of the University of Maryland, Mrs. Loretta T. D'Eustachio, Susan Robinson, and Mrs. Carolyn Banks.

222   Jackson R. Bryer

I. GENERAL

Abel, Lionel. "Beckett and Metatheatre." In his *Metatheatre*. New York: Hill and Wang, 1963, Pp. 83–85.

————. "Joyce the Father, Beckett the Son." *New Leader* 42 (14 December 1959) : 26–27. Reprinted in his *Metatheatre*, pp. 134–40.

A[birached], R[obert]. "Samuel Beckett." In Bernard Pingaud, ed., *Ecrivains d'aujourd'hui*. Paris: Grasset, 1960. Pp. 93–98.

————. "La Voix tragique de Samuel Beckett." *Etudes* 320 (January 1964) : 85–88.

Allsop, Kenneth. *The Angry Decade*. New York: British Book Centre, 1958. Pp. 37–40, and passim.

Amadou, Anne-Lisa. "Fra Jean-Paul Sartres roman verden til Samuel Becketts tragiske univers." In Terje Maerli, ed., *Samuel Beckett*, pp. 7–16.

Angus, William. "Modern Theatre Reflects the Times." *Queen's Quarterly* 70 (Summer 1963) : 255–63 [259–60].

Arrabal, Fernando. "In Connection with Samuel Beckett." In *Beckett at 60: A Festschrift*, p. 88.

Ashworth, Arthur. "New Theatre: Ionesco, Beckett, Pinter." *Southerly* 22, no. 3 (1962) : 145–54.

d'Aubarède, Gabriel. "Waiting for Beckett." Translated by Christopher Waters. *Trace*, no. 42 (Summer 1961), pp. 156–58. Originally appeared, in French, in *Nouvelles Littéraires*, 16 February 1961, pp. 1, 7. [Interview]

Bajini, Sandro. "Beckett o l'emblema totale." *Il Verri* 3 (April 1959) : 70–88.

Barbour, Thomas. "Beckett and Ionesco." *Hudson Review* 11 (Summer 1958) : 271–77 [Rev. art.: 271–75].

Barrett, William. "How I Understand Less and Less Every Year. . . ." *Columbia University Forum* 2 (Winter 1959) : 44–48.

————. "Samuel Beckett's World in Waiting: II. The Works of Beckett Hold Clues to an Intriguing Riddle." *Saturday Review* 40 (8 June 1957) : 15–16.

* *Beckett at 60: A Festschrift*. London: Calder and Boyars, 1967.

Beigbeder, Marc. "Le Théâtre à l'âge métaphysique." *L'Age Nouveau*, no. 85 (January 1954), pp. 30–41 [38–39].

————. *Le Théâtre en France depuis la Libération*. Paris: Bordas, 1959. Pp. 142–44.

Berlin, Normand. "Beckett and Shakespeare." *French Review* 40 (April 1967) : 647–51.

Bersani, Leo. "No Exit for Beckett." *Partisan Review* 33 (Spring 1966) : 261–67.

Bialos, Anne. "Samuel Beckett." *Studies in Literature* (Brooklyn College, New York), vol. 1 (Spring 1961), unpaginated.

Bjurström, C. G. "Samuel Beckett." *Bonniers Litterära Magasin* 23 (January 1954) : 27–33.

Blanchot, Maurice. "Where Now? Who Now?" Translated by Richard Howard. *Evergreen Review* 2 (Winter 1959) : 222–29. Reprinted in Richard Kostelanetz, ed., *On Contemporary Literature*. New York: Avon, 1964. Pp. 249–54. Originally appeared, in French, in *Nouvelle Nouvelle Revue Française* 2 (October 1953) : 676–86, and reprinted in Blanchot's *Le Livre à venir*. Paris: Gallimard, 1959. Pp. 256–64.

Blau, Herbert. "Counterforce II: Notes From the Underground." In his *The Impossible Theater: A Manifesto*. New York: Macmillan, 1964. Pp. 228–76 [228–51]. *Godot* section reprinted in Cohn, ed., *Casebook on "Waiting for Godot,"* pp. 113–21.

———. " 'Meanwhile, Follow the Bright Angels.' " *Tulane Drama Review* 5 (September 1960) : 89–101 [90–91].

———. "Politics and the Theater." *Wascana Review* 2, no. 2 (1967) : 5–23.

———. "The Popular, the Absurd, and the *Entente Cordiale*." *Tulane Drama Review* 5 (March 1961) : 119–51.

Boisdeffre, Pierre de. "Samuel Beckett ou l'au-delà" and "L'Antithéâtre total: Samuel Beckett ou la mort de l'homme." In his *Une Histoire vivante de la littérature d'aujourd'hui: 1938–1958*. Paris: Le Livre contemporain, 1958. Pp. 299–300, 678–80; see also passim.

Brée, Germaine. "L'Etrange Monde des 'grands articulés.' " In Melvin J. Friedman, ed., *Configuration critique de Samuel Beckett*, pp. 83–97.

Brée, Germaine, and Margaret Guiton. *An Age of Fiction: The French Novel From Gide to Camus*. New Brunswick, N.J.: Rutgers University Press, 1957. Pp. 236–37.

Briggs, Ray. "Samuel Beckett's World in Waiting: I. The Life of an Enigmatic New Idol of the Avant-Garde of Two Continents." *Saturday Review* 40 (8 June 1957) : 14.

Brooke-Rose, Christine. "Samuel Beckett and the Anti-Novel." *London Magazine* 5 (December 1958) : 38–46.

Brown, John Russell. "Mr. Pinter's Shakespeare." *Critical Quarterly* 5 (Autumn 1963) : 251–65 [255–57].

Bryer, J. R. "Critique de Samuel Beckett: Selection bibliographique." In Melvin J. Friedman, ed., *Configuration critique de Samuel Beckett*, pp. 169–84.

Calder, John. "Introduction." In *Beckett at 60: A Festschrift*, pp. 1–4.

Capone, Giovanna. *Drammi per voci: Dylan Thomas, Samuel Beckett, Harold Pinter.* Bologna: Pàtion, 1967.

Chambers, Ross. "Beckett's Brinkmanship." *AUMLA: Journal of the Australasian Language and Literature Association,* no. 19 (May 1963), pp. 57–75. Reprinted in Esslin, ed., *Samuel Beckett,* pp. 152–68.

————. "Samuel Beckett and the Padded Cell." *Meanjin Quarterly* 21 (December 1962) : 451–62.

Champigny, Robert. "Les Aventures de la première personne." In Melvin J. Friedman, ed., *Configuration critique de Samuel Beckett,* pp. 117–30.

————. *Le Genre dramatique.* Monaco: Regain, 1965. Pp. 58–61, 112, 129, 208–9.

Cleveland, Louise O. "Trials in the Soundscape: The Radio Plays of Samuel Beckett." *Modern Drama* 11 (December 1968) : 267–82.

Coe, Richard N. "God and Samuel Beckett." *Meanjin Quarterly* 24, no. 1 (1965) : 66–85.

* ————. *Samuel Beckett.* Edinburgh: Oliver and Boyd, 1964; New York: Grove Press, 1964.

Coffey, Brian. "Memory's Murphy Maker: Some Notes on Samuel Beckett." *Threshold,* no. 17 (1962), pp. 28–36.

Cohn, Ruby. "Acting for Beckett." *Modern Drama* 9 (December 1966) : 237.

————. "A Checklist of Beckett Criticism." *Perspective* 11 (Autumn 1959) : 193–96.

————. "The Comedy of Samuel Beckett: 'Something old, something new. . . .'" *Yale French Studies,* no. 23 (Summer 1959), pp. 11–17.

————. "A Note on Beckett, Dante, and Geulincx." *Comparative Literature* 12 (Winter 1960) : 93–94.

————. "Philosophical Fragments in the Works of Samuel Beckett." *Criticism* 6 (Winter 1964) : 33–43. Reprinted in Esslin, ed., *Samuel Beckett,* pp. 169–77.

————. "Play and Player in the Plays of Samuel Beckett." *Yale French Studies,* no. 29 (Spring–Summer 1962) , pp. 43–48.

————. "The Plays of Yeats through Beckett-Coloured Glasses." *Threshold,* no. 19 (Autumn 1965) , pp. 41–47.

————. "Preliminary Observations." *Perspective* 11 (Autumn 1959) : 119–31.

* ————. *Samuel Beckett: The Comic Gamut.* New Brunswick, N.J.: Rutgers University Press, 1962.

————. "Samuel Beckett: Self-Translator." *PMLA* 76 (December 1961) : 613–21.

————. "Still Novel." *Yale French Studies,* no. 24 (Summer 1959) , pp. 48–53.

————. " 'Theatrum Mundi' and Contemporary Theater." *Comparative Drama* 1 (Spring 1967) : 28–35 [30–31].

Cook, Albert S. "Language and Action in the Drama." *College English* 28 (October 1966) : 15–25 [21–25].

"The Core of the Onion." (London) *Times Literary Supplement,* 21 December 1962, p. 988 [Rev. art.].

Curtis, Anthony. "Mood of the Month—IV." *London Magazine* 5 (May 1958) : 60–65.

Davin, Dan. "Mr. Beckett's Everyman." *Irish Writing,* no. 34 (Spring 1956) , pp. 36–39.

* Delye, Huguette. *Samuel Beckett; ou, La Philosophie de l'absurde.* Aix-en-Provence: La Pensée universitaire, 1960.

Devine, George. "Last Tribute." In *Beckett at 60: A Festschrift,* p. 99.

Dreyfus, Dina. "Vraies et fausses énigmes." *Mercure de France,* no. 1130 (October 1957) , pp. 268–85 [276–85].

Driver, Tom F. "Beckett by the Madeleine." *Columbia University Forum* 4 (Summer 1961) : 21–25. [Interview]

Duckworth, Colin. "Introduction." In Duckworth, ed., *En attendant Godot.* London: George G. Harrap, 1966. Pp. xvii–cxxxv.

Ellmann, Richard. *James Joyce.* New York: Oxford University Press, 1959. Passim.

Elman, Richard M. "Beckett's Testament." *Commonweal* 80 (26 June 1964) : 416–18 [Rev. art.].

Erickson, John D. "Objects and Systems in the Novels of Samuel Beckett." *L'Esprit Créateur* 7 (Summer 1967) : 113–22.

Esslin, Martin. "Introduction." In Esslin, ed., *Samuel Beckett: A Collection of Critical Essays.* Englewood Cliffs, N.J.: Prentice-Hall, 1965. Pp. 1–15.

———. "Samuel Beckett." In John Cruickshank, ed., *The Novelist as Philosopher: Studies in French Fiction, 1935–1960.* London: Oxford University Press, 1962. Pp. 128–46.

———. "Samuel Beckett: The Search for Self." In his *The Theatre of the Absurd.* Garden City, N.Y.: Doubleday, Anchor Books, 1961. Pp. 1–46; see also passim.

———. "Samuel Beckett's Poems." In *Beckett at 60: A Festschrift,* pp. 55–60.

———. "The Theatre of the Absurd." *Tulane Drama Review* 4 (May 1960) : 3–15.

*———, ed. *Samuel Beckett: A Collection of Critical Essays.* Englewood Cliffs, N.J.: Prentice-Hall, 1965.

Evers, Francis. "Samuel Beckett: The Incurious Seeker." *Dublin Magazine* 7 (Spring 1968) : 84–88 [Rev. art.].

Fasano, Giancarlo. "Samuel Beckett." *Belfagor* 17 (31 July 1962) : 432–57.

Federman, Raymond. "Le Bonheur chez Samuel Beckett." *Esprit* 35 (July–August 1967) : 90–96.

*———. *Journay to Chaos: Samuel Beckett's Early Fiction.* Berkeley and Los Angeles: University of California Press, 1965.

Fitch, Brian T. "Narrateur et narration dans la trilogie romanesque de Samuel Beckett: *Molloy, Malone meurt, L'Innommable.*" *Bulletin des Jeunes Romanistes,* no. 3 (May 1961) , pp. 13–20.

Fletcher, John. "Action and Play in Beckett's Theater." *Modern Drama* 9 (December 1966) : 242–50.

———. "Beckett and the Fictional Tradition." *Annales Publiées par la Faculté des Lettres de Toulouse: Caliban* 2 (April 1965) : 147–58.

———. "Beckett et Proust." *Annales Publiées par la Faculté des Lettres de Toulouse: Caliban* 1 (January 1964) : 89–100.

———. "Beckett's Debt to Dante." *Nottingham French Studies* 4 (May 1965) : 41–52.

———. "Beckett's Verse: Influences and Parallels." *French Review* 37 (January 1964) : 320–31.

———. "In Search of Beckett." In *Beckett at 60: A Festschrift,* pp. 29–33.

———. "Le Cas Samuel Beckett." *Bulletin de l'Université de Toulouse* 72 (January 1963) : 405–6.

* ———. *The Novels of Samuel Beckett.* London: Chatto & Windus, 1964.

———. "Only New Understanding." *Journal of General Education* 17 (October 1965) : 246–48 [Rev. art.].

———. "The Private Pain and the Whey of Words: A Survey of Beckett's Verse." In Martin Esslin, ed., *Samuel Beckett,* pp. 23–32.

———. "Samuel Beckett and the Philosophers." *Comparative Literature* 17 (Winter 1965) : 43–56.

* ———. *Samuel Beckett's Art.* New York: Barnes & Noble, 1967.

———. "Samuel Beckett as Critic." *The Listener* 74 (25 November 1965) : 862–63.

———. "Samuel Beckett et Jonathan Swift: Vers une étude comparée." *Annales Publiées par la Faculté des Lettres de Toulouse* 11 (1962) : 81–117.

———. "Samuel Beckett; or, The Morbid Dread of Sphinxes." *New Durham,* June 1965, pp. 5–9.

Fowlie, Wallace. "Beckett (1906–)." In his *Dionysus in Paris.* New York: Meridian Books, 1960. Pp. 210–17; see also passim.

———. "The New French Theatre: Artaud, Beckett, Genet, Ionesco." *Sewanee Review* 67 (Autumn 1959) : 643–57 [Rev. art.: 648–51].

Friedman, Melvin J. "The Achievement of Samuel Beckett." *Books Abroad* 33 (Summer 1959) : 278–81.

———. "Beckett Criticism: Its Early Prime." *Symposium* 21 (Spring 1967) : 82–89.

———. "The Creative Writer as Polyglot: Valery Larbaud and Samuel Beckett." *Transactions of the Wisconsin Academy of Sciences, Arts and Letters* 49 (1960) : 229–36 [234–36].

Friedman, Melvin J. "A Note on Leibniz and Samuel Beckett." *Romance Notes* 4 (Spring 1963) : 93–96.

————. "The Novels of Samuel Beckett: An Amalgam of Joyce and Proust." *Comparative Literature* 12 (Winter 1960) : 47–58.

————. "Préface." In Friedman, ed., *Configuration critique de Samuel Beckett,* pp. 9–21.

————. "Les Romans de Samuel Beckett et la tradition du grotesque." In J. H. Matthews, ed., *Un Nouveau Roman?* Paris: M. J. Minard, 1964. Pp. 31–50.

————. "Samuel Beckett and the *Nouveau Roman.*" *Wisconsin Studies in Contemporary Literature* 1 (Spring–Summer 1960) : 22–36.

* ————, ed. *Configuration critique de Samuel Beckett.* Paris: M. J. Minard, 1964.

Frost, Tore. "Samuel Becketts romaner: En eftertanke." In Terje Maerli, ed., *Samuel Beckett,* pp. 81–92.

Frye, Northrop. "The Nightmare Life in Death." *Hudson Review* 13 (Autumn 1960) : 442–49 [Rev. art.].

Furbank, P. N. "Beckett's Purgatory." *Encounter* 22 (June 1964) : 69–72 [Rev. art.].

Geerts, Leo. "Samuel Beckett vertaald: De dramatiek van de herinnering." *Dietsche Warande & Belfort* 112 (September 1967) : 533–38.

Gerard, Martin. "Molloy Becomes Unnamable." *X, A Quarterly Review* 1 (October 1960) : 314–19.

* Gessner, Niklaus. *Die Unzulänglichkeit der Sprache: Eine Untersuchung über Formzerfall und Beziehungslosigkeit bei Samuel Beckett.* Zurich: Juris-Verlag, 1957.

Glicksberg, Charles I. "The Lost Self in Modern Literature." *The Personalist* 43 (Autumn 1962) : 527–38 [535–37].

————. "Samuel Beckett's World of Fiction." *Arizona Quarterly* 18 (Spring 1962) : 32–47. Reprinted, slightly revised, in his *The Self in Modern Literature.* University Park, Pa.: Pennsylvania State University Press, 1963. Pp. 121–33.

————. "*Waiting for Godot* and *Endgame.*" In his *The Self in Modern Literature,* pp. 117–21.

Gold, Herbert. "Beckett: Style and Desire." *The Nation* 183 (10 November 1956) : 397–99 [Rev. art.].

Goldberg, Gerald Jay. "The Search for the Artist in Some Recent British Fiction." *South Atlantic Quarterly* 62 (Summer 1963) : 387–401 [396–401].

Goth, Maja. *Franz Kafka et les lettres françaises (1928–1955)*. Paris: José Corti, 1956. Pp. 120–22.

Gregory, Horace. "Beckett's Dying Gladiators." *Commonweal* 65 (26 October 1956) : 88–92. Reprinted in his *The Dying Gladiators and Other Essays*. New York: Grove Press, 1961. Pp. 165–76.

Gresset, Michel. "Création et cruauté chez Beckett." *Tel Quel*, no. 15 (1963), pp. 58–65.

————. "Le 'parce que' chez Faulkner et le 'donc' chez Beckett." *Lettres Nouvelles*, no. 19 (November 1961), pp. 124–38.

Grossvogel, David I. "Samuel Beckett: The Difficulty of Dying." In his *Four Playwrights and a Postscript: Brecht, Ionesco, Beckett, Genet*. Ithaca, N.Y.: Cornell University Press, 1962. Pp. 85–131; see also pp. xi–xviii and 177–99.

————. *The Self-Conscious Stage in Modern French Drama*. New York: Columbia University Press, 1958. Pp. 324–34. Reprinted, with the same pagination, as *Twentieth Century French Drama*. New York: Columbia University Press, 1961.

Guggenheim, Marguerite. *Confessions of an Art Addict*. London: Andre Deutsch, 1960. P. 49, and passim.

————. *Out of This Century: The Informal Memoirs of Peggy Guggenheim*. New York: Dial Press, 1946. Passim.

Guicharnaud, Jacques, with the collaboration of June Beckelman. "Existence on Stage: Samuel Beckett." In their *Modern French Theatre From Giraudoux to Beckett*. New Haven: Yale University Press, 1961. Pp. 193–220. Reprinted in Richard Kostelanetz, ed., *On Contemporary Literature*. New York: Avon, 1964. Pp. 262–85.

————. "The 'R' Effect." *L'Esprit Créateur* 2 (Winter 1962) : 159–65.

Hainsworth, J. D. "Shakespeare, Son of Beckett?" *Modern Language Quarterly* 25 (September 1964) : 346–55 [Rev. art.].

Halldén, Ruth; Ingemar Hedenius; and Sandro Key-Åberg. "Ett samtal om Samuel Beckett." *Ord och Bild* 72, no. 2 (1963) : 93–104.

Hamilton, Carol. "Portrait in Old Age: The Image of Man in Beckett's Trilogy." *Western Humanities Review* 16 (Spring 1962) : 157–65.

Hamilton, Kenneth. "Boon or Thorn? Joyce Cary and Samuel Beckett on Human Life." *Dalhousie Review* 38 (Winter 1959) : 433–42 [437–42].

———. "Negative Salvation in Samuel Beckett." *Queen's Quarterly* 69 (Spring 1962) : 102–11.

Hartley, Anthony. "Samuel Beckett." *Spectator* (London) 191 (23 October 1953) : 458–59 [Rev. art.].

Harvey, Lawrence E. "Samuel Beckett: Initiation du poète." In Melvin J. Friedman, ed., *Configuration critique de Samuel Beckett,* pp. 153–68.

———. "Samuel Beckett on Life, Art, and Criticism." *Modern Language Notes* 80 (December 1965) : 545–62.

Hassan, Ihab. "The Literature of Silence: From Henry Miller to Beckett and Burroughs." *Encounter* 28 (January 1967) : 74–82 [80–81].

———. *The Literature of Silence: Henry Miller and Samuel Beckett.* New York: Alfred A. Knopf, 1967. Pp. 3–33, 111–219.

* Hayman, Ronald. *Samuel Beckett.* London: Heinemann, 1968.

Heppenstall, Rayner. *The Fourfold Tradition.* London: Barrie and Rockliff, 1961; Norfolk, Conn.: New Directions, 1961. Pp. 254–58, 259–65, and passim.

Herbert, Jocelyn. "A Letter." In *Beckett at 60: A Festschrift,* p. 98.

Hesse, Eva. "Die Welt des Samuel Beckett." *Akzente* 8 (June 1961) : 244–66.

Hicks, Granville. "Beckett's World." *Saturday Review* 41 (4 October 1958) : 14 [Rev. art.].

Higgins, Aidan. "Tribute." In *Beckett at 60: A Festschrift,* pp. 91–92.

Hobson, Harold. "Samuel Beckett, Dramatist of the Year." In Hobson, ed., *International Theatre Annual No. 1.* New York: Citadel Press, 1956. Pp. 153–55.

* Hoffman, Frederick J. *Samuel Beckett: The Language of Self.* Carbondale: Southern Illinois University Press, 1962. Sections on *Murphy, Watt, Molloy, Malone Dies,* and *The Unnamable* reprinted, in French, in Friedman, ed., *Configuration critique de Samuel Beckett,* pp. 23–53.

Hubert, Renée Riese. "The Couple and the Performance in Samuel Beckett's Plays." *L'Esprit Créateur* 2 (Winter 1962) : 175–80.

Hughes, Catharine. "Beckett and the Game of Life." *Catholic World* 195 (June 1962) : 163–68.

——. "Beckett's World: Wherein God Is Continually Silent." *The Critic* 20 (April–May 1962) : 40–42.

Hutchinson, Mary. "All the Livelong Way." In *Beckett at 60: A Festschrift,* pp. 93–95.

Iser, Wolfgang. "Beckett's Dramatic Language." Translated by Ruby Cohn. *Modern Drama* 9 (December 1966) : 251–59. Originally appeared, in German, in *Germanisch-Romanische Monatsschrift,* n.s., 11 (October 1961) : 451–67.

Jacobsen, Josephine, and William R. Mueller. "Beckett as Poet." *Prairie Schooner* 37 (Fall 1963) : 196–216.

——. "Samuel Beckett's Long Saturday: To Wait or Not to Wait?" In Nathan A. Scott, Jr., ed., *Man in the Modern Theatre.* Richmond, Va.: John Knox Press, 1965. Pp. 76–97.

* ——. *The Testament of Samuel Beckett.* New York: Hill and Wang, 1964.

* Janvier, Ludovic. *Pour Samuel Beckett.* Paris: Editions de Minuit, 1966.

Jolas, Maria. "A Bloomlein for Sam." In *Beckett at 60: A Festschrift,* pp. 14–16.

Kaiser, Joachim. "Am Rande dessen, was sagbar ist. Zum 60. Geburtstag des Dichters Samuel Beckett." *Universitas* (Stuttgart) 21 (June 1966) : 605–7.

Karl, Frederick R. "Waiting for Beckett: Quest and Re-Quest." *Sewanee Review* 69 (Autumn 1961) : 661–76. Reprinted in his *The Contemporary English Novel.* New York: Farrar, Straus and Cudahy, 1962. Pp. 19–39.

Kenner, Hugh. "The Absurdity of Fiction." *Griffin,* November 1959, pp. 13–16.

——. "The Beckett Landscape." *Spectrum* 2 (Winter 1958) : 8–24.

——. "Beckett: The Rational Domain." *Forum* (Houston) 3 (Summer 1960) : 39–47.

Kenner, Hugh. "The Cartesian Centaur." *Perspective* 11 (Autumn 1959) : 132–41. Reprinted in Esslin, ed., *Samuel Beckett*, pp. 52–61.

———. "Progress Report, 1962–65." In *Beckett at 60: A Festschrift*, pp. 61–77. Also in new edition of his *Samuel Beckett* (1968) .

———. "Samuel Beckett: Comedian of the Impasse." In his *Flaubert, Joyce and Beckett: The Stoic Comedians.* Boston: Beacon Press, 1962. Pp. 67–107.

* ———. *Samuel Beckett: A Critical Study.* New York: Grove Press, 1961.

———. "Samuel Beckett vs. Fiction." *National Review* 6 (11 October 1958) : 248–49 [Rev. art.].

———. "Voices in the Night." *Spectrum* 5 (Spring 1961) : 3–20.

Kermode, Frank. "Beckett, Snow, and Pure Poetry." *Encounter* 15 (July 1960) : 73–77 [Rev. art.]. Reprinted in his *Puzzles and Epiphanies.* London: Routledge & Kegan Paul, 1962. Pp. 155–63.

———. "The New Apocalyptists." *Partisan Review* 33 (Summer 1966) : 339–61 [354–55].

Kern, Edith. "Beckett and the Spirit of the Commedia dell'Arte." *Modern Drama* 9 (December 1966) : 260–67.

———. "Samuel Beckett et les poches de Lemuel Gulliver." In Melvin J. Friedman, ed., *Configuration critique de Samuel Beckett*, pp. 69–81.

Lamont, Rosette. "La Farce métaphysique de Samuel Beckett." In Melvin J. Friedman, ed., *Configuration critique de Samuel Beckett*, pp. 99–116.

Lappalainen, Armas. "Under Becketts presenning." *Ord och Bild* 71, no. 5 (1962) : 439–42.

Lebesque, Morvan. "Le Théâtre aux enfers: Artaud, Beckett et quelques autres." In his *Antonin Artaud et le théâtre de notre temps.* Paris: René Julliard, 1958. Pp. 191–96.

Lee, Warren. "The Bitter Pill of Samuel Beckett." *Chicago Review* 10 (Winter 1957) : 77–87 [Rev. art.].

Le Sage, Laurent. "Samuel Beckett." In his *The French New Novel.* University Park, Pa.: Pennsylvania State University Press, 1962. Pp. 47–54.

Leventhal, A. J. "The Beckett Hero." *Critique* 7 (Winter 1964–65) : 18–35. Reprinted in Esslin, ed., *Samuel Beckett*, pp. 37–51.

————. "Samuel Beckett, Poet and Pessimist." *The Listener* 57 (9 May 1957) : 746–47.

————. "The Thirties." In *Beckett at 60: A Festschrift,* pp. 7–13.

Lindon, Jerôme. "First Meeting With Samuel Beckett." In *Beckett at 60: A Festschrift,* pp. 17–19.

Loy, J. Robert. "*Things* in Recent French Literature." *PMLA* 71 (March 1956) : 27–41 [33].

Ludvigsen, Chr. "Samuel Beckett og Theodor Fontane: Ennspeciel kilde til visse temaer i Becketts senere dramatik." In Gustav Albeck, et al., eds., *Festskrift til Jens Kruuse den 6. april 1968.* Aarhus: Universitetsforlaget, 1968. Pp. 265–78.

Lumley, Frederick. "The Case Against Beckett." In his *New Trends in Twentieth Century Drama.* London: Barrie and Rockliff, 1967. Pp. 202–8.

MacGowan, Jack. "Working With Samuel Beckett." In *Beckett at 60: A Festschrift,* pp. 23–24.

* Maciel, Luis Carlos. *Samuel Beckett et a solidâo.* Porto Alegre, Brazil: Cadernos do Rio Grande, 1959.

Macksey, Richard. "The Artist in the Labyrinth: Design or *Dasein.*" *Modern Language Notes* 77 (May 1962) : 239–56 [248–53].

Mackworth, Cecily. "French Writing Today: Les Coupables." *Twentieth Century* 161 (May 1957) : 459–68 [463].

MacNeice, Louis. *Varieties of Parable.* Cambridge: At the University Press, 1965. Pp. 117–24, 128–29, 139–46, and passim.

* Maerli, Terje, ed. *Samuel Beckett.* Oslo: Universitetsforlaget, 1967.

Magnan, Jean-Marie. "Jalons I. Samuel Beckett ou les chaînes et relais du néant. II. Alain Robbe-Grillet ou le labyrinthe du voyeur." *Cahiers du Sud,* no. 371 (1963) , pp. 73–80 [73–76].

Magny, Olivier de. "Samuel Beckett et la farce métaphysique." *Cahiers de la Compagnie Madeleine Renaud-Jean Louis Barrault,* no. 44 (1963) , pp. 67–72.

————. "Samuel Beckett ou Job Abandonné." *Monde Nouveau: Paru,* no. 97 (February 1956) , pp. 92–99.

* Marissel, André. *Samuel Beckett.* Paris: Editions Universitaires, 1963.

————. "L'Univers de Samuel Beckett: Un noeud de complexes." *Esprit* 31 (September 1963) : 240–55.

Mauriac, Claude. "Samuel Beckett." In his *The New Literature*. Translated by Samuel I. Stone. New York: George Braziller, 1959. Pp. 75–90. Originally appeared, in French, in *Prevues*, no. 61 (March 1956), pp. 71–76. Reprinted in Mauriac's *L'Alittérature contemporaine*. Paris: Albin Michel, 1958. Pp. 77–92.

Mayoux, Jean-Jacques. "Beckett and Expressionism." Translated by Ruby Cohn. *Modern Drama* 9 (December 1966) : 238–41.

———. "Samuel Beckett and Universal Parody." Translated by Barbara Bray. In Martin Esslin, ed., *Samuel Beckett*, pp. 77–91. Originally appeared, in French, in *Les Lettres Nouvelles*, no. 6 (August 1960), pp. 271–91.

———. "The Theatre of Samuel Beckett." *Perspective* 11 (Autumn 1959) : 142–55. Originally appeared, in French, in *Etudes Anglaises* 10 (October–November 1957) : 350–66.

* ———. *Über Beckett*. Frankfurt: Suhrkamp, 1966.

* Mélèse, Pierre. *Samuel Beckett*. Paris: Seghers, 1966.

Mercier, Vivian. "Beckett and the Search for Self." *New Republic* 133 (19 September 1955) : 20–21 [Rev. art.].

———. "The Mathematical Limit." *The Nation* 188 (14 February 1959) : 144–45 [Rev. art.].

———. "Samuel Beckett and the Sheela-na-gig." *Kenyon Review* 23 (Spring 1961) : 299–324.

Metman, Eva. "Reflections on Samuel Beckett's Plays." *Journal of Analytic Psychology* 5 (January 1960) : 41–63. Reprinted in Esslin, ed., *Samuel Beckett*, pp. 117–39.

Miller, J. Hillis. "The Anonymous Walkers." *The Nation* 190 (23 April 1960) : 351–54 [Rev. art.: 353].

Miller, Karl. "Beckett's Voices." *Encounter* 13 (September 1959) : 59–61.

Mitgang, Herbert. "Waiting for Beckett: And His 'Happy Days' Premiere." New York *Times*, 17 September 1961, sec. 2, pp. 1, 3.

Monteith, Charles. "A Personal Note." In *Beckett at 60: A Festschrift*, p. 87.

Montgomery, Niall. "No Symbols Where None Intended." *New World Writing* 5 (April 1954) : 324–37.

Moore, Harry T. "The Mud and Ashcan World of Samuel Beckett." In his *Twentieth-Century French Literature Since World*

War II. Carbondale: Southern Illinois University Press, 1966. Pp. 165–76.

Moore, J. R. "Some Night Thoughts on Beckett." *Massachusetts Review* 8 (Summer 1967) : 529–39.

Morrissette, Bruce. "Les Idées de Robbe-Grillet sur Beckett." In Melvin J. Friedman, ed., *Configuration critique de Samuel Beckett*, pp. 55–67.

Morse, J. Mitchell. "The Case for Irrelevance." *College English* 30 (December 1968) : 201–11 [204–6].

————. "The Choreography of 'The New Novel.'" *Hudson Review* 16 (Autumn 1963) : 396–419 [414–17].

————. "The Contemplative Life According to Samuel Beckett." *Hudson Review* 15 (Winter 1962–63) : 512–24.

————. "The Ideal Core of the Onion: Samuel Beckett's Criticism." *French Review* 38 (October 1964) : 23–29.

Nadeau, Maurice. "Le Chemin de la parole au silence." *Cahiers de la Compagnie Madeleine Renaud-Jean Louis Barrault*, no. 44 (1963), pp. 63–66.

————. *Le Roman français depuis la guerre*. Paris: Gallimard, 1963. Pp. 155–59.

————. "Samuel Beckett: Humor and the Void." Translated by Barbara Bray. In Martin Esslin, ed., *Samuel Beckett*, pp. 33–36. Originally appeared, in French, in *Mercure de France* 312 (August 1951) : 693–97 [Rev. art.]. Reprinted in Nadeau's *Littérature présente*. Paris: Correa, 1952. Pp. 274–79.

————. "Samuel Beckett; ou, Le droit au silence." *Les Temps Modernes* 7 (January 1952) : 1273–82.

Norés, Dominique. "La Condition humaine selon Beckett." *Théâtre d'aujourd'hui*, no. 3 (1957), pp. 9–12.

Oates, J. C. "The Trilogy of Samuel Beckett." *Renascence* 14 (Spring 1962) : 160–65.

* Oliva, Renato. *Samuel Beckett: Prima del Silenzio*. Milan: U. Mursia, 1967.

Olles, Helmut. "Samuel Beckett." *Welt und Wort* 15 (June 1960) : 173–74. Reprinted in *Lexicon der Weltliteratur im 20. Jahrhundert*, vol. 1. Freiburg: Herder, 1960. Pp. 136–38.

O'Neill, Joseph P. "The Absurd in Samuel Beckett." *The Personalist* 48 (Winter 1967) : 56–76.

* Onimus, Jean. *Beckett.* Paris-Bruges: Desclée de Brouwer, 1968.

———. "Samuel Beckett, le clochard et l'aisle." *Revue Générale Belge* 103, no. 2 (1968) : 5–17.

Palmer, Tony. "Artistic Privilege." *London Magazine* 8 (May 1968) : 47–52 [Rev. art.: 50–52].

"Paradise of Indignity." (London) *Times Literary Supplement,* 28 March 1958, p. 168 [Rev. art.].

Parker, R. B. "The Theory and Theatre of the Absurd." *Queen's Quarterly* 73 (Autumn 1966) : 421–41.

Peyre, Henri. *French Novelists of Today.* New York: Oxford University Press, 1967. Pp. 401–2.

Picchi, Mario. "Samuel Beckett: Introduzione." *La Fiera Letteraria,* 29 June 1958, p. 7.

Pinget, Robert. "My Dear Sam." In *Beckett at 60: A Festschrift,* pp. 84–85.

Pinter, Harold. "Beckett." In *Beckett at 60: A Festschrift,* p. 86.

Popkin, Henry. "Williams, Osborne, or Beckett?" *New York Times Magazine,* 13 November 1960, pp. 32–33, 119–21.

Poulet, Robert. "Samuel Becket [*sic*]." In his *La Lanterne magique.* Paris: Debresse, 1958. Pp. 236–42.

Pritchett, V. S. "An Irish Oblomov." *New Statesman,* n.s., 59 (2 April 1960) : 489 [Rev. art.]. Reprinted in his *The Living Novel and Later Appreciations.* New York: Random House, 1964. Pp. 315–20.

Pronko, Leonard C. "Beckett, Ionesco, Schéhadé: The Avant-Garde Theatre." *Modern Language Forum* 42 (December 1958) : 118–23.

———. "Samuel Beckett." In his *Avant-Garde: The Experimental Theater in France.* Berkeley and Los Angeles: University of California Press, 1962. Pp. 22–58.

* Reid, Alec. *All I Can Manage, More Than I Could: An Approach to the Plays of Samuel Beckett.* Chester Springs, Pa.: Dufour Editions, 1968.

———. "Beckett and the Drama of Unknowing." *Drama Survey* 2 (Fall 1962) : 130–38.

Ricks, Christopher. "Beckett and the Lobster." *New Statesman*, n.s., 67 (14 February 1964) : 254–55 [Rev. art.].

————. "The Roots of Samuel Beckett." *The Listener* 72 (17 December 1964) : 963–64, 980 [Rev. art.].

Robbe-Grillet, Alain. "Samuel Beckett, or 'Presence' in the Theatre." Translated by Barbara Bray. In Martin Esslin, ed., *Samuel Beckett*, pp. 108–16. Originally appeared, in French, in *Pour un nouveau roman*. Paris: Gallimard, 1964. Pp. 121–36. Also translated into English as *For a New Novel*, trans. Richard Howard. New York: Grove Press, 1965. *Godot* section of latter reprinted in Cohn, ed., *Casebook on "Waiting for Godot,"* pp. 15–21.

Roll-Hansen, Diderik. "Harold Pinter og det absurde drama." *Samtiden* 74 (September 1965) : 435–40 [437–38].

Rousseaux, André. "L'Homme désintégré de Samuel Beckett." In his *Littérature du vingtième siècle*. 5th ser. Paris: Albin Michel, 1955. Pp. 105–13.

Rowe, Kenneth Thorpe. *A Theater in Your Head*. New York: Funk and Wagnalls, 1960. Pp. 242–43, and passim.

Schneider, Alan. "Waiting for Beckett: A Personal Chronicle." *Chelsea Review*, no. 2 (Autumn 1958) , pp. 3–20. Reprinted, abridged, in Cohn, ed., *Casebook on "Waiting for Godot,"* pp. 51–57, and in *Beckett at 60: A Festschrift*, pp. 34–52.

Schoell, Konrad. "The Chain and the Circle: A Structural Comparison of *Waiting for Godot* and *Endgame*." *Modern Drama* 11 (May 1968) : 48–53.

* ————. *Das Theater Samuel Becketts*. Munich: Allach, 1966.

Schramm, Ulf. "Samuel Beckett." In his *Fiktion und Reflexion: Überlegungen zu Musil und Beckett*. Frankfort on the Main: Suhrkamp, 1967. Pp. 171–229.

Scott, Nathan A., Jr. "The Recent Journey Into the Zone of Zero: The Example of Beckett and His Despair of Literature." *Centennial Review* 6 (Spring 1962) : 144–81 [160–81].

* ————. *Samuel Beckett*. London: Bowes, 1965; Toronto: Queenswood, 1965; New York: Hillary House, 1965.

Seaver, Richard. "Samuel Beckett: An Introduction." *Merlin* 1 (Autumn 1952) : 73–79.

* Seipel, Hildegard. *Untersuchungen zum experimentellen Theater von Beckett und Ionesco.* Bonn: Romanisches Seminar der Universität Bonn, 1963.

Serreau, Genevieve. "Samuel Beckett." In her *Histoire du "Nouveau Théâtre."* Paris: Gallimard, 1966. Pp. 83–116. Section on *Godot* reprinted in Cohn, ed., *Casebook on "Waiting for Godot,"* pp. 171–75.

Shenker, Israel. "Moody Man of Letters." New York *Times,* 6 May 1956, sec. 2, pp. 1, 3. [Interview]

S[imon], A[lfred]. "Le Degré zéro du tragique." *Esprit* 31 (December 1963) : 905–9.

* Simpson, Alan. *Beckett and Behan and a Theatre in Dublin.* London: Routledge & Kegan Paul, 1962; New York: Hillary House, 1966. Part of section on *Godot* reprinted in Cohn, ed., *Casebook on "Waiting for Godot,"* pp. 45–49.

———. "Samuel Beckett." In *Beckett at 60: A Festschrift,* pp. 96–97.

Staib, Philippe. "A Propos Samuel Beckett." In *Beckett at 60: A Festschrift,* pp. 89–90.

Stamirowska, Krystyna. "The Conception of a Character in the Works of Joyce and Beckett." *Kwartalnik Neofilologiczny* 14, no. 4 (1967) : 443–47.

Steiner, George. "Of Nuance and Scruple." *New Yorker* 44 (27 April 1968) : 164–74 [Rev. art.].

S[tolpe], J[an]. "Samuel Beckett: Att vara konstnär." *Ord och Bild* 72, no. 2 (1963) : 91–92.

Strauss, Walter A. "Dante's Belacqua and Beckett's Tramps." *Comparative Literature* 11 (Summer 1959) : 250–61

Styan, J. L. *The Dark Comedy.* Cambridge: At the University Press, 1962. Pp. 226–31.

Suvin, Darko. "Beckett's Purgatory of the Individual." *Tulane Drama Review* 11 (Summer 1967) : 23–36.

Sypher, Wylie. "The Anonymous Self: A Defensive Humanism." In his *Loss of the Self in Modern Literature and Art.* New York: Random House, 1962. Pp. 147–65 [147–58]; see also passim.

Tagliaferri, Aldo. "Il concreto e l'astratto in Beckett." *Verri,* no. 20 (1966) , pp. 29–54.

"Talk of the Town." *New Yorker* 40 (8 August 1964) : 22–23.
[Interview]

Tassing, Einar. "Samuel Beckett." In Sven M. Kristensen, ed.,
Fremmede digtere i det 20. århundrede, vol. 3. Copenhagen:
G. E. C. Gads, 1968. Pp. 427–44.

Thiel, André. "La condition tragique chez Samuel Beckett." *La
Revue Nouvelle* 45 (15 May 1967) : 449–63.

Tindall, William York. "Beckett's Bums." *Critique* 2 (Spring–
Summer 1958) : 3–15.

* ———. *Samuel Beckett.* New York: Columbia University Press,
1964.

Ulriksen, Solveig Schult. "Beckett og den 'absurde tradisjon' (Jarry,
Apollinaire, Antonin Artaud)." In Terje Maerli, ed., *Samuel
Beckett,* pp. 17–30.

Unterecker, John. "Samuel Beckett's No-Man's Land." *New Leader*
42 (18 May 1959) : 24–25 [Rev. art.].

Vold, Jan Erik. "Samuel Becketts romaner." *Samtiden* 74
(September 1965) : 441–47.

Walker, Roy. "Samuel Beckett's Double Bill: Love, Chess and
Death." *Twentieth Century* 164 (December 1958) : 533–44.

Webb, Eugene. "Critical Writings on Samuel Beckett: A
Bibliography." *West Coast Review* 1 (Spring 1966) : 56–70.

Wellershoff, Dieter. "Failure of an Attempt at De-Mythologization:
Samuel Beckett's Novels." Translated by Martin Esslin. In Martin
Esslin, ed., *Samuel Beckett,* pp. 92–107. Originally appeared, in
German, in *Merkur* 17 (June 1963) : 528–46, and incorporated into
Wellershoff's *Der Gleichgültige.* . . .

———. "Samuel Beckett." In his *Der Gleichgültige: Versuche über
Hemingway, Camus, Benn und Beckett.* Cologne: Kiepenheuer &
Witsch, 1963. Pp. 97–127.

Wellwarth, G. E. "Life in the Void: Samuel Beckett." *University of
Kansas City Review* 28 (Autumn 1961) : 25–33. Reprinted in his
The Theatre of Protest and Paradox. New York: New York
University Press, 1964. Pp. 37–51.

Wendler, Herbert W. "Graveyard Humanism." *Southwest Review*
49 (Winter 1964) : 44–52.

Wernick, Robert. "The Three Kings of Bedlam." *Life* 64 (2
February 1968) : 60–69 [62A–65].

"Why Samuel Beckett Writes in French." *Books Abroad* 23 (Summer 1949) : 247–48. Originally appeared in *Transition Forty-eight.*

Wilson, Colin. "Samuel Beckett." In his *The Strength to Dream: Literature and the Imagination.* Boston: Houghton, Mifflin, 1962. Pp. 86–91.

Winther, Truls. "Samuel Beckett om kunstnere og deres verk." In Terje Maerli, ed., *Samuel Beckett,* pp. 93–107.

Worth, Katharine J. "Yeats and the French Drama." *Modern Drama* 8 (February 1966) : 382–91 [384–91].

Yerlès, Pierre. "Le Théâtre de Samuel Beckett." *La Revue Nouvelle* 33 (15 April 1961) : 401–7.

II. STUDIES OF INDIVIDUAL WORKS

Acts Without Words, I and II. Cohn, *Samuel Beckett*, 247–48;
Fletcher, "Action and Play . . . ," 246–47; Hassan, *The
Literature of Silence*, 192–93; Mélèse, 115–17; Pronko, "Samuel
Beckett," 47–49; Reid, *All I Can Manage*, 74–75, 79–80; Reid,
"Beckett . . . ," 134.
Tynan, Kenneth. *Curtains*. New York: Atheneum, 1961. P. 403
[Repr. rev.].

All That Fall. Barbour, 274–75; Capone, 101–30; Cleveland,
271–77; Coe, *Samuel Beckett*, 99–102; Cohn, *Samuel Beckett*,
243–47; Esslin, "Samuel Beckett: The Search for Self," 40;
Grossvogel, "Samuel Beckett," 120–22; Hassan, *The Literature of
Silence*, 189–91; Hayman, 39–44; Janvier, 118–22; Kenner,
Samuel Beckett: A Critical Study, 168–74; Mélèse, 90–100;
Metman, 60–62; Karl Miller, 59–61; Pronko, "Samuel Beckett,"
49–50; Reid, *All I Can Manage*, 68–70; Reid, "Beckett . . . ,"
133–34; Scott, *Samuel Beckett*, 114–18; Seipel, 242–47; Serreau,
106–7; Styan, 229–30.
Alpaugh, David J. "The Symbolic Structure of Samuel Beckett's *All
That Fall*." *Modern Drama* 9 (December 1966) : 324–32.
Davie, Donald. "Kinds of Comedy." *Spectrum* 2 (Winter 1958) :
25–31.
O'Brien, Justin. "Samuel Beckett and André Gide: An Hypothesis."
French Review 40 (February 1967) : 485–86.

Cascando. Capone, 148–53; Cleveland, 280–81; Hayman, 66–67;
Janvier, 161–66; Kenner, "Progress Report . . . ," 67–69; Mélèse,
108–13; Reid, *All I Can Manage*, 88–89.

Come and Go. Kenner, "Progress Report . . . ," 76–77; Reid, *All I
Can Manage*, 93–94.

Dante . . . Bruno. Vico . . Joyce. Friedman, "The Novels of
Samuel Beckett," 47–48; Hassan, *The Literature of Silence*, 121;
Strauss, 252.

Dis Joe. Hayman, 72–74; Janvier, 170–71; Kenner, "Progress Report
. . . ," 71–72; Mélèse, 113–14; Reid, *All I Can Manage*, 92.

Dream of Fair to Middling Women. Federman, 209–11; Fletcher,
The Novels of Samuel Beckett, 21–37.

Echo's Bones. Cohn, *Samuel Beckett,* 40–44.

Embers. Capone, 137–47; Cleveland, 277–79; Cohn, "Play and
Player . . . ," 46–47; Cohn, *Samuel Beckett,* 250–51; Esslin,
"Samuel Beckett: The Search for Self," 42–43; Grossvogel,
"Samuel Beckett," 122–23; Hassan, *The Literature of Silence,*
191–92; Hayman, 51–56; Janvier, 125–30; Kenner, *Samuel
Beckett: A Critical Study,* 174–76; Mélèse, 101–7; Karl Miller,
60–61; Pronko, "Samuel Beckett," 51–53; Reid, *All I Can
Manage,* 86; Reid, "Beckett . . . ," 136; Scott, *Samuel Beckett,*
119–21; Seipel, 247–53; Serreau, 107.

Endgame. Abel, "Joyce the Father . . . ," 26–27; Barbour, 271–74;
Blau, "Counterforce II . . . ," 240–51; Blau, "Politics . . . ,"
11–13; Boisdeffre, 679–80; Coe, *Samuel Beckett,* 95–99; Cohn,
"Play and Player . . . ," 44–46; Cohn, *Samuel Beckett,* 226–42;
Cook, 23–24; Esslin, "Samuel Beckett: The Search for Self,"
27–39; Fowlie, "Beckett," 214–16; Fowlie, "The New French
Theatre . . . ," 650–51; Glicksberg, "*Waiting for Godot* and
Endgame," 120–21; Grossvogel, "Samuel Beckett," 109–18;
Grossvogel, *The Self-Conscious Stage,* 331–34; Hassan,
The Literature of Silence, 183–88; Hayman, 22–38; Hoffman,
153–55; Hubert, 176–78; Catharine Hughes, "Beckett and the
Game of Life," 166–67; Catharine Hughes, "Beckett's World,"
41–42; Iser, 252–54; Janvier, 104–14, 250–51; Kenner, *Samuel
Beckett: A Critical Study,* 155–65; Lumley, 206–7; MacNeice,
120–21; Mayoux, "The Theatre of Samuel Beckett," 142–55;
Mélèse, 49–65; Metman, 55–60; Pronko, "Samuel Beckett," 39–47;
Reid, *All I Can Manage,* 71–73; Robbe-Grillet, 113–16;
Schneider, 10–19; Schoell, "The Chain and the Circle"; Scott,
Samuel Beckett, 94–98; Seipel, 213–32; Serreau, 97–104; Styan,
230–31; Walker, 538–44; Wernick, 62B; Yerlés, 402–6.

Atkinson, Brooks. "Abstract Drama." New York *Times,* 16
February 1958, sec. 2, p. 1 [Rev. art.].

"Beckett's Letters on *Endgame:* Extracts from His Correspondence
With Director Alan Schneider." In Daniel Wolf and Edwin
Fancher, eds., *The Village Voice Reader.* Garden City, N.Y.:
Doubleday, 1962. Pp. 182–86 [Repr. from *Village Voice*].

Brick, Allan. "A Note on Perception and Communication in
Beckett's *Endgame.*" *Modern Drama* 4 (May 1961) : 20–22.

Chambers, Ross. "Vers une interprétation de 'Fin de partie.' " *Studi
Francesi* 11 (January–April 1967) : 90–96.

Clurman, Harold. *Lies Like Truth.* New York: Macmillan, 1958. Pp. 224–25 [Repr. rev.].

Cohn, Ruby. "The Beginning of *Endgame.*" *Modern Drama* 9 (December 1966) : 319–23.

———. "*Endgame:* The Gospel According to Sad Sam Beckett." *Accent* 20 (Autumn 1960) : 223–34.

———. "Tempest in an Endgame." *Symposium* 19 (Winter 1965) : 328–34.

Deming, Barbara. "John Osborne's War Against the Philistines." *Hudson Review* 11 (Autumn 1958) : 411–19 [416–17].

Despard, Annabelle. "Sluttspill?" In Terje Maerli, ed., *Samuel Beckett,* pp. 43–50.

Dobrée, Bonamy. "The London Theatre." *Sewanee Review* 66 (Winter 1958) : 146–60 [Rev. art.: 149–52].

Easthope, Anthony. "Hamm, Clov, and Dramatic Method in *Endgame.*" *Modern Drama* 10 (February 1968) : 424–33.

Eastman, Richard M. "The Strategy of Samuel Beckett's *Endgame.*" *Modern Drama* 2 (May 1959) : 36–44.

Frisch, Jack E. "*Endgame:* A Play as Poem." *Drama Survey* 3 (Fall 1963) : 257–63.

Gassner, John. "Beckett's *Endgame* and Symbolism." In his *Theatre at the Crossroads.* New York: Holt, Rinehart and Winston, 1960. Pp. 256–61.

Kott, Jan. "*King Lear* or *Endgame.*" Translated by Boleslaw Taborski. *Evergreen Review,* no. 33 (August–September 1964), pp. 53–65. Reprinted in his *Shakespeare Our Contemporary.* Garden City, N.Y.: Doubleday, 1964. Pp. 87–124. Originally appeared, in French, in *Temps Modernes,* no. 194 (July 1962), pp. 48–77, and reprinted in Kott's *Shakespeare notre contemporain.* Paris: René Julliard, 1962. Pp. 115–58.

Lamont, Rosette C. "The Metaphysical Farce: Beckett and Ionesco." *French Review* 32 (February 1959) : 319–28 [324–28].

Lemarchand, Jacques. "*Fin de partie.*" *Nouvelle Nouvelle Revue Française* 5 (June 1957) : 1085–89 [Rev. art.].

Leventhal, A. J. "Close of Play: Reflections on Samuel Beckett's New Work for the French Theatre." *Dublin Magazine,* n.s., 32 (April–June 1957) : 18–22 [Rev. art.].

Lyons, Charles R. "Beckett's *Endgame:* An Anti-Myth of Creation."
     Modern Drama 7 (September 1964) : 204–9.
Mercier, Vivian. "How to Read *Endgame.*" *Griffin,* June 1959, pp.
     10–14.
Sheedy, John J. "The Comic Apocalypse of King Hamm." *Modern
     Drama* 9 (December 1966) : 310–18.
Tallmer, Jerry. "Beckett's *Endgame.*" In Daniel Wolf and Edwin
     Fancher, eds., *The Village Voice Reader.* Garden City, N.Y.:
     Doubleday, 1962. Pp. 180–82 [Repr. rev. from *Village Voice*].
Tynan, Kenneth. *Curtains.* New York: Atheneum, 1961. Pp. 225–28,
     401–3 [Repr. revs.].
Weales, Gerald. "The Language of *Endgame.*" *Tulane Drama
     Review* 6 (June 1962) : 107–17.
West, Alick. "How Shall We Judge?" *Zeitschrift für Anglistik und
     Amerikanistik* 15, no. 4 (1967) : 341–42.

Film. Hayman, 74; Janvier, 166–70; Kenner, "Progress Report
     . . . ," 69–71; Mélèse, 118–19; Reid, *All I Can Manage,* 90–91.
Edström, Mauritz. "Ansiktet pa väggen." *Ord och Bild* 75 (1966) :
     19–24.
Hampton, Charles C., Jr. "Samuel Beckett's *Film.*" *Modern Drama*
     11 (December 1968) : 299–305.

From an Abandoned Work. Capone, 130–37; Cohn, *Samuel Beckett,*
     179–81; Mélèse, 100; Reid, "Beckett . . . ," 134–35.

Happy Days. Coe, *Samuel Beckett,* 105–10; Cohn, "Play and Player
     . . . ," 47–48; Cohn, *Samuel Beckett,* 251–59; Grossvogel,
     "Samuel Beckett," 128–31; Hassan, *The Literature of Silence,*
     196–98; Hayman, 57–63; Hubert, 179–80; Catharine Hughes,
     "Beckett and the Game of Life," 167–68; Catharine Hughes,
     "Beckett's World," 42; Janvier, 149–57; Kern, "Samuel Beckett et
     les poches . . . ," 76–79; Lumley, 207–8; Mélèse, 71–81; Reid, *All
     I Can Manage,* 81–82; Reid, "Beckett . . . ," 136; Scott, *Samuel
     Beckett,* 121–23; Serreau, 107–14; Worth, 385–89.
Alpaugh, David J. "Negative Definition in Samuel Beckett's *Happy
     Days.*" *Twentieth Century Literature* 11 (January 1966) : 202–10.
Brustein, Robert. "Déjà vu." In his *Seasons of Discontent.* New
     York: Simon & Schuster, 1965. Pp. 53–56 [Repr. rev.].
Clurman, Harold. *"Happy Days."* In his *The Naked Image.* New
     York: Macmillan, 1966. Pp. 40–42 [Repr. rev.].

Eastman, Richard M. "Samuel Beckett and *Happy Days*." *Modern Drama* 6 (February 1964) : 417–24.

Ellingsen, Olav M. "*Happy Days:* Som et drama om uforløst kjaerlighet, liv og død." In Terje Maerli, ed., *Samuel Beckett,* pp. 51–63.

Kern, Edith. "Beckett's Knight of Infinite Resignation." *Yale French Studies,* no. 29 (Spring–Summer 1962) , pp. 49–56.

Kott, Jan. "A Note on Beckett's Realism." Translated by Boleslaw Taborski. *Tulane Drama Review* 10 (Spring 1966) : 156–59.

Lamont, Rosette. "Death and Tragi-Comedy: Three Plays of the New Theatre." *Massachusetts Review* 6 (Winter–Spring 1965) : 381–402 [385–91].

Lyons, Charles R. "Some Analogies between the Epic Brecht and the Absurdist Beckett." *Comparative Drama* 1 (Winter 1967–68) : 297–304. [*Mother Courage* and *Happy Days*]

M[arowitz], C[harles]. "A View From the Gods." *Encore* 10 (January–February 1963) : 6–7 [Rev. art.].

Renaud, Madeleine. "Beckett the Magnificent." In *Beckett at 60: A Festschrift,* pp. 81–83.

Tynan, Kenneth. *Tynan Right and Left.* London: Longmans, Green, 1967. Pp. 105–6 [Rev. art.].

How It Is. Coe, *Samuel Beckett,* 82–87; Cohn, *Samuel Beckett,* 182–207; Esslin, "Samuel Beckett," 143–44; Federman, 3–13; Fletcher, *The Novels of Samuel Beckett,* 209–22; Furbank, 69–72; Hassan, *The Literature of Silence,* 168–73; Janvier, 133–45, 245–48; Scott, *Samuel Beckett,* 76–79.

Cohn, Ruby. "*Comment c'est:* De quoi rire." *French Review* 35 (May 1962) : 563–69.

Federman, Raymond. "Beckett and the Fiction of Mud." In Richard Kostelanetz, ed., *On Contemporary Literature.* New York: Avon, 1964. Pp. 255–61.

———. " 'How It Is' : With Beckett's Fiction." *French Review* 38 (February 1965) : 459–68.

Fournier, Edith. "Pour que la boue me soit contée. . . ." *Critique* 17 (May 1961) : 412–18 [Rev. art.].

Genêt. "Letter From Paris." *New Yorker* 38 (4 March 1961) : 95–100 [100].

"Novels of 1964: Samuel Beckett: *How It Is* (21 May) ." In *T.L.S.: Essays and Reviews From the Times Literary Supplement, 1964.* London: Oxford University Press, 1965. Pp. 45–47 [Repr. rev.].

Imagination Dead Imagine. Kenner, "Progress Report . . . ," 66–67.

Krapp's Last Tape. Brown, 255; Coe, *Samuel Beckett,* 102–5; Cohn, *Samuel Beckett,* 248–50; Esslin, "Samuel Beckett: The Search for Self," 41–42; Fletcher, "Action and Play . . . ," 246; Grossvogel, "Samuel Beckett," 123–27; Hassan, *The Literature of Silence,* 193–95; Hayman, 45–50; Hoffman, 155–59; Hubert, 178–79; Janvier, 122–25; Lumley, 207; Mélèse, 65–71; Pronko, "Samuel Beckett," 51; Reid, *All I Can Manage,* 21–24, 76–78; Reid, "Beckett . . . ," 135–36; Scott, *Samuel Beckett,* 118–19; Seipel, 232–41; Serreau, 104–6; Walker, 533–36; Yerlés, 406–7.

Atkinson, Brooks. "Village Vagrants." New York *Times,* 31 January 1960, sec. 10, p. 1 [Rev. art.].

Brustein, Robert. "Listening to the Past." In his *Seasons of Discontent.* New York: Simon & Schuster, 1965. Pp. 26–29 [Repr. rev.].

Clurman, Harold. *"The Zoo Story* and Beckett's *Krapp's Last Tape."* In his *The Naked Image.* New York: Macmillan, 1966. Pp. 13–15 [Repr. rev.].

Gilbert, Sandra M. " 'All the Dead Voices': A Study of *Krapp's Last Tape." Drama Survey* 6 (Spring 1968) : 244–57.

Mihalovici, Marcel. "My Collaboration With Samuel Beckett." In *Beckett at 60: A Festschrift,* pp. 20–22.

Oberg, Arthur K. *"Krapp's Last Tape* and the Proustian Vision." *Modern Drama* 9 (December 1966) : 333–38.

Tynan, Kenneth. *Curtains.* New York: Atheneum, 1961. Pp. 225–28 [Repr. rev.].

Malone Dies. Bjurström, 30; Blanchot, 223–24; Chambers, "Samuel Beckett and the Padded Cell," 457–58; Coe, *Samuel Beckett,* 62–68; Cohn, *Samuel Beckett,* 114–68; Cohn, "Samuel Beckett: Self-Translator," 619–20; Cohn, "Still Novel," 51; Esslin, "Samuel Beckett," 138–39; Fletcher, *The Novels of Samuel Beckett,* 151–76; Frye, 446–47; Glicksberg, "Samuel Beckett's World of Fiction," 39–41; Goldberg, 398–400; Carol Hamilton, 157–61;

Hassan, *The Literature of Silence*, 158–62; Hoffman, 127–32; Jacobsen and Mueller, *The Testament of Samuel Beckett*, 88–99; Janvier, 64–73, 236–41; Karl, 672–74; MacNeice, 141–46; Scott, "The Recent Journey . . . ," 173–74; Scott, *Samuel Beckett*, 64–66; Tassing, 439–41; Tindall, "Beckett's Bums," 11–13; Wellershoff, "Failure of an Attempt . . . ," 98–101.

Cmarada, Geraldine. "*Malone Dies:* A Round of Consciousness." *Symposium* 14 (Fall 1960) : 199–212.

Picchi, Mario. "Beckett: *Malone muore.*" *La Fiera Letteraria,* 30 November 1958, p. 2 [Rev. art.].

Vold, Jan Erik. "Malones blyant." In Terje Maerli, ed., *Samuel Beckett,* pp. 65–79.

Mercier and Camier. Cohn, *Samuel Beckett,* 95–98; Duckworth, xlvi–lxxv; Federman, 135–76; Fletcher, *The Novels of Samuel Beckett,* 110–18; Janvier, 39–43.

Molloy. Bjurström, 29–30; Blanchot, 222–23; Chambers, "Samuel Beckett and the Padded Cell," 454–56; Coe, *Samuel Beckett,* 54–62; Cohn, *Samuel Beckett,* 114–68; Cohn, "Samuel Beckett: Self-Translator," 618–19; Cohn, "Still Novel," 49–51; Davin, 36–39; Esslin, "Samuel Beckett," 135–38; Fasano, 441–46; Fletcher, *The Novels of Samuel Beckett,* 119–50; Friedman, "A Note on Liebniz . . . ," 94–96; Friedman, "The Novels of Samuel Beckett," 53; Frye, 445–46; Glicksberg, "Samuel Beckett's World of Fiction," 35–39; Goldberg, 396–98; Carol Hamilton, 157–61; Kenneth Hamilton, "Boon or Thorn?" 439–42; Hassan, *The Literature of Silence,* 152–58; Hoffman, 121–27; Janvier, 48–61, 231–36; Karl, 668–71; Kermode, "Beckett, Snow . . . ," 74–75; Kern, "Samuel Beckett et les poches . . . ," 75–76; Lee, 84–86; Nadeau, "Samuel Beckett: Humor and the Void," 33–36; Scott, "The Recent Journey . . . ," 170–73; Scott, *Samuel Beckett,* 62–64; Strauss, 254; Tassing, 437–39; Tindall, "Beckett's Bums," 7–12; Wellershoff, "Failure of an Attempt . . . ," 93–98.

Bataille, Georges. "Le Silence de Molloy." *Critique* 7 (15 May 1951) : 387–96 [Rev. art.].

Bowles, Patrick. "How Samuel Beckett Sees the Universe." *The Listener* 59 (19 June 1958) : 1011–12.

Boyle, Kevin. "Molloy: Icon of the Negative." *Westwind* 5 (Fall 1961) .

Chanan, Gabriel. "The Plight of the Novelist." *Cambridge Review* 89A (26 April 1968) : 399–401 [401].

Friedman, Melvin J. "Molloy's 'Sacred' Stones." *Romance Notes* 9 (Autumn 1967) : 8–11.

Hayman, David. "Quest for Meaninglessness: The Boundless Poverty of Molloy." In William O. S. Sutherland, ed., *Six Contemporary Novels: Six Introductory Essays in Modern Fiction*. Austin: University of Texas, Department of English, 1962. Pp. 90–112. Reprinted, in French, in Friedman, ed., *Configuration critique de Samuel Beckett,* pp. 131–51.

Kern, Edith. "Moran-Molloy: The Hero as Author." *Perspective* 11 (Autumn 1959) : 183–93.

———. "Samuel Beckett: Dionysian Poet." *Descant* 3 (Winter 1959) : 33–36.

Lancelotti, Mario A. "Observaciones sobre Molloy." *Sur*, no. 273 (November–December 1961) , pp. 50–52.

Pingaud, Bernard. "*Molloy*." *Esprit* 19 (September 1951) : 423–25 [Rev. art.].

———. "*Molloy,* douze ans après." *Les Temps Modernes* 18 (January 1963) : 1283–1300.

Solomon, Philip Howard. "Samuel Beckett's *Molloy*: A Dog's Life." *French Review* 41 (October 1967) : 84–91.

More Pricks Than Kicks. Cohn, *Samuel Beckett,* 18–40; Esslin, "Samuel Beckett," 130–31; Federman, 33–55, 211–14; Fletcher, *The Novels of Samuel Beckett,* 18–21; Hoffman, 101–3; Leventhal, "The Beckett Hero," 19–22; Scott, *Samuel Beckett,* 38–40; Strauss, 252–53.

Federman, Raymond. "Beckett's Belacqua and the Inferno of Society." *Arizona Quarterly* 20 (Autumn 1964) : 231–41.

Murphy. Barrett, "Samuel Beckett's World in Waiting . . . ," 15–16; Bjurström, 28–29; Coe, *Samuel Beckett,* 20–35; Cohn, *Samuel Beckett,* 45–64; Cohn, "Samuel Beckett: Self-Translator," 613–16; Davin, 37; Esslin, "Samuel Beckett," 131–33; Fasano, 438–41; Federman, 56–93; Fletcher, *The Novels of Samuel Beckett,* 38–55; Friedman, "The Novels of Samuel Beckett," 51–52; Frye, 443–44; Glicksberg, "Samuel Beckett's World of Fiction," 32–35; Hassan, *The Literature of Silence,* 140–45; Hoffman, 105–14; Jacobsen and Mueller, *The Testament of*

Samuel Beckett, 67–72, 80–82; Janvier, 25–31, 219–24; Karl, 665–66; Kenner, *Samuel Beckett: A Critical Study,* 49–58; Scott, "The Recent Journey . . . ," 162–64; Scott, *Samuel Beckett,* 41–47; Strauss, 253–54; Tassing, 431–33; Tindall, "Beckett's Bums," 5–6; Wilson, 88.

Cooney, Séamus. "Beckett's *Murphy*." *Explicator,* vol. 25 (September 1966), item 3.

Mintz, Samuel I. "Beckett's *Murphy*: A 'Cartesian' Novel." *Perspective* 11 (Autumn 1959) : 156–65.

* Harrison, Robert. *Samuel Beckett's "Murphy": A Critical Excursion.* Athens: University of Georgia Monographs, no. 15, 1968.

Les Nouvelles ("L'Expulse," "La Fin," "Le Calmant," "Premier amour"). Cohn, *Samuel Beckett,* 101–13; Federman, 177–99; Janvier, 43–48, 230–31.

Ping. Lodge, David. "Some Ping Understood." *Encounter* 30 (February 1968) : 85–89.

Play. Cohn, " 'Theatrum Mundi' . . . ," 31; Hayman, 68–71; Janvier, 157–61; Kenner, "Progress Report . . . ," 63–66, 72–76; Mélèse, 82–88; Reid, *All I Can Manage,* 36–48, 83–84; Serreau, 114–16; Worth, 387–90.

Brustein, Robert. "Déjà vu." In his *Seasons of Discontent.* New York: Simon & Schuster, 1965. Pp. 53–56 [Repr. rev.: 56].

Clurman, Harold. "The Lover and Beckett's *Play*." In his *The Naked Image.* New York: Macmillan, 1966. Pp. 112–14 [Repr. rev.].

Dukore, Bernard F. "Beckett's Play, *Play*." *Educational Theatre Journal* 17 (March 1965) : 19–23.

Hubert, Renée Riese. "Beckett's *Play* between Poetry and Performance." *Modern Drama* 9 (December 1966) : 339–46.

Proust. Friedman, "The Novels of Samuel Beckett," 49–51; Hassan, *The Literature of Silence,* 121–22; Jacobsen and Mueller, *The Testament of Samuel Beckett,* 59–67; Scott, *Samuel Beckett,* 35–38.

Texts for Nothing. Coe, *Samuel Beckett,* 79–82; Cohn, *Samuel Beckett,* 169–79; Fletcher, *The Novels of Samuel Beckett,* 196–205; Janvier, 86–87, 242–44; Scott, *Samuel Beckett,* 74–76.

The Unnamable. Bjurström, 30–31; Blanchot, 224–29; Chambers, "Samuel Beckett and the Padded Cell," 458–62; Coe, *Samuel Beckett,* 69–79; Cohn, *Samuel Beckett,* 114–68; Cohn, "Samuel Beckett: Self-Translator," 620–21; Cohn, "Still Novel," 52–53; Esslin, "Samuel Beckett," 139–43; Fletcher, *The Novels of Samuel Beckett,* 179–94; Frye, 447–48; Glicksberg, "Samuel Beckett's World of Fiction," 41–47; Goldberg, 400; Carol Hamilton, 162–63; Hassan, *The Literature of Silence,* 162–67; Heppenstall, 261–63; Hoffman, 132–37; Janvier, 74–81, 240–41; Karl, 674–76; Mercier, "The Mathematical Limit," 145; Scott, "The Recent Journey . . . ," 174–75; Scott, *Samuel Beckett,* 66–67; Tassing, 441–44; Tindall, "Beckett's Bums," 13–15; Wellershoff, "Failure of an Attempt . . . ," 101–4.

Fanizza, Franco. "La parola e il silenzio ne 'L'Innomable' di Samuel Beckett." *Aut Aut,* no. 60 (November 1960) , pp. 380–91.

Hayman, David. "Introduction to an Extract from *The Unnamable.*" *Texas Quarterly* 1 (Spring 1958) : 127–28.

Raes, Hugo. "Samuel Beckett im Amerika." *Vlaamse Gids* 43 (July 1959) : 495–96.

Rickels, Milton. "Existential Themes in Beckett's 'Unnamable.' " *Criticism* 4 (Spring 1962) : 134–47.

Waiting for Godot. Abel, "Joyce the Father . . . ," 26–27; Bjurström, 31–33; Blau, "Counterforce II . . . ," 229–40; Blau, "Politics . . . ," 9–11, 13, 15–17; Boisdeffre, 678–79; Brown, 255–57; Coe, *Samuel Beckett,* 88–95; Cohn, "Play and Player . . . ," 43–44; Cohn, *Samuel Beckett,* 208–25; Cohn, "Samuel Beckett: Self-Translator," 616–17; Cohn, " 'Theatrum Mundi' . . . ," 30–31; Cook, 21–23; Duckworth, xlv–cxxxi; Esslin, "Samuel Beckett: The Search for Self," 13–27; Fletcher, "Action and Play . . . ," 243–48; Fowlie, "Beckett," 210–14; Fowlie, "The New French Theatre . . . ," 648–50; Frye, 444–45; Glicksberg, "*Waiting for Godot* and *Endgame,*" 118–20; Grossvogel, "Samuel Beckett," 88–109; Grossvogel, *The Self-Conscious Stage,* 324–31; Guicharnaud, "Existence on Stage . . . ," 193–212; Hassan, *The Literature of Silence,* 175–83; Hayman, 4–21; Hoffman, 138–53; Hubert, 175–76; Catharine Hughes, "Beckett and the Game of Life," 163–65; Catharine Hughes, "Beckett's

World," 40–41; Iser, 254–59; Janvier, 96–104, 248–50; Kenner, *Samuel Beckett: A Critical Study*, 133–55; Kermode, "Beckett, Snow . . . ," 74; Kern, "Beckett and the Spirit of the Commedia dell'Arte," 261–67; Lee, 80–84; Lumley, 203–6; MacNeice, 117–20; Mayoux, "The Theatre of Samuel Beckett," 142–55; Mélèse, 21–49; Metman, 44–55; O'Neill, 69–72; Pronko, "Samuel Beckett," 25–39; Reid, *All I Can Manage*, 50–58, 65–67; Reid, "Beckett . . . ," 130–33; Robbe-Grillet, 108–13; Schneider, 3–9; Schoell, "The Chain and the Circle"; Scott, *Samuel Beckett*, 83–94; Seipel, 181–212; Serreau, 85–97; Strauss, 255–61; Styan, 227–29; Wernick, 62B; Wilson, 89–90; Worth, 387–88; Yerlès, 401–5.

A., S. "Balzac, a-t-il inspiré *En attendant Godot?*" *Le Figaro Littéraire*, 17 September 1955, p. 12.

Anders, Günther. "Being without Time: On Beckett's Play *Waiting for Godot.*" Translated by Martin Esslin. In Martin Esslin, ed., *Samuel Beckett*, pp. 140–51. Originally appeared, in German, in Anders' *Die Antiquiertheit des Menschen: Über die Seel im Zeitalter der zweiten industriellen Revolution*. Munich: C. H. Beck, 1956. Pp. 213–31.

Ashmore, Jerome. "Philosophical Aspects of *Godot.*" *Symposium* 16 (Winter 1962) : 296–304.

Atkins, Anselm. "Lucky's Speech in Beckett's *Waiting for Godot:* A Punctuated Sense-Line Arrangement." *Educational Theatre Journal* 19 (December 1967) : 426–32.

———. "A Note on the Structure of Lucky's Speech." *Modern Drama* 9 (December 1966) : 309.

Bagby, Philip H. *"Waiting for Godot."* (London) *Times Literary Supplement*, 23 March 1956, p. 181 [Letter to the Editor].

Ball, Patricia M. "Browning's Godot." *Victorian Poetry* 3 (Autumn 1965) : 245–53.

Beckett, Jeremy. *Meanjin* 15 (Winter 1956) : 216–18 [Rev. art.].

Belmont, Georges. "Un Classicisme retrouvé." *La Table Ronde,* no. 62 (February 1953) , pp. 171–74 [Rev. art.].

Bentley, Eric. *The Life of the Drama*. New York: Atheneum, 1964. Pp. 99–101, 347–51.

———. "The Talent of Samuel Beckett." *New Republic* 134 (14 May 1956) : 20–21 [Rev. art.]. Reprinted, with "Postscript 1967," in Cohn, ed., *Casebook on "Waiting for Godot,"* pp. 59–66.

Bonczek, J[ane] C. "Being and Waiting: A Sign of Our Times." *Lit,* no. 5 (1964), pp. 6–10.

Brée, Germaine, and Eric Schoenfeld. "Introduction." In Brée and Schoenfeld, eds., *En attendant Godot.* New York: Macmillan, 1963. Pp. 1–7.

Broch, Kirsten. "Når stillstanden blir drama." In Terje Maerli, ed., *Samuel Beckett,* pp. 31–41.

Brooks, Curtis M. "The Mythic Pattern in *Waiting for Godot.*" *Modern Drama* 9 (December 1966) : 292–99.

Brown, John Russell. "Mr. Beckett's Shakespeare." *Critical Quarterly* 5 (Winter 1963) : 310–26.

Brown, Robert McAfee. "The Theme of Waiting in Modern Literature." *Ramparts* 3 (Summer 1964) : 68–75 [69–70].

Bull, Peter. "*Waiting for Godot.*" In his *I Know the Face, But. . . .* London: Peter Davies, 1959. Pp. 166–91. Reprinted, abridged, in Cohn, ed., *Casebook on "Waiting for Godot,"* pp. 39–43.

Butler, Harry L. "Balzac and Godeau, Beckett and Godot: A Curious Parallel." *Romance Notes* 3 (Spring 1962) : 13–17.

Butler, Michael. "Anatomy of Despair." *Encore* 8 (May–June 1961) : 17–24.

Case, Sue-Ellen. "Image and Godot." In Ruby Cohn, ed., *Casebook on "Waiting for Godot,"* pp. 155–59.

Chadwick, C. "*Waiting for Godot:* A Logical Approach." *Symposium* 14 (Winter 1960) : 252–57.

Champigny, Robert. "*Waiting for Godot:* Myth, Words, Wait." Translated by Ruby Cohn. In Ruby Cohn, ed., *Casebook on "Waiting for Godot,"* pp. 137–44. Originally appeared, in French and in slightly different form, in *PMLA* 75 (June 1960) : 329–31.

Chase, N. C. "Images of Man: *Le Malentendu* and *En Attendant Godot.*" *Wisconsin Studies in Contemporary Literature* 7 (Autumn 1966) : 295–302.

Chiari, Joseph. *The Contemporary French Theatre: The Flight From Naturalism.* London: Rockliff, 1958. P. 226.

———. *Landmarks of Contemporary Drama.* London: Herbert Jenkins, 1965. Pp. 68–80.

Christie, Erling. "Det absurde drama: Tanker omkring Samuel Becketts 'Waiting for Godot.'" *Samtiden* 66 (1957) : 578–84.

Clurman, Harold. "Samuel Beckett." In his *Lies Like Truth*. New York: Macmillan, 1958. Pp. 220–22 [Repr. rev.].

Cohen, Robert S. "Parallels and the Possibility of Influence Between Simone Weil's *Waiting for God* and Samuel Beckett's *Waiting for Godot*." *Modern Drama* 6 (February 1964) : 425–36.

Cohn, Ruby. "The Absurdly Absurd: Avatars of Godot." *Comparative Literature Studies* 2, no. 3 (1965) : 233–40.

————. "Waiting Is All." *Modern Drama* 3 (September 1960) : 162–67.

* ————, ed. *Casebook on "Waiting for Godot."* New York: Grove Press, 1967.

Cole, Connelly. "A Note on *Waiting for Godot*." *Icarus,* January 1957, pp. 25–27.

"Comment: *Waiting for Godot*." *Meanjin* 15 (Winter 1956) : 132.

Corrigan, Robert W. "The Theatre in Search of a Fix." *Tulane Drama Review* 5 (June 1961) : 21–35 [23–24].

Dimié, Moma. "Godou." *Delo* (Belgrade) 14 (1968) : 543–48.

D[ort], B[ernard]. "*En attendant Godot:* Pièce de Samuel Beckett." *Les Temps Modernes,* no. 90 (May 1953) , pp. 1842–45 [Rev. art.].

Douglas, Dennis. "The Drama of Evasion in *Waiting for Godot*." *Komos* 1 (1968) : 140–46.

Drews, Wolfgang. "Die Grossen Unsichtbaren, VII: Godot." *Theater und Zeit* 6 (February 1959) : 107–9.

Dubois, Jacques. "Beckett and Ionesco: The Tragic Awareness of Pascal and the Ironic Awareness of Flaubert." Translated by Ruby Cohn. *Modern Drama* 9 (December 1966) : 283–91.

Duckworth, Colin. "The Making of *Godot*." *Theatre Research* 8, no. 3 (1966) : 123–45.

Dukore, Bernard F. "Controversy: A Non-Interpretation of *Godot*." *Drama Survey* 3 (Spring–Summer 1963) : 117–19.

————. "Gogo, Didi, and the Absent Godot." *Drama Survey* 1 (Winter 1962) : 301–7.

————. "The *Other* Pair in *Waiting for Godot*." *Drama Survey* 7 (Winter 1968–69) : 133–37.

Empson, William. " 'Waiting for Godot.' " (London) *Times Literary Supplement,* 30 March 1956, p. 195 [Letter to the Editor].

Esslin, Martin. "The Absurdity of the Absurd." *Kenyon Review* 22 (Autumn 1960) : 670–73 [672–73].

———. "Godot and His Children: The Theatre of Samuel Beckett and Harold Pinter." In William A. Armstrong, ed., *Experimental Drama*. London: G. Bell, 1963. Pp. 128–46.

Fertig, Howard. "*Waiting for Godot:* A Review." In Daniel Wolf and Edwin Fancher, eds., *The Village Voice Reader*. Garden City, N.Y.: Doubleday, 1962. Pp. 67–69 [Repr. rev. from *Village Voice,* 11 April 1956].

Fletcher, John. "Beckett and Balzac Revisited." *French Review* 37 (October 1963) : 78–80.

———. "Roger Blin at Work." *Modern Drama* 8 (February 1966) : 403–8. Reprinted in Cohn, ed., *Casebook on "Waiting for Godot,"* pp. 21–26.

Flood, Ethelbert. "A Reading of Beckett's *Godot*." *Culture* 22 (September 1961) : 257–62.

Francis, Richard Lee. "Beckett's Metaphysical Tragicomedy." *Modern Drama* 8 (December 1965) : 259–67.

Fraser, G. S. " 'Modernity' in the Drama." In his *The Modern Writer and his World: Continuity and Innovation in Twentieth-Century Literature*. New York: F. A. Praeger, 1965. Pp. 50–69 [61–64].

———. "They Also Serve." (London) *Times Literary Supplement,* 10 February 1956, p. 84 [Rev. art.]. Reprinted in Derek Hudson, ed., *English Critical Essays: Twentieth Century: Second Series*. London: Oxford University Press, 1958, pp. 324–32, and in Cohn, ed., *Casebook on "Waiting for Godot,"* pp. 133–37.

Friedman, Melvin J. "Crritic!" *Modern Drama* 9 (December 1966) : 300–308.

Gascoigne, Bamber. *Twentieth-Century Drama*. London: Hutchinson, 1962; New York: Barnes & Noble, 1966. Pp. 184–88.

Gassner, John. "Beckett: *Waiting for Godot*." In his *Theatre at the Crossroads*. New York: Holt, Rinehart and Winston, 1960. Pp. 252–56 [Repr. rev.].

Gray, Ronald. " 'Waiting for Godot': A Christian Interpretation." *The Listener* 57 (24 January 1957) : 160–61.

Grenier, Jean. "*En attendant Godot*." *Le Disque Vert* 1 (July–August 1953) : 81–86.

Harvey, Lawrence E. "Art and the Existential in *En attendant Godot*." *PMLA* 75 (March 1960) : 137–46. Reprinted, abridged, in Cohn, ed., *Casebook on "Waiting for Godot,"* pp. 144–54.

Hobson, Harold. "The First Night of 'Waiting for Godot.'" In *Beckett at 60: A Festschrift*, pp. 25–28.

————. "Foreword to 'Waiting for Godot.'" In Colin Duckworth, ed., *En attendant Godot*. London: George G. Harrap, 1966. Pp. vii–ix.

Hooker, Ward. "Irony and Absurdity in the Avant-Garde Theatre." *Kenyon Review* 22 (Summer 1960) : 436–54 [444–54].

"Hurry, Godot, Hurry." *Time* 69 (18 March 1957) : 108 [Rev. art.].

Jessup, Bertram. "About Beckett, Godot and Others." *Northwest Review* 1 (Spring 1957) : 25–30.

Johnston, Denis. "Waiting With Beckett." *Irish Writing,* no. 34 (Spring 1956), pp. 23–28 [Rev. art.]. Reprinted in Cohn, ed., *Casebook on "Waiting for Godot,"* pp. 31–38.

Josbin, Raoul. "*Waiting for Godot*." Translated by Joseph E. Cunneen. *Cross Currents* 6 (Summer 1956) : 204–7. Originally appeared, in French, in *Etudes,* no. 150 (July–August 1953), pp. 77–83.

Kern, Edith. "Drama Stripped for Inaction: Beckett's *Godot*." *Yale French Studies,* no. 14 (Winter 1954–55), pp. 41–47.

Killinger, John. *The Failure of Theology in Modern Literature*. New York: Abingdon Press, 1963. Pp. 215–17.

Knight, G. Wilson. "The Kitchen Sink: On Recent Developments in Drama." *Encounter* 21 (December 1963) : 48–54 [51].

Kolve, V. A. "Religious Language in *Waiting for Godot*." *Centennial Review* 11 (Winter 1967) : 102–27.

Korg, Jacob. "The Literary Esthetics of Dada." *Works* 1 (Spring 1968) : 43–54.

Leventhal, A. J. "Mr. Beckett's *En Attendant Godot*." *Dublin Magazine,* n.s., 29 (April–June 1954) : 11–16.

Levy, Alan. "The Long Wait for Godot." *Theatre Arts* 40 (August 1956) : 33–35, 96. Reprinted in Cohn, ed., *Casebook on "Waiting for Godot,"* pp. 74–78.

Lewis, Allan. "The Theatre of the 'Absurd': Beckett, Ionesco, Genet." In his *The Contemporary Theatre*. New York: Crown, 1962. Pp. 259–81 [259–65].

"The Long Wait." (London) *Times Literary Supplement,* 5 May 1961, p. 277.

Luchs, Fred E. *"Waiting for Godot." Christianity Today* 4 (6 June 1960) : 6–8.

McCoy, Charles. *"Waiting for Godot:* A Biblical Appraisal." *Florida Review,* no. 2 (Spring 1958) , pp. 63–72. Reprinted in *Religion in Life* 28 (Fall 1959) : 595–603.

Mailer, Norman. "A Public Notice on *Waiting for Godot."* In his *Advertisements for Myself.* New York: G. P. Putnam's, 1959. Pp. 320–25; see also pp. 315–16 [Rev. art.]. "A Public Notice" reprinted in Cohn, ed., *Casebook on "Waiting for Godot,"* pp. 69–74.

Marinello, Leone J. "Samuel Beckett's *Waiting for Godot:* A Modern Classic Affirming Man's Dignity and Nobility and Ultimate Salvation." *Drama Critique* 6 (Spring 1963) : 75, 81.

Markus, Thomas B. "Controversy: Bernard Dukore and *Waiting for Godot." Drama Survey* 2 (February 1963) : 360–63.

Mercier, Vivian. "A Pyrrhonian Eclogue." *Hudson Review* 7 (Winter 1955) : 620–24 [Rev. art.].

Mihályi, Gábor. "Beckett's 'Godot' and the Myth of Alienation." *Modern Drama* 9 (December 1966) : 277–82. See also *New Hungarian Quarterly,* no. 24 (Winter 1966) .

Moore, John R. "A Farewell to Something." *Tulane Drama Review* 5 (September 1960) : 49–60.

O'Meara, John J. " 'Waiting for Godot.' " (London) *Times Literary Supplement,* 6 April 1956, p. 207 [Letter to the Editor].

Packard, William. "Poetry in the Theatre—V." *Trace,* no. 66 (Fall 1967) , pp. 447–55.

Paris, Jean. "The Clock Struck Twenty-nine." *The Reporter* 15 (4 October 1956) : 39–40 [40].

Politzer, Heinz. "The Egghead Waits for Godot." *Christian Scholar* 42 (March 1959) : 46–50.

Portal, Georges. "Pour l'amour de Dieu." *Ecrits de Paris,* nos. 195–96 (July–August 1961) , pp. 139–46.

"Puzzling About Godot." (London) *Times Literary Supplement,* 13 April 1956, p. 221.

Radke, Judith J. "The Theatre of Samuel Beckett: 'Une Durée à animer.' " *Yale French Studies,* no. 29 (Spring–Summer 1962), pp. 57–64.

Rainoird, Manuel. *"En attendant Godot." Monde Nouveau* 11 (August–September 1956) : 115–17 [Rev. art.].

Rechtien, Brother John. "Time and Eternity Meet in the Present." *Texas Studies in Literature and Language* 6 (Spring 1964) : 5–21.

Rexroth, Kenneth. "Samuel Beckett and the Importance of Waiting." In his *Bird in the Bush.* Norfolk, Conn.: New Directions, 1959. Pp. 75–85 [Repr. rev.].

Rhodes, S. A. "From Godeau to Godot." *French Review* 36 (January 1963) : 260–65.

Robbe-Grillet, Alain. "Samuel Beckett, auteur dramatique." *Critique* 9 (February 1953) : 108–14.

Sastre, Alfonso. "Siete notas sobre 'Esperando a Godot.' " *Primer acto,* no. 1 (April 1957), pp. 46–52.

Schechner, Richard. "There's Lots of Time in *Godot." Modern Drama* 9 (December 1966) : 268–76. Reprinted in Cohn, ed., *Casebook on "Waiting for Godot,"* pp. 175–87.

Schumach, Murray. "Why They Wait for Godot." *New York Times Magazine,* 21 September 1958, pp. 36, 38, 41.

Schwarz, Karl. "Die Zeitproblematik in Samuel Becketts *En attendant Godot." Die Neueren Sprachen,* n.s., 16 (May 1967) : 201–9.

Scott, Bernard E. "The Press of Freedom: Waiting for God." In Daniel Wolf and Edwin Fancher, eds., *The Village Voice Reader.* Garden City, N.Y.: Doubleday, 1962. Pp. 79–84 [82–83: repr. from *Village Voice*].

Sheedy, John J. "The Net." In Ruby Cohn, ed., *Casebook on "Waiting for Godot,"* pp. 159–66.

Tallmer, Jerry. "Godot on Broadway" and "Godot Still Waiting." In Daniel Wolf and Edwin Fancher, eds., *The Village Voice Reader.* Garden City, N.Y.: Doubleday, 1962. Pp. 69–76 [Repr. revs. from *Village Voice*].

Todd, Robert E. "Proust and Redemption in *Waiting for Godot." Modern Drama* 10 (September 1967) : 175–81.

Tompkins, J. M. S. *"Waiting for Godot."* (London) *Times Literary Supplement,* 24 February 1956, p. 117 [Letter to the Editor].

Torrance, Robert M. "Modes of Being and Time in the World of *Godot." Modern Language Quarterly* 28 (March 1967) : 77–95.

Trousdale, Marion. "Dramatic Form: The Example of *Godot." Modern Drama* 11 (May 1968) : 1–9.

Tynan, Kenneth. *Curtains.* New York: Atheneum, 1961. Pp. 101–3, 272 [Repr. revs.].

Vahanian, Gabriel. "The Empty Cradle." *Theology Today* 13 (January 1957) : 521–26.

Via, D. O., Jr. *"Waiting for Godot* and Man's Search for Community." *Journal of Bible and Religion* 30 (January 1962) : 32–37.

Walsh, J. S. " 'Waiting for Godot.' " (London) *Times Literary Supplement,* 9 March 1956, p. 149 [Letter to the Editor].

Webner, Hélène L. *"Waiting for Godot* and the New Theology." *Renascence* 21 (Autumn 1968) : 3–9, 31.

Whittick, Arnold. *Symbols, Signs and Their Meaning.* London: Leonard Hill, 1960. Pp. 372–74.

Williams, Raymond. "Tragic Deadlock and Stalemate: Chekhov, Pirandello, Ionesco, Beckett." In his *Modern Tragedy.* Stanford, Calif.: Stanford University Press, 1966. Pp. 139–55 [153–55].

Wilson, Katharine M. " 'Waiting for Godot.' " (London) *Times Literary Supplement,* 2 March 1956, p. 133 [Letter to the Editor].

Watt. Brooke-Rose, 39–44; Coe, *Samuel Beckett,* 36–53; Cohn, *Samuel Beckett,* 65–94; Esslin, "Samuel Beckett," 133–35; Federman, 94–132; Fletcher, *The Novels of Samuel Beckett,* 59–89; Friedman, "The Novels of Samuel Beckett," 52–53; Frye, 444; Hassan, *The Literature of Silence,* 145–51; Hoffman, 114–19; Jacobsen and Mueller, *The Testament of Samuel Beckett,* 73–77, 82–87; Janvier, 31–39; Karl, 666–68; Mercier, "The Mathematical Limit," 144–45; Morse, "The Choreography of 'The New Novel,' " 415–17; Scott, "The Recent Journey . . . ," 164–69; Scott, *Samuel Beckett,* 48–59; Tassing, 433–34; Tindall, "Beckett's Bums," 6–7.

Brée, Germaine. "Beckett's Abstractors of Quintessence." *French Review* 36 (May 1963) : 567–76.

Brick, Allan. "The Madman in His Cell: Joyce, Beckett, Nabokov and the Stereotypes." *Massachusetts Review* 1 (Fall 1959) : 40–55 [45–49].

Cohn, Ruby. "*Watt* in the Light of *The Castle.*" *Comparative Literature* 13 (Spring 1961) : 154–66.

Greenberg, Alvin. "The Death of the Psyche: A Way to the Self in the Contemporary Novel." *Criticism* 8 (Winter 1966) : 1–18.

Hesla, David H. "The Shape of Chaos: A Reading of Beckett's *Watt.*" *Critique* 6 (Spring 1963) : 85–105.

Hoefer, Jacqueline. "*Watt.*" *Perspective* 11 (Autumn 1959) : 166–82. Reprinted in Esslin, ed., *Samuel Beckett,* pp. 62–76.

Lombardi, Thomas W. "Who Tells Who *Watt.*" *Chelsea,* no. 22–23 (June 1968), pp. 170–79.

Seaver, Richard. "Samuel Beckett." *Nimbus* 2 (Autumn 1953) : 61–62 [Rev. art.].

Senneff, Susan Field. "Song and Music in Samuel Beckett's *Watt.*" *Modern Fiction Studies* 11 (Summer 1964) : 137–49.

Warhaft, Sidney. "Threne and Theme in *Watt.*" *Wisconsin Studies in Contemporary Literature* 4 (Autumn 1963) : 261–78.

Whoroscope. Cohn, *Samuel Beckett,* 11–16; Hassan, *The Literature of Silence,* 122–23.

Words and Music. Capone, 153–57; Cleveland, 279–80; Hayman, 64–66; Mélèse, 107–8; Reid, *All I Can Manage,* 87.

Index

MELVIN J. FRIEDMAN is professor of
comparative literature at the University of
Wisconsin-Milwaukee. He has been a
Fulbright fellow, a Sterling Fellow at Yale,
and a senior fellow of the American Council
of Learned Societies. He was editor of two
journals, *Wisconsin Studies in Contemporary
Literature* and *Comparative Literature
Studies,* and was associate editor of *Yale
French Studies.* Mr. Friedman is now an
assistant editor of *Modern Language
Journal.* He has published a great deal of
work concerned with twentieth-century
literature.